Seven Theories of Hun

TOM CAMPBELL

Seven Theories of Human Society

CLARENDON PRESS   OXFORD
1981

Oxford University Press, Walton Street, Oxford OX2 6DP
London Glasgow New York Toronto
Delhi Bombay Calcutta Madras Karachi
Kuala Lumpur Singapore Hong Kong Tokyo
Nairobi Dar es Salaam Cape Town
Melbourne Auckland

and associate companies in
Beirut Berlin Ibadan Mexico City

Published in the United States by
Oxford University Press, New York

British Library Cataloguing in Publication Data

Campbell, Tom
Seven theories of human society.
1. Social sciences
I. Title
301   H61

ISBN 0–19–876104–X
ISBN 0–19–876105–8 Pbk

Typeset by Macmillan India Ltd., Bangalore 25
Printed in the United States of America

TO MY MOTHER

Preface

This book is designed to introduce the reader to a wide range of contrasting theories of society. The material is set out so as to facilitate the analysis and assessment of each type of theory. The objective is to encourage further informed and critical study of social thought.

Particular care has been taken to spell out the moral and political significance of the theories discussed. The theorists selected are important for a number of social sciences, including economics, psychology, history, and law. Although the seven theories are presented in terms of individual thinkers, each theorist is used as a vehicle for the study of a particular type of social theory. The chronological order of the presentation demonstrates the development of social theory and the way in which it is affected by historical change, but this is not the main purpose of the book. Overall the approach is philosophical rather than empirical in that more attention is given to clarifying the logical structure and methodological assumptions of the theories than to assessment of their detailed factual content.

I have received a great deal of assistance from many people in the preparation of this book. Peter Lamarque helped with the initial planning. Michael Lessnoff read and commented most helpfully on the entire manuscript. Stephen Clark and Paddy O'Donnell performed the same service for Chapter 3 and 9 respectively. I am indebted to Sheila MacLean for very many stylistic improvements. My thanks are also due to my editors at Oxford University Press; and to Helen Matthew and Ruby Burgess for their swift and sure typing.

Grogport   TOM CAMPBELL
September 1980

Contents

PART ONE Introduction

CHAPTER 1

Theories of Society

HUMAN life is unthinkable outside society. Individuals cannot exist in complete and permanent isolation. Men need each other to survive and to live as human beings. This mutual dependence makes some form of regular co-operation, and hence some form of society, a necessity. Man is a social being, that can scarcely be doubted. But what exactly is society? This question is just as basic and just as perplexing as the more traditional question 'what is man?'. It is one of those innocent-sounding but troublesome queries about the nature of things with which we are all utterly familiar but about which we are embarrassingly inarticulate, despite their undoubted importance for our daily lives and for our self-understanding. To answer it we need a theory of society.

In our own day the nature of society is a problem to which an entire science, that of sociology, addresses itself, but it is an issue which spills over into all the social sciences, including history, and is inseparable from some of the major concerns of philosophy. There is therefore a multiplicity of different and rather unco-ordinated sources to look to for leads into the understanding of social life. But this saturation of attention has not produced an established theory of society. For all the wealth of accumulated data concerning particular societies in different periods and cultures there are still radical disagreements about which sort of social phenomena are fundamental to our understanding of social processes and how these phenomena are to be accounted for. An introduction to social theory cannot therefore proceed on the basis of the sort of uncontroversial elementary knowledge to be found in, for instance, the natural sciences. It is necessary, instead, to present a survey of alternative theoretical approaches and contributions to the ordering and understanding of social relationships. Moreover there is no compelling reason for restricting such a survey to purely modern theories, for it is by no means clear that earlier attempts to provide comprehensive accounts of social life have been superseded, and there is some advantage in taking seriously the ideas of major thinkers who lived in types of society far removed from the complex industrial states which have provided the context for modern theories.

This book contains sketches, assessments, and comparisons of seven competing attempts by major thinkers to give a systematic account of what is distinctive and significant about the ways in which human beings relate to each other in societies. Ranging from Aristotle's influential analysis of the small city-state of classical Greece to the twentieth-century work of Alfred Schutz which has inspired some recent adventurous ideas about social phenomena, each theorist has been selected for the intrinsic interest of his views and as an example of a distinguishable type of social theory. Together they provide us with an overview of man's most successful attempts to understand his human environment.

Selecting only seven theories of society has not been an easy matter. Sociology as the self-conscious scientific study of social life as a whole is relatively recent and I have therefore chosen a predominance of modern theorists, in particular the three whose ideas embody the main competing schools of contemporary social theory, each with its characteristic concepts: Marx (conflict and power), Durkheim (structure and function), and Weber (social action and rational bureaucracy). However these modern giants need to be set against a wider perspective. Reflection on the nature of social life goes back at least as far as ancient Greece, and Aristotle's account of the natural sociableness of man is still influential. This serves as a contrast to the work of Thomas Hobbes which, despite its obvious flaws, sets many of the problems which more modern theories seek to answer, such as the basis of social order. A transitional figure, representing the mature thought of the eighteenth-century Enlightenment, is Adam Smith, who, despite his association with economic individualism, brings to the fore in his concept of the 'invisible hand' the idea of society as an integrated system. Finally the work of Alfred Schutz is included as the inspiration of some recent development in the study of society—particularly ethnomethodology—which cast doubt on the whole idea of 'society' as a distinct unitary entity open to detached scientific study.

In Part I I prepare the ground for the study of the seven theories which have been selected as illustrative of the central divergent tendencies in social thought. This chapter deals with the nature of social theory, raising, through an introductory discussion of Hobbes and Durkheim, the question of what it is to offer a theory as distinct from merely a description of social life. The following chapter outlines the most important ways in which social theories differ from each other, giving a framework of parameters which will assist us in comparing social theories and suggesting criteria for their assessment.

THE NATURE OF HUMAN SOCIETY

The absence of an agreed social theory is not just a matter for intellectual and academic concern. Some ideas about what constitutes a society and how societies retain their unity and continuity through various historical transformations are assumed in all the major practical concerns of life, including private morality and public decision-making. We cannot know how to act unless we know how our projects are affected by the existence and activities of other people around us. We cannot join with others to make reasoned choices about matters of common interest without entertaining beliefs about the essential features of co-operative existence. All reflective practical activity presupposes a view of social life, and the success of such activity depends, among other things, on the correctness of that view.

Our conception of society is also fundamental to understanding ourselves. Is the society in which we live simply a very important association that helps us to achieve certain personal objectives, such as material security, as Thomas Hobbes suggests? Or is there a more fundamental social reality which enters into the very essence of our nature as human beings, as Marx and Durkheim would have us believe? Man may be, in Aristotle's words, a social animal, in that he cannot live permanently outside a social group, but are we dependent on our society only as an external support for the maintenance of our personal life or is it that we have no genuine existence apart from our social relationships? However we answer these questions, the image we have of ourselves is inseparable from the picture we have of society.

But even if we allow that our view of society is important, both for self-understanding and for practical decision-making, is society really such a puzzling phenomenon? Perhaps society is not at all the mystifying, intangible thing that it is often said to be. Is our society not simply all those other people among whom we live and work and with whose ways we have an easy familiarity? It may be that when we speak of 'society' we mean simply any large number of people inhabiting the same geographical area among whom there is a degree of daily interaction.

Well, certainly there cannot be a society without people, and a reasonable number of them at that; several families would be the very minimum that anyone would be prepared to contemplate as sufficient to make up even a very simple society. And equally clearly a society must have some sort of physical location, although this need not be a permanent one. Both features—individual people and a common territory— are necessary for the existence of a society, but they are certainly not sufficient in themselves to constitute social existence. A society cannot be *just* a territorial collection or aggregate of people. A large number of persons fortuitously deposited in the same location would not thereby constitute a society, although they might in time become part of one. The fact that human beings are always to be found in societies does not mean that a society can simply be analysed as any collection of people, for not all connections between individuals are to be regarded as social relationships.

To form a society individuals must be related in a certain manner. For instance, if people do not communicate with each other, if they are perpetually in aggressive physical combat, if they do not co-operate with each other, and do so routinely over a period of time, then their interactions are not social and they do not constitute a society. But although it is clear that not just any aggregate of persons form a society, it is not easy to say just how people must be 'grouped' before we can say that their relationships are social. We can agree that it is not enough for them simply to be classified as being similar types, since very similar people can live in different societies. Nor is physical proximity a guarantee of social interaction as the relationship between warring tribes makes evident. We can say that social relationships are orderly interactions involving mutual awareness and symbolic communication, but beyond this it is extremely difficult to be precise about what is required to make a mere collection of people into a socially organized group.

Nevertheless, granted that something has to be added to the initial idea of a territorial collection of interacting individuals if we are to arrive at an adequate conception of a society, this no-nonsense approach of regarding a society as a number of interacting people with a common geographical location is attractively simple and straightforward. Moreover it can readily be developed by specifying that the people concerned share a common co-operative organization which enables them to live together in some sort of order and perhaps harmony. After all, we sometimes use the word 'society' to refer to a number of people who have formed themselves into an association or club through which they pursue certain aims or purposes which they all share. A society for the protection of rare animals or a motor-cycling club are examples of such 'societies'. Thinking along these lines we can conceive of society as a whole as a rather big association for the furtherance of a large and disparate set of common purposes, a sort of glorified club or all-purpose association with an extensive, territorially based membership and a complex set of rules and regulations.

There must, of course, be differences between society as a whole and associations or clubs within a society. If society is an association it is normally one into which we are born rather than one which we join and from which we can readily withdraw. It must be an indispensable club, which we cannot very well get on without, and one whose purposes are rather hard to list in an exhaustive manner. But these things may be true to an extent of many associations, particularly those which are central to the manner in which we provide for our material requirements. And in any case there is no need to deny that society is an unusual type of association in order to hold that societies are best understood as associations or clubs. What matters is whether or not it is helpful to regard a society as an organization created by individuals to serve their particular private purposes. If so, then we can proceed to theorize about society by identifying these purposes and examining how social organization helps to further them.

This common-sensical approach to the understanding of society is not without its advocates among the classical social philosophers. Thomas Hobbes, the tough-minded and incisive founder of the social theory of post-medieval Europe, is prepared to carry the analogy between a society and an association to its logical conclusion. He suggests that we think of social life as preceded by a 'state of nature' in which there was no social organization, no rules, no regulations for orderly interaction and no sustained co-operation. Due to the uncertainties, inconveniences and straightforward dangerousness of this imagined asocial existence, men had reason to come together and set up a society in the same way as those already living in a social environment might meet to set up an association or establish a business enterprise. Hobbes argues that it would be rational for man to escape from the hazardously unpredictable state of nature by agreeing on the basic rules of their association and promising each other to obey the rulings of a single political authority. In this way they would ensure their individual safety by pledging joint support to a body powerful enough to curb the destructive tendencies in human nature. This became the model for all 'social contract' theories of society.

For Hobbes, although not for all contract theorists, to create a society is at the same time to create a state or 'commonwealth', for the authority in question is given sovereign power—that is, the right to make rules backed by physical compulsion. But even for Hobbes society is more than the state. Once the original contract of society is made there arise other subsidiary groupings which are not directly the creatures of the political sovereign, although they are made possible by the existence of an absolute political authority. Thus economic, religious, and educational organizations are able to develop within a political society, enabling men to move towards the attainment of a satisfying material and cultural existence. These organizations are themselves contractually based so that the idea of an explicit agreement or contract between individual persons is for Hobbes the fundamental social relationship.

Not many contemporary sociologists are followers of Hobbes, although many make passing references to his work. This is partly on account of his dated language and inadequate scientific method. But it is also due to the fact that Hobbes is an 'individualistic' theorist in that he believes there to be a fixed and universal human nature, independent of the effects of social conditioning, which is the ultimate explanation for social life. In contrast the standard modern view is that society is a phenomenon which is presupposed by the activities and attributes of individual human beings, an underlying and ongoing reality which cannot be reduced to the product of individual human conduct and nature. Thus although Emile Durkheim—an early twentieth-century theorist whose work we shall also be examining—believes, with Hobbes, that society involves the control of individuals, he thinks that this is accomplished by a natural process whereby a collective or group consciousness emerges, prior to the conduct and choices of any individual or number of individuals, and determines the individual's beliefs, emotions and behaviour. Through this process the individual becomes fitted to take part in a complex pattern of relationships which form an integrated whole with the behaviour of other members of his society.

According to this theory it is not that men form a society but that society forms men. Society is a pre-existing set of interconnected ways of behaving which becomes incorporated into the psychology and behaviour of individual human beings and controls all that is distinctively human about them. Their language, their morality, their religion, their economic activities, even their reasoning, are all social products. On this 'holistic' view of society, understanding the behaviour of individuals requires knowledge of the nature of their society and their place in it. Thus, in his well-known study of suicide, Durkheim sets out to demonstrate that this seemingly most personal of acts is in fact an expression of social and not individual factors (see pp. 159–60). For this reason suicide is not to be studied by examining the motives of individual suicides but by showing how the suicide rate is determined by the type and stage of society in question, in particular by the sort of 'solidarity' which holds people together in their social groupings.

To make the point that society contributes so much and individual human nature so little to the formation of human behaviour, Durkheim sometimes draws on biological analogies and speaks of the social 'organism', a recurring concept in social theory, and one which, as we shall see, is to be found as far back as Aristotle. And, in order to bring out the overwhelming importance for the individual of his social relationships, he also suggests that we can regard society as being a sort of god, for 'Society' creates and sustains men as individuals and calls for their loyalty, commitment and even worship. But, since a society cannot be literally a biological organism or a god, Durkheim, like every other non-individualistic social theorist, has the difficult task of stating his theory of society in a clear and unambiguous manner.

Durkheim's theory is one version of a general trend in contemporary social theory, and Durkheim, unlike Hobbes, is a major figure within modern 'sociology', by which is meant the scientific study of society in all its aspects, economic, religious, political and educational. Although few sociologists would want to speak of society as a god, they do have what might be regarded as a professional interest in stressing the significance of society as an object of study and this involves countering what they regard as the naive assumption that individuals are somehow more real and therefore more important in the explanatory scheme of things than the society to which men owe their existence and from which they derive their particular natures.

But Hobbes, for all his emphasis on the individual, is just as much a theorist of society as is Durkheim. His ideas compete with those of Durkheim in a systematic way and lead to different and competing outlooks on such matters of common concern as the rights and duties of persons, the basis of community life and political organization, and the sort of social existence for which it is realistic to strive. The orderly way in which their theories come into conflict indicates an underlying similarity in the formal structure of their ideas and shows that they are, to an extent, presenting rival explanations for the same phenomena. These underlying similarities are as significant for our present purposes as their obvious disagreements, and it will help us to anticipate what we may expect of a theory of society if we look in a little more detail at what is common to their intellectual endeavours. At the same time I will introduce into the discussion references to others of the chosen seven theorists to illustrate the range of different views about the nature of social theory. This will help to prepare the way for the analysis of conflicting trends in theories of society which is presented in chapter two, where I shall discuss further the contrast between individualism and holism.

THE NATURE OF SOCIAL THEORY

The most significant thing which Hobbes and Durkheim have in common which marks them out as theorists of society is that they do not merely describe social existence or narrate the history of social development for its own sake. Rather they endeavour to get us to see human society in a certain way so that what we derive from reading their works is not just more information about social life but something much more important, a better understanding of the nature of human social relationships. Their shared objective is to provide greater social insight and comprehension, not to present a mass of raw social data. They do this by setting up models of how societies operate, breaking them down into their constituent parts and indicating their working relationships. For Hobbes this means analysing the nature of contracts entered into by rational and self-interested individuals. For Durkheim it involves demonstrating the functional interdependence of the great occupational groups within the social organism. In so doing both purport to tell us not only what happens in social relationships, but also why societies operate in one way rather than another. They seek to further our understanding as much as our knowledge of social phenomena, to explain as well as describe.

This is true of all genuine social theorists. Aristotle, for instance, invites us to see that communal civic living is 'natural' to man. Adam Smith, on the other hand, presents us with a model of society as an immense and intricate machine designed by a benevolent and rather cunning creator, while Marx claims to exhibit the hidden reality of social existence by bringing to light the economic necessities underlying class conflict. Weber and Schutz also, in their own way, present a certain perspective on social life, the former teaching us to see social relationships in terms of different types of 'action', the latter enticing us with the idea that there is really no such thing as 'society' if this is thought of as a reality existing outside the experience of interacting individuals. Despite the many differences between our seven representative theorists it can be said of them all that they are intellectual visionaries. This is what makes them social theorists rather than mere fact gatherers.

The main elements of a theory are definition, description and explanation. I shall say something about each of these elements in turn.

Definitions tell us how the writer is going to use his key terms. Any theorist of society must, for instance, clarify what he means by the word 'society', and offer some account of his central terminology, such as 'contract' or 'solidarity'. The process of defining such general terms is often referred to as the analysis of concepts. This is normally accomplished by indicating the features which an entity must have if the term in question is to be correctly used to refer to it. Thus, in this book, when we speak of 'society' we are not speaking of the world of upperclass social gatherings, nor are we thinking of particular associations, such as a trades union or political party. 'Society', for our purposes, is a term which refers to a more inclusive phenomenon, namely the whole complex network of human relationships within large-scale groups or collectivities which share a common culture and way of life. One thing we will be looking for from our theorists is a more precise definition of 'society' than this. Often this is provided by bringing in and analysing other fundamental terms which the theorist considers to be closely related to our concept of society. Thus Hobbes tells us, for example, that 'society' is 'the condition of living together in peace' and goes on to spell out what that means by contrasting it with a state of war, arguing that the existence of a society must be coterminous with the operation of a coercive political sovereign, thus bringing together the ideas of society and state. In contrast to this relatively 'external' or physical definition of a society, Durkheim's initial definition of 'society' refers to a normative or moral order which has a psychic reality in the consciousness of individuals and no necessary connection with the state, while Marx defines 'society' as 'the ensemble of social relationships' which he then traces to what he calls 'the relations of production' (see p. 123).

Definitions are not particularly important in themselves. They are valuable as aids to clear thinking and the merits and demerits of particular definitions are therefore relative to the purposes for which they are used. Most frequently a theorist uses his key concepts, once analysed, as instruments for conveying significant facts about the world. Thus Hobbes, who is particularly keen on definitions, uses them to assert that society—or the condition of living together in peace—involves the making and keeping of contracts. This is a factual or empirical assertion in so far as it purports to convey information about the world which we can test by observation and experience. Durkheim, who is not so rigorous as Hobbes in his definitions, places greater emphasis on accurate descriptive statements. Using many of the methods of modern social science, including official statistical data, Durkheim presents extensive accounts of men's economic practices, religious beliefs and rites, professional organization, and so on. He is more sensitive than Hobbes to the variety of ways of life in different types of society and takes description of these disparate phenomena as a prime sociological task, as do Aristotle, Smith, Marx and Weber whose approaches are thus much more empirical or less '*a priori*' (independent of experience) than that of Hobbes. However, all theorists are, to some extent, in the business of deploying a set of carefully defined terms (or analysed concepts) to describe social life as they observe it.

While definitions can be short and sharp, description is an endless and open-ended activity to which there is no logical limit. There is an infinity of facts to be discovered, investigated, proved or disputed. Even for such voluminous writers as Marx, Weber and Durkheim some selection of material is always necessary. This takes us to what is characteristic of a 'theoretical' as distinct from a narrowly 'empirical' approach which sticks to relating particular facts. A theory is an attempt to impose some order on the endless multiplicity of descriptions by selecting and yet summarizing the crucial facts about the phenomena in question. Selection in itself does not constitute a theoretical approach for a theory must have something to say about *all* relevant phenomena. The need to be both comprehensive and selective can be met only by the processes of abstraction and generalization, that is by picking out from the mass of observable phenomena certain recurrent features which are claimed to be present in and central to many or all social relationships. This is what Hobbes does by fastening on the notions of contract and sovereignty, Durkheim's equivalent being his conception of solidarity and its relationship to other significant social phenomena, such as the division of labour, a concept also much used by Smith and Marx, the former relating it to the idea of social cohesion based on mutual sympathy in contrast to the latter who takes the division of labour to be both cause and effect of social conflict. In Aristotle a similar role is played by his concept of friendship which in one form or another is present in all normal social relationships, whereas for Weber the concept of social action serves as the basis for abstraction and generalization. Each theorist thus develops his particular cluster of key concepts around which he organizes the raw material which he gathers from the observation of social reality.

Abstraction and generalization are indispensable to any systematic theory, indeed they are to a large extent what theorizing amounts to. But, in looking for a theory of an entity as complex and intangible as society, these processes can result in something so vague and imprecise as to be hopelessly uninformative. To be fully comprehensive is often to miss what is really interesting in the phenomena in question, in this case the significant differences between types of social relationships. One main objective of a social theory is therefore to summarize the most important differences between social phenomena, so providing a classification or taxonomy of types of society.

Hobbes's ambition is to provide a genuinely universal theory which applied to all societies, but even he develops various distinctions between, for instance, sovereignty which comes about through conquest and sovereignty based on voluntary agreement. In Durkheim's case a great deal of his work is concerned with the difference between two types of solidarity, the 'mechanical' and the 'organic'. Indeed the fame of many theorists rests on their suggestions as to the ways in which societies and social relationships may be distinguished and classified.

For instance, Aristotle contrasts three 'good' forms of civil society (kingship, aristocracy and polity) with three 'bad' forms (tyranny, oligarchy and democracy). Adam Smith is renowned as a pioneer of the idea that societies pass through the four stages of hunting, pasturage, agriculture and commerce. Marx's most acute analysis occurs in his contrast between feudalism and capitalism, Weber's equivalent being the transition from traditional to rational-bureaucratic social organization.

Distinguishing types of society is still a matter of description rather than explanation. An explanation has to go beyond saying *what* is the case to offer us some understanding of *why* these things are as they are, for instance why it is that one type of society should change, either rapidly by revolution or slowly by evolution, into another type. In any adequate theory, description must, therefore, be joined to and culminate in some form of explanation.

The notion of what it is to explain something is extremely elusive. It is a topic which will occupy us again in chapter 2 p. 38) and throughout the book. In the end explanation is a highly subjective matter in that what satisfies one person's curiosity or intellectual puzzlement may not do the same for others. Aristotle feels the need to establish what is 'natural' to each type of being. Hobbes likes to trace all social phenomena to what he regards as their roots in the pre-existing motives of the individuals involved. This procedure does not entirely satisfy Adam Smith or Durkheim for whom the existence of certain motives in human behaviour is one of the things that requires explanation; they are uneasy in their minds until they have shown how a particular form of behaviour is 'functional' for a society in that it contributes to the operation of its other parts. Durkheim, for instance, explains religious ritual, in part at least, by its function in promoting the social cohesion on which other aspects of social life depend.

Hobbes, Smith, Durkheim and Marx have the common characteristic that the major part of their sociological explanations involve causal statements. They assume that if two types of events are observed to occur regularly in a certain temporal order and spatial proximity, then there is a natural necessity to their conjunction and we may explain the occurrence of a particular instance of a type of phenomenon by showing that it was preceded by the sort of event with which it is linked in such a causal generalization. Aristotle also investigates social causes (and functions) but in a rather different sense of 'cause'. But other theorists reject this approach to social explanation and argue that, since human behaviour is free it cannot be causally determined. What we have to do instead, according to these theorists, is seek understanding of human motivations and reasons. This can be done by sympathetic and imaginative observation, and perhaps also by introspectively examining our own attitudes, beliefs, emotions and reasons. In this way, it is thought, we can reach intellectual satisfaction by social explanations which reveal the meaning of behaviour rather than its alleged causes. We have a hint of this approach in Smith but it is more characteristic of Weber and serves as the foundation of Schutz's whole approach to social theory. We will see (p. 40) that this is one of the major divergences in theories of society.

All these elements of theorizing—definition, description and explanation—are closely related and often hard to distinguish. Moreover, despite Hobbes's attempt to do something of this sort, it is not a simple matter of starting with a set of definitions and working upwards *via* description to explanation, for a theorist's preconceptions about what constitutes a good explanation will affect his selection of facts and this in turn will affect his use of key words. Nevertheless, although it is not an easy task, it is enormously helpful in the exposition and understanding of a theory to sort out these three elements as far as it is possible to do so, and this is one of the things attempted in this book.

Perhaps the most important but often the least visible of these elements is explanation, in that a theorist's idea of what counts as a good explanation is often left obscure. For this reason we will start our account of each theory with a discussion of the *approach* adopted by the theorist in question before going on to present the substance of his theory.

As far as their approach goes both Hobbes and Durkheim regard themselves as scientific within the assumptions of their day, but differ radically in their ideas as to what scientific method is, Hobbes modelling himself on geometry and mechanics, Durkheim being more empirical and biological in his method. They differ also in how their scientific interest is motivated, and have different ideas about what they hope to achieve through their studies. Neither is a purely detached observer of social life and both combine scientific interest with practical concerns, seeking to apply their knowledge to the problems of their day as they see them. Hobbes is preoccupied with the danger of anarchy which he experienced in the violence and confusion of the English Civil War. Durkheim is also concerned with social order, but his focus of interest is not on physical conflict but on the disintegration of modern industrial society through the decline of moral community and hence individual discipline. The whole of his scientific enterprise could be said to lead up to recommendations for curing 'anomie', as he calls the collapse of social order.

Thus both our illustrative social theorists have their anxieties and hopes about the societies they attempt to define, describe and explain, and this is broadly true of all social theorists. Marx, for instance, eagerly anticipates the collapse of the type of liberal society which Smith seeks to justify and consolidate. (This is one respect in which Marx is a theorist of social change in contrast to Hobbes, Durkheim and most other social theorists who are concerned with social order and stability.) So our first task when dealing with our seven theories will be to outline the method of studying society adopted by the theorist in question and indicate his motivation for undertaking that study, in short, to indicate his approach to social theory.

As far as the content of social theories is concerned, point for point comparisons will be facilitated by starting with an account of their *theory of man*. It is impossible to conceive of a theory of society without a conception of human nature. We cannot comprehend Hobbes's analysis of society, for instance, without knowing that he sees human beings as complicated and relatively self-sufficient machines impelled to seek their own survival and endowed with reason as an instrument for discovering how to satisfy their appetites. His social theory consists largely in listing these universal appetites and showing how rational men enter society to satisfy their presocial desires. The same is true in a very much less extreme way for Aristotle and Adam Smith, although neither adopt Hobbes's antisocial view of man; whereas for Durkheim man is little more than a conglomeration of unregulated, uncontrolled and unspecific desires which the individual is powerless to direct or limit, and he has to look to society to provide the linguistic, reasoning and institutional requirements for ordering human life. This holds to a lesser extent for Marx who has little patience with the idea of a human nature which is independent of particular social contexts. Thus a basic constituent of each theory is its view of man, or theory of human nature.

Once we have an idea of what man is like, it becomes much easier to identify the functions attributed by each theorist to social life. This constitutes, in the narrow sense, the *theory of society*. For Hobbes, society has the limited but important function of protecting the individual from the harmful acts of his fellows and enforcing contacts, leaving man relatively free to provide for his own material and spiritual needs with only 'external' or contractual relations with other men. (Smith accepts this as at least part of the truth although he argues that Hobbes omits that aspect of social life which is based on mutual sympathy.) But Durkheim's society must provide men with language, with rationality, with morality, with religion and everything else which is necessary to enable such an otherwise amorphous being to fit into a complex social organization. Out of this comes a social reality in which individuals are 'internally' related in that they share a common outlook with their fellows in virtue of which they feel and actually are united by their mutual participation in the same social reality. (This approximates to Aristotle's ideal of the best form of civic community and has something in common with Marx's projected communist society.)

Within these broad limits both Hobbes and Durkheim proceed to develop a view of the characteristic forms of social relationship and how these knit together. Hobbes stresses the struggle for power, glory and wealth and the way in which these relate to mutual destructiveness on the one hand and to contractual agreements on the other, all social situations being a mixture of these two elements. Durkheim, on the other hand, argues that if men were as Hobbes thought them to be, then no effective agreements could be made. All contracts, he thinks, presuppose an under-lying social consensus about the moral duty of keeping agreements. Durkheim's object is to elucidate the basis of this moral consensus on which all social relationships depend.

There is no need for us to trace further at this stage how Hobbes, Durkheim and the other theorists distinguish between types of social relationships and build up their explanations of the social phenomena they describe. We have noted how Hobbes traces everything back to the universal nature of man and Durkheim works out the part which each social phenomenon plays in the total complex social organism. These and other themes will be taken up in subsequent chapters. Enough has been said already to illuminate what we should look for at the heart of a social theory.

But it would be incomplete to leave the matter there, for each theorist seeks to draw some *practical implications* from his analysis of society, implications which are closely related to his reasons for undertaking the study in the first place. Aristotle outlines in some detail the closest approximation to his ideal community which he considers to be practicable. Hobbes implicitly advises the rational individual to subject himself to the authoritative rules of the sovereign. Smith seeks the removal of restrictions on industry and commerce, while Durkheim calls for the development, through education, ritual and political organization, of a group consciousness based on the functional divisions of economic life and co-ordinated by the overall control of a 'collective conscience' as the basis for the unity and direction of the social organism. Marx, of course, looks to the revolutionary overthrow of the

capitalist system. Weber's aspirations are less easy to summarize but they involve admiration for both rational organization and charismatic leadership.

Despite what some theorists claim, their recommendations
do not follow in strict logic from the rest of their theories. For
instance, it would be possible for Hobbes and Durkheim to be
indifferent to the anarchy or anomie they forsee as the natural
consequence of certain elements in their societies, and thus to
avoid drawing any practical conclusions. But although political and social recommendations are not in any tight sense
implications of descriptive and explanatory contributions, the
force of these recommendations does often depend in large
part on the preceding sociological analysis and certainly in the
cases of Hobbes and Durkheim there is a close affinity between
their descriptions and their prescriptions.

Most of this chapter has been taken up with a discussion of
the similarities and differences in the basic ingredients of all
social theories, particularly those of Hobbes and Durkheim
between whom the contrasts are most pronounced. The object
has been to illustrate the characteristic interlocking patterns of
ideas to be found in the form of all social theories despite the
fact that they vary in substance according to the period, the
social experience, personal interests, intellectual outlook and
general expertise of the theorist.

In accordance with our analysis of the various elements of
social theories, after the context of each theorist's life and work
has been outlined, his ideas will be presented in terms of (1) his
approach to society, (2) his theory of man, (3) his theory of
society, (4) the implications of the theory for practical
concerns, and finally (5) an assessment of the theory as a whole
and, where relevant, an indication of later or related developments in social theory. The aims are to provide a map locating
the characteristic features of differing theories of society and to
erect some signposts for further study.

Before going on to consider in more detail just what sort of
thing a theory of society is and how theories may be compared
and criticized, we should note two important related points
about social theories. The first is their 'self-fulfilling' and 'self-

refuting' nature and the second is their ideological status.

A theory of society is unlike a theory of non-human entities in that its truth or falsity may be to a degree affected by whether or not it is believed. Actual social relationships can be radically altered by the social theories which are held by the participants in such a way as to make the theories self-fulfilling or self-refuting. For instance, if a person believes that conflict underlies all social interaction, then he will tend to look for signs of conflict in his social relationships and thereby help to create or intensify conflicts which might have been absent or less pronounced had he believed in the possibility of harmonious social relationships. Similarly if a social theory predicts certain changes, such as a trend towards more equality of opportunity in industrial societies, this may lead men to anticipate, and so further, developments in this direction, or to do their best to thwart the emergence of a change of which they disapprove.

We should be aware, therefore, that social theories, while they cannot of themselves produce radical social changes— and the extent to which they can influence social change is a hotly disputed question—often affect the reality which they describe and explain. This is because social relations are in part constituted by people's beliefs about their societies and their place within these societies. Theories of society are thus in the complicated position of being part of the reality they purport to analyse. This means that we cannot afford to ignore entirely any theory that is liable to be believed and so enter into the fabric of social relationships.

Secondly, social theories are ideological in that even the most neutral-looking factual claims about social phenomena can be taken up and used in the competition between social groups for positions of power, wealth and influence, so that all major social theories are associated, at least in many people's minds, with different political outlooks. The work of Adam Smith, for instance, as the classic expression of modern liberal economics, is clearly connected with the ideology of western capitalism, while Marx's social theory is part and parcel of his analysis of exploitation in the capitalist system and his anticipation of the harmony and freedom which is possible in a communist society. Hobbes has been seen as an early advocate of bourgeois individualism, with its emphasis on possessiveness and acquisitiveness, while the corporatist ideas of Durkheim have been said to foreshadow certain aspects of state socialism, or even fascism.

The ideological origins and uses of social theories together with their self-fulfilling and self-refuting character, make their objective and neutral assessment extremely difficult. This accounts for at least some of the continuing disagreements about the nature of society and highlights the need to look at a range of social theories. But by distinguishing carefully between a theory and its alleged implications, and noting the possible ideological prejudices of its author and supporters, we shall at least have made a move in the direction of rational criticism.

Having noted these difficulties we can now pass to a more systematic examination of what can be done by way of the comparison and critical assessment of theories of society.

FOR FURTHER READING

There are many good introductions to sociology which discuss what it is to theorize about society. Particularly recommended are *Introducing Sociology*, ed: Peter Worsley (Penguin Books: Harmondsworth, 2nd edition, 1977) and Peter L. Berger and Brigitte Berger, *Sociology: A Biographical Approach* (Penguin Books: Harmondsworth, 1976).

For a more abstract treatment of social theory see Vernon Pratt, *The Philosophy of the Social Sciences* (Methuen: London, 1978). Lucid discussions of the nature of social explanation and the relation of social science to ideology are to be found in Michael Lessnoff, *The Structure of Social Science* (Allen and Unwin: London, 1974).

On theories of human nature see Martin Hollis, *Models of Man* (Cambridge University Press: Cambridge, 1977).

Reading on Hobbes and Durkheim will be recommended at the end of chapters 4 and 7 respectively. A wide ranging presentation of the sort of contrasts we have noted between Hobbes and Durkheim is contained in an article by Alan Dawe, 'The Two Sociologies', *British Journal of Sociology*, Vol. xxi, No. 2, June 1970.

CHAPTER 2

Comparing and Assessing Theories

IN Chapter 1 I discussed the puzzling nature of social reality and set out a scheme for analysing theories of society by splitting them up into manageable parts for exposition and discussion. In Part Two we will find that this scheme fits some theories better than others since each theory has its own particular emphasis and presuppositions, but it will prove a useful expository device to consider first the general approach and method of each theorist, then his view of human nature, his characteristic descriptions and explanations of social processes, following this with an examination of the implications the theory may have for practical concerns. Imposing this framework on each theory in turn will help us to compare them and assess their relative merits. As there is little point in identifying differences in theories of society if we are at a loss as to how to choose between them I will complete my treatment of each theory with some remarks about its strengths and weaknesses and the extent to which it may be defended against its critics, mentioning how it has been put aside, modified or developed in the light of criticism.

In this second introductory chapter I shall outline the main ways in which theorists diverge from each other and present certain scales or parameters of divergence in which we can locate each theory. I will then prepare for the critical element in our task by setting out the criteria which we would expect a good theory to satisfy and mention some of the common errors into which theorists tend to fall. Thus armed with some comparative and critical tools I will then proceed with the analysis and assessment of the theories of human society.

SOCIOLOGICAL PARAMETERS

A society—and indeed a group within society—is a form of order: it involves regularly repeated patterns of interactions between human beings. This order need not be without conflict or even without violence, and its extent clearly varies from society to society. But if human interactions are not in some way patterned then they do not form part of a society. I have expressed this by saying that a society is not just an aggregate or collection of human beings but an orderly grouping with discernible regularities of interaction.

Beyond such very general assertions there is very little agreement among theorists on the nature of social phenomena. A large majority of theorists contend that human, as distinct from animal, societies depend very little on genetically inherited patterns of behaviour (but see the discussion of sociobiology, pp. 88–91). Many theorists stress the social significance of distinctive human capacities, such as speech and rationality, which make it possible for men to learn and alter the standards of expected behaviour and attitudes prevalent in their own particular group. This leads to the view that a society is constituted by the rules or norms which are expressed in its moral and legal codes, social conventions and religious precepts. This view is expressed by saying that human society is based on culture not instinct. But although this provides common ground for many social theorists the idea that a society is essentially a socially transmitted normative order of prohibitions and prescriptions is disputed by those who view social norms as of minor significance or as the products of other, allegedly basic, factors, such as biological needs or economic forces.

The existence of such radical disagreement over fundamentals makes it difficult and unfruitful to attempt the formulation of a common core of sociological doctrines. There is no consensus social theory. It is, however, possible, to indicate a few dimensions or parameters in terms of which theories may be compared with each other. This does not commit us to the view that the 'correct' theory must be some sort of compromise between the polarities of each dimension. In this section I will adopt this approach and suggest some parameters which can be deployed to bring out the main differences between social theories.

I use the term 'parameter' to refer to a broad axis or area within which we can place a specific factor or element in a theory and so determine the extent to which it approximates to either of two extreme positions which represent the opposite ends of a single but broad dimension. Parameters are helpful in social theory for three reasons. First, few social theories can be pigeon-holed into sharply distinguished compartments. They present us with few 'either-ors' and many 'more or lesses'. (For instance, most theories are 'individualistic' to a certain extent.) It is therefore beneficial to have a scheme of interpretation which takes this for granted. Second, social theories cannot be located on a simple scale or 'narrow' dimension which could be represented as a straight line between two clearly defined polarities. This is because of the variety of different sub-types which occur. (For instance, there are many different versions of 'individualism' and 'holism' so that there cannot be any simple, straightforward opposition between these two generally conflicting positions). The concept of a parameter is intended to capture this idea of logical space in which the elements of a theory can be positioned. Third, the concept of sociological parameters enables us to bring out the fact that theories which differ in some respects are very similar in other ways. Many sociological variables are relatively independent of each other. It is therefore better to think of a social theory in terms of a number of distinct divergencies rather than to rest content with a crude label for the theory as a whole. This helps us to draw attention to some unexpected similarities as well as obvious differences between theories.

My choice of parameters is a personal one. Certainly it would be easy to add many more to the list that I have chosen. But those that I have selected provide at least an initial basis for the analysis, comparison and assessment of social theories. We have touched on some of them already in chapter 1 but with others we shall be breaking new ground.

(1)   The Idealist-Materialist Parameter

One of the most fundamental divergences in social theory is between those who regard human societies as an expression of mind or consciousness and those who think of societies in terms of physical or material properties. The former may be called sociological idealists, the latter sociological materialists. The labels 'idealist' and 'materialist' are not being used here in their moral or evaluative senses in which an 'idealist' is someone who has high moral aspirations and a 'materialist' someone who is concerned only with money and possessions. For our purposes these labels describe in the one case those who view social reality as consisting primarily of ideas (the 'idealists') and in the other, those who think of it as a form of matter (the 'materialists').

One of the most puzzling features of human experience is the apparent dichotomy between mind and matter. Thought, feelings and choices—the contents of consciousness—appear to be utterly different sorts of things from material entities, be they solids, fluids, gases or electronic particles. For instance, we cannot imagine what it is to touch a thought, measure the size of a feeling or determine the mass of a choice. We are conscious of material objects but consciousness itself does not seem to be a tangible object. Hence the apparent chasm between subjective experience or awareness and the objective world of material objects.

Human beings have bodies and are thus part of the realm of matter but they also have minds, feelings and wills and are, therefore, also part of what appears to be an entirely different, spiritual type of reality. This apparent dualism of human nature underlies the disputes between philosophical idealists and philosophical materialists; the latter argue that, in the end, everything, including consciousness can be reduced to the characteristics of material objects which are in effect the only real things in the universe. Philosophical idealists take the opposite line and contend that matter exists only in the mind of some perceiving or thinking being, be he god or man, so that ultimately only minds can properly be said to exist.

Common-sense would seem to favour a compromise position (called philosophical dualism) which admits the reality of both mind and matter. But dualism comes up against the difficulty of explaining how such very different types of entity as mind and matter can interact with each other. How can an invisible, unquantifiable and intangible thing like a feeling affect a visible, measureable and touchable substance like a muscle, and vice versa? What mutual influence could there be between two such very different types of being?

If the common-sense dualist simply accepts as an undeniable fact that there is such interaction between mind and matter this leaves unresolved another important question, namely the relative importance of the two different types of reality in their mutual interplay. Does mind dominate matter, or matter mind? Or are we dealing with two equally important and influential entities? In answering such questions dualists move either towards idealism by making mind the controlling factor, or towards materialism by stressing the power of matter over mind. In this respect we can see that there is a variety of possible positions between pure idealism and pure materialism.

The contrast between idealism and materialism appears in social theory in the split between those who think of society primarily as a mental phenomenon to be analysed in terms of thoughts, feelings and divisions (the sociological idealists) and those who look upon social relationships as an expression of physical facts such as climate, economic goods, physical power or biochemical reactions (the sociological materialists). More specifically the sociological idealist often fastens on those mental phenomena which are referred to as social norms, that is those rules of which members of a society are aware and by which they govern their conduct towards each other. He tends to regard social order as rule-governed and therefore as a mental rather than a physical phenomenon.

In its most general sense, a rule is any statement that in a certain type of situation a certain type of behaviour is appropriate, or correct, or required, of certain types of persons. A rule is therefore said to be 'prescriptive' rather than descriptive of behaviour in that it says what is to be done rather than what has been done. This does not mean that it is a prediction about what will be done, for it states what ought to happen, and this leaves open the possibility that this may not happen; rules may be ignored, broken or violated, as well as followed, without their status as rules being in any way undermined. To disobey a rule is not in itself to deny the existence or justification of that rule. Rules are not, therefore, generalizations, like scientific laws, which can be disproved by showing that they do not describe actual events. Rules purport to state what is correct, not necessarily what is the case. But standards of correctness, and the notions of right and wrong which they employ, appear, on the face of it, to be mental rather than material entities. This means that to visualize society as a normative order of rules is to see it in idealist terms.

It will be useful at this point to say a little more about this normative social order as the sociological idealist conceives it. Rules, it is said, are central to every human activity. Most obvious are the rules of morality and law which prohibit, require or allow all sorts of actions, but less obvious rules govern all learned behaviour. There are rules of games as well as of intellectual activities such as arithmetic, and learning would not be possible at all without the rules which govern the use of words. Language, as much as property, government, sexuality and economics, depends on accepted standards of correct behaviour (in this case speech). Indeed the rules of language are illustrative of the majority of rules on which social order rests, in that they are normally followed unthinkingly and automatically as the result of a long process of learning and habituation.

While the content and scope of rules vary enormously and the degree of conformity to rules differs from society to society, the idealist argues that such order as exists in human societies is rule-based in that it involves awareness by members of a society of what it is correct to do, or what is required of them in different types of situation and a readiness to conform to such rules on most occasions. Those rules which relate directly to interactions between persons are called 'social' norms if they have the function of regulating standard types of interaction. The characteristic content of social norms can be expressed in the language of rights and duties. If there is a rule indicating that persons of type A in situation type S are required to act or refrain from acting towards persons of type B in a certain manner, then A is then said to have a duty or obligation to B, and B has a right that A act or refrain from acting in the way specified. Thus land owners may have a right either in law or social convention that others do not enter their land without permission, so we say that these others have a duty not to trespass.

Using the concept of a social norm the idealist can build up a picture of society as a set of rules, roles and institutions. Some social norms, such as prohibitions against killing other human beings or stealing their property, usually apply to all members of a society, but in others the rights and duties involved apply only to a certain class or type of person, such as parents, land owners or car drivers. When a number of social norms apply to a certain type of person then it is common to speak of a social 'role', by which is meant a position occupied by an individual to which is attached a set of rights and duties. Thus land owners normally have certain obligations in relation to their land, as well as rights to use, alter or sell it. Children, as they grow up, come to be in the position of having certain duties within the family, as well as rights, such as the right to an education. So for soldiers, for postmen, politicians, managers, schoolteachers, and so forth, each has his own characteristic cluster of rights and duties.

The idea of a role as a part played by persons who occupy a particular type of position in society is the conception on which a sociological idealist can build the notion of social structure—the term given to the normative framework into which individuals fit in so far as they are part of a social order. The cluster of rights and duties attached to each position are complementary and so provide a basis for collaboration between those occupying different but related positions. Children, mothers, fathers, aunts, uncles and so on, have positions whose rights and duties dovetail to form the 'institution' of the family, for each have a part to play in a pattern of relationships which sustains a form of coexistence and co-operation in single households. The same applies to other institutions such as the business company (made up of the roles of manager, worker, shareholder, etc.), and the club (with its members, committee members, chairmen, etc.).

Starting, therefore, from the idea of a single person conforming to, or being obliged by, a rule and extending this to cover the idea of a person occupying a position or role with various rights and duties, and thus playing a part which involves him in directing his actions in a rule-governed manner towards the occupants of other roles which are inter-connected with his role in such a way as to form an institution, a sociological idealist can arrive at the conception of social structure as the totality of such institutional arrangements. An example which approximates to this is to be found in Talcott Parsons's synthesis of the views of Durkheim and Weber, which is discussed on pp. 189–96.

Sociological idealists are not alone in deploying the notions of social norms, social roles and social institutions. The distinctiveness of their position is in the contention that this normative structure has to be understood as part of a mental, moral or spiritual realm which has a life and nature of its own. This involves the 'ontological' claim that social norms have a non-material existence and the explanatory thesis that such social norms make a major, perhaps overwhelming contribution to the workings of human societies.

In this they oppose two sorts of materialists. First there is the 'behaviourist' who argues that statements about supposedly mental entities are really about observable behaviour: thus a motive becomes a disposition to behave in a certain way and a feeling, like happiness, is equated with muscular contractions, such as those involved in smiling for instance. For the behaviourist social norms consist of regular patterns of publicly observable behaviour, particularly the regular application of psychological pressure or physical punishment to those individuals who break the normal patterns. This removes social norms from the ideal sphere.

A second, weaker position, which can still be called materialist (and remember we are dealing with parameters not compartments), does not reduce social norms to material categories, but by-passes the normative order by arguing either that social norms are mere expressions of underlying material factors (a position which is called 'epiphenomenalism' in the dispute between the philosophical versions of idealism and materialism), or that they have little importance so far as the decisive determinants of social behaviour are concerned. This is to accept the ontological standing of idealist social norms but to deny their explanatory significance for social theory.

Thus Marx (at least on Engels's interpretation, see pp. 118f) is definitely a materialist but only in the weaker sense in that he regards all moral, religious and legal rules as the expression of the material interests of the dominant social class. But he does not deny the existence of consciousness and the ideality of normative beliefs. Hobbes is, as we shall see (pp. 73f), a thorough-going materialist in the strong sense (at least in aspiration) since he attempts to account for everything, including psychological processes, as 'matter in motion'. But Adam Smith, for instance, although he attempts something similar to Hobbes in showing that mental and emotional processes are governed by principles very similar to the laws of motion, does not identify the laws which govern the physical and the mental world. He is not therefore committed to what I have called strong materialism, but, on the other hand, he does at least tend towards the weaker version of materialism in the type of factors to which he gives weight in sociological explanation (such as economic interest and physical force).

At the other extreme Schutz, building on some of Weber's insights, comes the closest of our seven theorists to the idealist position, at least as regards the primacy of consciousness, although in so far as Aristotle believes in an objective moral order which is known to the trained consciousness of the wise individual he is more typical of traditional idealism with its stress on the existence of a spiritual realm existing outside and beyond human consciousness. But in this he does not go as far as his predecessor Plato. Durkheim too, in his concept of the collective conscience gives a central role to the mental—or, in his terms, 'moral'—aspect of social relationships. But, as we shall see, he, like Weber, attributes to the moral order only a relative independence from natural economic factors, physical geography and population size.

(2) The Descriptive-Normative parameter

Most theories attempt not only to tell us what society is but also to make recommendations for its improvement. The former is the factual or 'descriptive' element in a theory, the latter the 'normative', prescriptive or evaluative one. Theories differ in the degree of emphasis that they place on the one as against the other, and for this reason, we may speak of a descriptive–normative parameter.

The term 'normative' has to be used with care. For the idealist society is by definition a normative order, and all theories to some extent concern norms. Social theorists, we have noted, differ about what norms are: whether for instance, they are to be construed as threats (as some materialists argue) or as the objects of rational intuitions (an idealist position), but they must all go some way towards describing the nature, content and operation of norms, and they must give us information about the social norms which are followed in particular societies. In this sense all social theories are normative. But, for this reason, it is unhelpful to use 'normative' to cover any theory which deals with norms, even descriptively.

To describe norms is not the same thing as to make a normative statement any more than to describe a game is to play it. I shall therefore reserve the term 'normative' for the assertion (or criticism and evaluation) of norms and behaviour of the sort that occurs when we are not engaged in talking about morality, for instance, but asking ourselves what we ought to do, when this involves asking not what is in fact expected of us, but what ought to be expected of us. Such questions cannot be answered without adopting some standard or ideal of what social relationships or individual behaviour should be like. Morality, in this sense, is a critical activity since it involves opening up questions about the correctness of social norms.

It is a complicated question of practical philosophy to know exactly where to draw the boundary between descriptive and normative assertions. The most common way is to distinguish between statements of verifiable fact and any form of recommendation. But some recommendations are really in part factual claims as they merely tell us how best to achieve our desired objectives, that is, they are about the best means to assumed ends, and are, in technical terms, 'hypothetical' rather than 'categorical'. We might say that genuine evaluations or prescriptions are about the choice of the ends or ultimate objectives of human activities. This is often said to be the sphere of morality. But there are clearly values other than moral ones which feature in our evaluation of ends; aesthetic values, for instance, or judgements of beauty, are clearly just as normative as moral judgements. And in social theory it can be claimed that legal, political and religious judgements, for instance, are not reducible to moral ones and yet are clearly evaluative or prescriptive.

The difficulty of determining exactly where the boundary between descriptive and normative assertions is to be drawn, however, increases rather than diminishes the importance of distinguishing between the two types of assertion since the type of evidence which is relevant to the proof of descriptive statements is quite different from that which goes to justify normative assertions; observations about what is or has been the case do not in themselves establish what ought to be done or what situations are desirable in themselves. To argue that what ought to be the case follows logically from a statement about what is the case, is a common error which is called the 'naturalistic fallacy'. We will see that this is a trap into which many social theorists fall.

Pre-modern social theorists such as Aristotle, Hobbes and Smith do not attach great significance to the descriptive-normative parameter and happily incorporate a measure of prescription into their theories. But because of the controversial nature of the appropriate method for justifying any normative assertions and the incorrigibility of evaluative disagreements, modern theorists such as Marx, Durkheim and Weber attempt to purge their theories of all normative elements and present a purely descriptive system of thought. Indeed it is the boast of many modern social thinkers that the content of their theories is, in Weber's phrase, 'value-free', although few if any are entirely successful in making good this claim. We have, therefore, to locate each theory along the descriptive-normative parameter, both according to its stated intentions and in the light of its actual performances. It is an important fact about a social theorist's approach that he is endeavouring to confine himself to descriptive and explanatory enterprises, for this alerts us to the type of evidence which is relevant to his material, but we also have to be aware of the ease with which normative elements encroach into such theories, often without the supporting argumentation which is present in more overtly normative theories.

(3)   *The Individualistic-Holistic parameter*

Perhaps the most fundamental and persistent difference between social theories is the significance attributed to the characteristics of the human individual in contrast to the qualities of groups or of society as a whole in the explanation of behaviour.

We have noted, in comparing Hobbes and Durkheim, that Hobbes is an 'individualist' in that he deduces all social organization from the properties of individual human beings who are autonomous, fully-formed persons independently of the social relationships into which they enter, whereas Durkheim is a 'holist' in that he sees society as an independent force that gives form and substance to the life of the individual person. This is simply one manifestation of an ancient contrast between the individual and society which takes many forms and which presents all the complexities of a chicken-and-egg conundrum, since in any actual social situation it seems hard to tell whether the characteristics of individuals are the causes or the effects of the type of group or society in which they live. Adam Smith perhaps best exemplifies the compromise position here since he accepts an underlying basic uniformity of human nature which is, however, moulded to a limited extent by the individual's social experience.

The distinction between individualistic and holistic theories cuts across that between description and evaluation in that individualism may be either a descriptive or an evaluative thesis. Evaluatively the individualist holds that only individuals matter: the interests, wishes and happiness of individuals are what count in the determination of moral and political priorities. In itself this is hardly controversial unless the evaluative thesis is made more specific by saying that what is important about individuals is their 'individualism', by which is meant having the qualities of distinctiveness, of being different from and independent of others, or being self-sufficient and successful in competitive situations. It is, however, possible to accept—as probably even Marx does—the general view that only individuals count in moral terms without espousing the values of what might be called the competitive or 'rugged' individualism of extreme 'liberal' ideology in contrast to the more socialist individualism which stresses the essentially co-operative nature of human self-fulfilment. In these terms both Hobbes and Durkheim are evaluative individualists in the broad sense, with Hobbes tending towards the competitive and Durkheim towards the co-operative versions of the thesis. But there are also elements in Durkheim (and some would say in Aristotle and Marx) of evaluative holism, that is the thesis that the interests of society as a whole take precedence over those of individuals, particularly where those individuals are 'anti-social' in that they do not fit into the organic unity of society. In its extreme form—as in fascism or totalitarian socialism—evaluative holism requires the complete subordination of the individual to society or the state without this being justified in turn by the benefits derived by individuals from social and political institutions.

In its descriptive form, individualism is rather complex. Its central thesis is that the behaviour of individuals is ultimately explicable in terms of a theory of human nature rather than by reference to a theory of society. There are really two central issues involved here. The first is the question of whether or not society can in the end be described without reference to social categories. Thus, can we say what it is for a person to play the role of a father or economist without bringing in reference to the institution of the family or the existence of professional groups? In the case of fatherhood, it might be thought that this can be done by citing the facts about biological paternity which in themselves make no reference to the social institution of the family, but it may be that we cannot actually say what it is to be a father in a particular society without reference to the social norms of fatherhood which pertain there.

It is a separate question, however, how far such behaviour, once described, is to be explained in terms of individual or social characteristics. The central contention of what is called 'methodological individualism' is that social phenomena, however described, are explicable only by reference to the intentions, motives and attributes of individuals, whereas 'methodological holism', in its extreme form at any rate, takes the opposite view and asserts that all social explanations terminate in facts about societies, such as population size, the extent of the division of labour, and so on. It is on this issue that we have the clearest contrast between the individualism of Hobbes and Smith on the one hand and the holism of Durkheim and Marx on the other.

(4) The Conflict-Consensus parameter.

On this parameter, at one extreme are those theories according to which a society is organized conflict and competition—either between individuals or groups—the outcome of which is determined by various forms of power or coercion, economic, political or 'spiritual' (that is through the manipulation of beliefs and feelings). At the other extreme are those theories which view conflict as only a surface matter obscuring large areas of agreement or consensus on basic values and the prime modes of social organization.

The continued existence of any society requires a degree of adherence to shared norms, but this need not amount to consensus in the sense of willing endorsement of the norms in question. Conformity can be the result of sanctions, either of the brute physical sort which is threatened against 'law-breakers' or the more subtle pressures of public opinion and social ostracism. And it is, of course, the 'sanction' of economic necessity that leads many people to act as if they shared the values of the controlling individuals or groups within a social organization. Conflict theories stress these elements of coercion and power, while consensus theories tend to assume that the use of sanctions can only be peripheral in the attainment of social order.

This parameter also has an evaluative as well as a descriptive form, since the elimination of conflict and domination is often presented as a social ideal—as in Aristotle and Marx—whereas there are those who regard competitive conflict, resolved in terms of the relative power of the contestants, as being an inevitable or even a welcome expression of the values of forcefulness, aggression and achievement, something that all men desire and which is to be admired. These evaluations can be separated from the factual argument about the degree of consensus which exists in actual societies.

Hobbes has a descriptive individualistic theory, which assumes a major element of conflict in all social relationships, while Durkheim is a descriptive (and perhaps normative) holist theorist who dwells on consensual harmony, but the extent to which societies are seen as arenas of conflict does not always vary with the individualistic-holistic parameter. Marx, for instance, has a holistic theory which has become the classic descriptive theory of social conflict, in his case the struggle being between social classes.

The conflict-consensus parameter is closely tied to the concept of power or the capacity to obtain compliance to one's wishes in the face of opposition to those wishes. Obvious examples of this are in the use of force, or of money. But conceptual difficulties arise over the 'power' to mould opinion, belief or values and so to bring about a consensus which would not otherwise have existed. If this is a form of power then an apparently willing consensus can still be seen as the consequence of the exercise of power. Hence the importance of concepts such as 'socialization' and 'false-consciousness' (see p. 124) in social theories, for the extent to which the learning process is seen as a matter of the free exchange of ideas and knowledge or as the manipulation of socially relevant beliefs and values is one of the key variables which tends to get lost in any crude distinction between conflict and consensus theories.

While conflict theories stress power (the capacity to obtain compliance to one's will in the face of opposition), consensus theories dwell more on the idea of authority (the right to create rules and require obedience to them). Where this right is based not on the threat of sanctions but on the willing and informed agreement of the members of a society, authority may be contrasted with power. At their most extreme, consensus theories hold not simply that 'law' defined as general rules backed by physical coercion cannot be the basis of social order, but that we should see legal systems themselves and a fortiori non-legal social norms, as expressing a social consensus to which the use of coercion has only a marginal relevance.

(5) *The Positivist-Interpretative parameter*

This parameter has to do with the assumptions made by theorists about the type of explanation suited to social phenomena. I have touched on this issue already in chapter 1 in relation to the nature of social theory. Positivists, it will be remembered, consider that the approach to social phenomena should be no different in principle from that adopted to natural or non-social pheomena. They believe that society can be studied scientifically and that science has to do with establishing interlocking sets of causal generalizations, so that to explain a phenomenon is to show that it is of type X which is constantly associated temporally and spatially with other phenomena of type Y; an event is explained when it is shown to be an instance of a causal law of the form 'whenever event type Y (the cause) occurs, there follows event type X (the effect)'. When *x* and *y* are observable phenomena the causal generalization can be disproved by seeing that there are *y*s which are not followed by *x*s. Such observations falsify causal generalizations which must then be abandoned or modified to take account of the observed exceptions. Causal generalizations or laws are themselves explained by subsuming them under yet more general causal correlations.

Such explanations are, for the positivist, intellectually satisfying and provide valuable knowledge, for they can be used to predict the future and so anticipate or control events. Social knowledge of this sort is a form of power which can be used to alter social phenomena by intervening in the causal process in such a way as to obtain more desirable outcomes. For instance, the knowledge that density of population increases the level of crime can be used to reduce crime through the dispersal of population. The positivist regards such causal knowledge as both illuminating and useful.

The positivist intellectual ideal draws its inspiration from the development of natural science. We will see that it plays an important part in social theory from the time of Hobbes, although the term 'positivism' is most closely associated with eighteenth-century Frenchman Auguste Comte (see p. 140). No doubt if positivist sociologists had been as successful as natural scientists their approach to social explanation would be without serious rivals. But, whatever the reason may be— whether it is the ideal nature of social phenomena, their complexity or the fact that individuals have a freedom of choice which eludes causal explanation—the results of positivism have been less than satisfactory according to the strict canons of scientific logic which require precise testable causal correlations. Such causal hypotheses as have been put forward in social 'science' tend to be too localized or too imprecise to be serious candidates for the status of causal laws.

This lack of success may, of course, be due to the immaturity of the scientific study of society, but it does give rival types of explanation the chance of challenging the appropriateness of the positivistic approach to social phenomena. We have seen that one alternative is the more common-sense approach of interpreting social behaviour in the light of the meaning which is attributed to it by the participants. This involves noting the intentions, motives and reasons of social agents and explaining why they behave as they do in terms of their beliefs and values. This is alleged to help us to understand social phenomena without reducing them to a causal straight-jacket, for we can appreciate someone's reasons or motives for action without holding that he was caused to behave in that way. This rival mode of explanation which draws on the meaningfulness of human behaviour is called 'interpretative'. It is closely associated with the methodology of Max Weber, although he is by no means an extreme example of this approach. Its objective is to describe social phenomena in such a way as to give us the sort of understanding of them which is, at least in principle, available to the agents themselves but cannot be in any straightforward way 'observed' by the onlooker.

This emphasis on the subjective meaningfulness of social interactions gives interpretative explanatory approaches an affinity with idealism; similarly there is an obvious tie-up between positivism and materialism since the sociological positivists seeks to follow the methods of the natural sciences, which deal with the material realm. But the overlap between the two parameters is by no means complete. Many of those who tend to idealism by believing in an autonomous field of socially fundamental mental phenomena are also positivists in seeking to follow the causal model of the natural sciences in their sociological explanations. Durkheim, and probably Adam Smith, fall into this category. It is therefore a mistake to assume that those whom I have called sociological idealists necessarily tend towards interpretative explanations in social theory.

Taken to their logical extreme (as Schutz, for instance, tends to do), interpretative explanations can be offered only of particular historical occurrences. This is unsatisfactory so far as providing a theory of society is concerned, for we are not then able to generalize in a way which fulfils the theoretical goals of abstraction and comprehensiveness. As in Max Weber's case, interpretative schemes tend, therefore, to be conjoined to some sort of causal programme. Moreover it is hard for even the most committed positivist to exclude from his repertoire explanations which gain their force from interpretative understanding. This gives the positivist-interpretative contrast the characteristic of a parameter. It is a parameter on which it is often very hard to locate a particular theorist as the endless debates concerning the proper exegesis of Marx's methodology demonstrates (see p. 116). But it is important to be as clear as we can on where each theorist stands on this parameter for this determines the ultimate objective of his theoretical endeavours.

Many other contrasts could be drawn and other parameters suggested for the purposes of comparing theories of society: the emphasis placed on the similarities rather than the differences between societies, the degree of stress placed on political factors in social theory, the relative attention given to the static or unchanging elements of societies as against the causes or reasons for social change and development, and within theories of social change, the contrast between those that are evolutionary and those that are revolutionary. All these are important theoretical divisions which could have been dealt with at length. But we have now sufficient parameters to be going on with and I will now turn to the topic of the assessment of theories of society.

CRITICAL CRITERIA

Within the confines of this book we shall be dealing with the broad sweep of major social theories which illustrate the main types of theory from which we may choose in order to establish a satisfactory theoretical approach to the study of society. At this level of generality, selection and criticism do not typically call for straightforward judgements of truth and falsity as would be the case if theories consisted merely of simple descriptive statements. Each theorist evolves his own abstract conceptual framework in the light of which he picks out and presents the social facts he considers significant, and formulates the sort of explanations and recommendations which provide him with intellectual and moral satisfaction. Theories are always open to criticism in term of counter evidence in so far as they involve empirical generalizations, but detailed empirical failures may not be of crucial importance for a theory as a whole, and the general approach to the study of society may be completely unaffected by new empirical evidence which can usually be fitted into the theory by making minor modifications. No one, for instance, is going to put aside the Hobbesian theory simply because it conflicts in some detail with the findings of modern psychology, for theories of a Hobbesian type can readily be erected on empirical evidence which is not obviously deficient by modern standards.

Instead of looking for neat empirical proofs and disproofs of a general social theory, it is often better to think in terms of the fruitfulness of each theoretical approach in helping us to sort out and understand social life. Theorists tend to do this by identifying a familiar aspect of social life in their own society and attempting to see social phenomena as being reducible to the same sort of thing. We shall encounter many examples of the resulting parochialism which oversimplifies, by ignoring and distorting that which does not fit into the favoured type of relationship, be it dominance (power), exchange (self-interest) or communalism (fraternity).

The opposite danger in a social theory is extreme generality amounting to vacuity when ill-defined and amorphous concepts are used to cover very many different things to no significant explanatory benefit. This happens, for instance, when all the ills of modern industrial society are lumped together as manifestations of man's 'alienated' condition.

It may be that any over-arching theory of society is going to fall between these two errors of parochialism and vacuity and that in the end they can be tested only by seeing how they work out in generating particular detailed empirical studies which prove to have relevance to current human interests. Nevertheless it is possible to list some criteria and common faults for which we can be on the look-out when examining each theory and which will help us at least to develop some rationally grounded attitudes towards them.

(1) Clarity

Clarity is the first requirement of a social theory since what is unclear can be neither fully understood nor properly assessed. It is a requirement which is often missing in those social theories which employ the rather loose terminology of everyday life. Other social theories are beset by jargon and technical terms. This is not necessarily a vice since we need to refine the language of untrained social comment if we are to achieve precision, and, once important distinctions have been made, these have to be labelled in order that we should not slip back into the imprecisions of everyday language. It is, however, a grave defect in a theory of society if its key terms are poorly defined or its central contentions obscurely stated.

Much of our critical efforts will therefore be directed towards expounding the specialist terminology of our social theorists, particularly those used by holists like Durkheim who speak of such entities as the 'collective conscience'. But less obscure terms such as Adam Smith's 'impartial spectator' also need to be examined with care and we must also be suspicious of the unexplained adoption of everyday language, which is often too ambiguous to serve as an adequate vehicle for theoretical analysis. Clarity is, therefore, the first requirement of a social theory. What is not clear cannot be a candidate for rational assessment.

(2) Consistency

If clarity is needed to gain entry to the fold of viable social theories, consistency is required to remain there. The whole point of a theoretical approach is to present a view of society which coheres. This means, in the first place, internal coherence. A theory must not contradict itself by asserting or denying in one place what it denies or asserts in another.

Obviously theorists may properly change their views over time but persistent contradictions are a grave source of weakness in a theory. One example is to be found in Hobbes who appears to presuppose concepts and activities as existing in the state of nature, at the point at which the contract is made, which cannot *ex hypothesi*, arise until society has been established by the contract (see p. 86). Similarly we need to look carefully at the possible inconsistency in Marx's rejection of all objective values in his analysis of capitalist societies since he apparently goes on to assume some of these values when he welcomes the freedom and community which are to be features of communist society.

Even if internal contradictions can be avoided, a theory is also judged by how well it hangs together as a mutually supporting set of assumptions. For instance, it is a strength, so far as consistency goes, that Smith's economic theory dovetails with his utilitarian ethics and his theological beliefs, although this of course presents problems if we wish to develop a non-theological version of Smithian economics.

(3) Empirical Adequacy

For the positivist, the key test of a theory is the extent to which it is corroborated, or, perhaps, not falsified, by repeatable observations. Certainly no theory can stand which is based on factual assertions which are plainly false. In dealing with general theories the disproof of some of the factual claims embodied in its particular applications may not be very serious. No social theory ever met its end over a minor error of fact. But persistent failure to produce empirical statements which correspond with observed social phenomena in areas of central concern to a theory undermines the credibility of a whole approach. No Marxist theory could survive clear evidence of the absence of conflict in the capitalist economic systems, and the empirical foundation of Weber's thesis that there is a correlation between protestantism and the emergence of capitalism obviously affects the credibility of his theory as a whole.

The most common error of social theorists is over-hasty generalization from limited empirical evidence. Thus Durkheim passes too readily from observations about the religious practices of Australian aborigines to pronouncements about religion in general. The same can be said about Marx's extrapolation of his findings concerning the early stages of capitalism to other radically different economic situations.

The assessment of the empirical element in social theories is a difficult matter. Much depends on historical facts which are no longer available to us. Other difficulties relate to the nature of the phenomena in question. Rule-following behaviour, which, as we have seen, sociological idealists regard as central to social behaviour, cannot be directly observed in the physical movements of participants but must always be to an extent inferred or imputed on the basis of observation. Moreover, it is usually impossible to conduct social experiments to test empirical hypotheses, especially when these relate to large-scale social changes over long periods.

Despite these difficulties, the appeal to the observed facts of human social interactions provides the most objective test available of the descriptive content of social theories, and any social theory, even an interpretative one, whose hypotheses are consistently falsified by empirical evidence, must be rejected.

(4) Explanatory Adequacy

Theories must not only fit the facts of social life, they must also explain them. At this point there is an inevitable circularity in assessing social theories, for each theorist appeals to his own standards of what constitutes a good explanation and uses his own selection of what he considers needs explanation. Very often a theorist can cope well with his chosen data using his own model of explanation but this may not be adequate beyond these confines. Thus, even if Weber's analysis of rational action is convincing it does not help us so much with the many examples of non-rational 'action' which, as he allows, are a feature of social interactions. Because these non-rational elements are more difficult to render meaningful, they tend to fit less readily into Weber's picture of society.

In testing explanatory adequacy, therefore, we need to look at the theory in the light of data which it does *not* present and in terms of explanatory ideals which are foreign to it, and not simply view it against its own selected data and its own standards of explanation.

(5)   Normative rationality

Any values or norms presented or endorsed within a theory of human society constitute its most 'subjective' aspect and, in the end, assessment of the evaluative content of a theory is a matter for personal moral judgement which cannot be tested except by reference to the individual's own moral standards.

What can be expected of the social theory, however, is that its values and prescriptions, and their implications, be correctly identified, clearly expounded and consistently maintained. Where this is achieved it is possible for us at least to compare them with our own value assumptions. Moreover, theorizing about alternative social organizations and rival ways of life can act as a stimulus to moral reflection so that the evaluative content of a theory of society may lead the individual to revise his own normative assumptions. The study of social theories can thus be taken up into the development of the individual's own moral ideas.

There are many pitfalls in the path towards clarity, consistency, empirical corroboration, explanatory adequacy and normative rationality. Often some of these standards are met at the expense of others. Consistency may be achieved at the price of vagueness or on the basis of biased selection of empirical evidence. Apparently illuminating explanations can collapse before the demand for more clarity of expression. Other types of pitfall occur in the confusion of the various types of assertion which go to make up a theory. Definitions (e.g. stating what the word 'capitalism' means) are passed off as descriptions of what goes on in actual societies (e.g. in economies which we customarily call capitalist). And descriptions of what is the case are mysteriously transformed into assertions about what ought to be the case (the 'naturalistic fallacy'). In the examination of our theories of human society we must keep an eye open for such lapses in argumentation as well as noting the more obvious ways in which theories fail to match up to our five critical criteria.

I will conclude this introductory part of the book with a word about the chronological order in which the theories are presented in Part Two. This mode of presentation is not intended to suggest that there is a clear line of progress in social theory from the earliest to the most recent. It is nearer the truth to say that there are fashions in social theory which derive in part from the social problems of the time and which throw up recurrent themes. However every major theorist introduces ideas and approaches of such significance that they have at least to be taken into account by those who come after them. For this reason there is something approaching an orderly development in social theorizing in that each theorist to an extent responds to the work of his predecessors. This is true even in the case of the historical leap which I have made from Aristotle to Hobbes and Smith. Greek thought was rediscovered in the Renaissance so that Hobbes, for instance, is very conscious of where he disagrees with Aristotle. And many of the eighteenth-century Enlightenment thinkers were steeped in Aristotle's ideas, as Smith's use of the concept of 'nature' illustrates.

Similarly a great deal of Smith's social theory is a conscious refutation of Hobbesianism (in fact he absorbs as much as he rejects of Hobbes's individualism) although it was the novelty of Smith's emphasis of the concept of society itself and the notion of a social system that had most impact on later theorists. This combination of overt criticism and substantial borrowing is a feature of the relationship between many theorists. Marx scorns Adam Smith for his 'bourgeois individualism' but uses much of Smith's analysis of capitalism and develops Smith's idea of historical stages. Weber, in turn, has to be read in the light of his criticisms and accommod-

ations to Marxism, while Schutz's contribution is a deployment of selected themes from Weber's work.

There is thus a dialectic process of argument and counter-
argument in the history of social thought which justifies the
historical order employed in Part Two. To what extent this
dialectical process has resulted in theoretical progress students
of social theory must judge for themselves.

FOR FURTHER READING

For the standard concepts used in most social theories consult the
books recommended at the end of chapter 1. In addition R. M.
McIver and C. H. Page, *Society* (Macmillan: London, 1950) is still
useful, if a little dated. See also Percy Cohen, *Modern Social Theory*
(Heinemann: London, 1968); Ralph Dahrendorf, *Essays in Social
Theory* (Routledge: London, 1968): Stephen Mennell, *Sociological
Theory* (Nelson: London, 1974); Dorothy Emmet, *Rules, Rôles and
Relations* (Macmillan: London, 1966); and Robert A Nisbet, *The
Sociological Tradition* (Heinemann: London, 1967).

On idealism and materialism in social theory see Vernon Pratt, *The
Philosophy of the Social Sciences* (Methuen: London, 1978).

For the distinction between description and prescription see R. M.
Hare, *The Language of Morals* (Oxford University Press: London,
1952). There is a good collection of articles on individualism and
holism, *Modes of Collectivism and Individualism* (Heinemann: London,
1973), ed. by John O'Neill. See also Philip Pettit, *Judging Justice*
(Routledge: London, 1980), Part II, and Steven Lukes
'Methodological Individualism Reconsidered', *British Journal of
Sociology*, Vol. 19 (1968) pp. 119–29; this is reprinted in Dorothy
Emmet and Alistair McIntyre, (eds.), *Sociological Theory and Philosophical Analysis* (Macmillan: London, 1970) which contains other
relevant articles.

PART TWO   Seven theories

CHAPTER 3

Aristotle: The Civic
Community

ARISTOTLE views human society as an ethical enterprise,
rooted in man's natural sociability, which is directed at the
realization, in a political community, of moral goodness and
intellectual excellence.

Aristotle was not primarily a social theorist but, as the
originator of the 'Aristotelian' philosophy which dominated the
thinking of medieval Europe and hence Catholic theology to
the present day, his ideas underlie a long and far from extinct
tradition in social theorizing according to which society is an
expression of, and a requirement for, man's particular type of
nature or 'being'.

Aristotle attended Plato's Academy in Athens for twenty
years and later set up his own school, the Lyceum, in that same
city-state. But he was not himself an Athenian. He was born in
384 B.C. into a medical family at Stagira, a small oligarchy
which was taken into the expanding feudal kingdom of
Macedonia. He spent many of his mature years also outside
Athens. For a while he was under the protection of the
philosophically minded 'tyrant' Hermias at Atarneus where
he studied marine biology. Later he was tutor to the young
Alexander before his pupil became the famous king of
Macedonia. Aristotle never fully accepted the democratic
practices of the Athenians who expelled him, during a wave of
anti-Macedonian feeling, shortly before his death at the age of
sixty-five. He thus narrowly escaped the fate of his illustrious
predecessor Socrates.

The writings of Aristotle, most of which are in the form of
lecture notes, cover natural science, metaphysics, ethics, logic,
rhetoric, aesthetics and politics. The most important from the
point of view of social theory are the *Nicomachean Ethics* and the
Politics. If his writings have a common theme it is that each

type of natural object, or being, has an inherent potentiality which explains its characteristic development or movement towards its particular end or 'telos'. In the case of man, a species of animal, this telos involves the full flowering of his social nature in the friendship between equal citizens within a properly constituted city-state. He can therefore be seen as the theorist of society as a civic or political community.

ARISTOTLE'S APPROACH

Aristotle's philosophy is naturalistic and teleological. It is naturalistic firstly in that it is empirical, at least to the extent that Aristotle is much more concerned than Plato, for instance, to apply to all spheres of thought the methods of observation and classification which he was taught as a medical student and carried on in his biological fieldwork. Thus, at the Lyceum, he set his students to study over 150 types of political constitution. His approach is also naturalistic in a further sense: he believes that the universe consists of a hierarchy of beings each with a nature or essence whose full development represented its own standard of excellence, so that his empirical observations of movement and growth merges with a form of evaluation according to which what is natural is good. In this teleological form of naturalism each type of being has a 'final' cause which makes it develop towards its appointed telos, this being both an empirical and a normative idea.

Aristotle's naturalistic view of the universe does not depend on theological beliefs. It is designed to explain change and development in natural terms (although he does bring in an 'unmoved mover'). But he retains elements of the theory of 'forms' or 'ideas' which Plato uses to explain similarities between things: thus everything which is beautiful is said to participate in the 'form' or 'idea' of beauty; this is what gives them their unity and explains their beauty. Plato is an idealist (see p. 28) and his 'forms' are transcendental entities lying beyond ordinary experience in a spiritual or heavenly world known only to the purified mind of the true philosopher, but

Aristotle thinks that the forms can be studied empirically by observing the physical world, analysing its constituent parts and noting the processes of growth. Aristotle thinks that it is possible to discover the final causes which determine the end towards which a thing moves or develops. He also investigates efficient causes, that is the immediate causes of events (nearer but not quite equivalent to the modern sense of cause), and also material causes, that is the stuff of which things are made. Thus as the result of an efficient cause, say mating, there comes about the existence of an embryo which has the same raw material as some other entities (the material cause) but has its own particular form which determines into what sort of being it develops, given the right conditions (the final cause). Whether studying embryos or political constitutions Aristotle is always concerned to examine existing phenomena, but his assumption is that each type of thing has a 'natural' perfection which might not be realized in any particular case but which can nevertheless be discovered by looking at its normal development.

Aristotle's way of approaching objects is clearly medical and biological in that it uses ideas of the growth of organisms towards maturity and the conception of health as normal functioning. He applies this method to ethics by thinking of virtue as consisting in the proper working of man's characteristic features, which he equates with happiness ('eudaimonia'). He relates this to social and political theory by observing that these functions involve participating in the telos of a larger whole, the society-state. For this reason he regards politics as the master science (*Ethics*, Book I, Chapter 2). By studying how to achieve the good life political science determines the subordinate place of other branches of thought, like medicine, military science or household management, which are of value only for the contribution they make to the overall good of the community. It is, therefore, to the organization of the total community that Aristotle looks for his standards of normative judgement and it is the good of the community as a whole to which he gives priority over the desires and well-being of particular individuals, lending some substance to the view that there is a touch of normative holism in his approach. This gives his ideal civic community an authoritarian aspect and goes with his distrust of pure democracy which he considers to be an unstable form of society.

ARISTOTLE'S THEORY OF MAN

Aristotle's biological approach involves analysing entities into their parts and classifying them by species and genus. Thus man is an animal with certain distinctive elements, particularly reason and speech. They are important because they give him the capacity to conform to ethical standards. These qualities are superimposed on non-rational elements, common to all animals, such as the processes of unconscious organic growth, and emotions or appetites, like sexual desire and instinct, which tend towards some fulfilment or 'good', particularly the avoidance of pain and the search for pleasure. The rational part is conscious and deliberative. It is divided into practical reason which has the function of controlling appetites (for, unlike animals which are governed by habit, men can consciously control their non-rational impulses) and theoretical reason, which is able to grasp the workings of the universe and understand its operations. The latter constitutes man's highest and most distinctive activity: the life of contemplation.

The basic appetites of man are social to an extent, in that they include the desire for a sexual partner, a natural affection for others and a desire for their company for its own sake. But the pursuit of pleasure, the pride of power over others and the passion for unlimited acquisition, make man overall, at least in his uneducated and unsocialized state, wicked. Men in general are greedy and cowardly, and since they have the power to act at will (unlike the animals) they are, when separated from the law of justice, which Aristotle equates with reason, 'the worst of animals' (*Politics*, Book I, Chapter 2). This slavery to the lower pleasures is the condition of most men, but Aristotle, believing in man's potential to discover and prefer the higher pleasures of moral and mental activity, looks to the life of a well-ordered community, for which man has in any case a certain affinity, to develop his true nature. Society is therefore natural to man because he has within him the efficient causes of social existence, sexual desire and the need for the companionship, and also because it is only with a social group that his nature can develop.

A central part of man's rational nature is the capacity to follow standards of conduct. Aristotle maintains that moral standards represent a 'mean' or balance between certain extremes and deficiencies in human feeling and behaviour. Thus courage is a mean between cowardice and rashness and generosity is a balance between being stingy and being prodigal (*Ethics*, Book II, Chapter 6). The same is true of other moral virtues such as justice, magnanimity, good temper and temperateness. Aristotle considers that the precise level of feeling and type of action which exhibits the mean is hard, perhaps impossible, to determine, so that much has to be left to the judgement of the man of practical reason who has experience of all pleasures. But virtue consists primarily in the disposition to conform to such general standards and this comes about principally through a thorough and strict education which renders virtuous conduct habitual.

Virtue is not, however, the only aspect of the good life which is made possible by, and helps to further, social existence. Social co-operation is also necessary for the security and material prosperity which is required for the flourishing of the higher human capacities, particularly the life of theoretical contemplation, the self-sufficient and therefore the most satisfying and worth-while of human activities.

Man's natural sociability takes many forms. Aristotle brings them together under the heading of friendship ('philia') by which he means a lasting affectionate bond between individuals that involves a desire for co-operation (*Ethics*, Books VIII and IX, and *Politics*, Book II, Chapter 4). As with many of Aristotle's concepts, friendship has both a sociological and a normative function. Some form of friendship is an element at every level of community life: sexual and paternal affection are bonds in the family life, and in the wider sphere mutual benevolence arises when people find each other pleasant (as with young people), or useful, (as in commercial relationships). But the highest form of friendship is one in which those who are equal love each other because of their goodness: this, the most lasting, satisfying and unifying human relationship, is possible only between mature, moderately wealthy citizens of a small city community. The friendship of equals is at once a major unifying force in this community and the telos of human relationships. It is a model of perfect consensus. But since only a few men can ever attain to that perfect friendship which could by itself sustain consensual community life, actual societies are marred by a degree of conflict and must be organized according to rules of justice inculcated by state-directed education and backed by considerable compulsion. The human capacity to understand and follow rules, which arises from man's rationality, is therefore as important in making social life possible as is the human potential for forming affectionate relationships. To this extent an element of Plato's idealism remains in Aristotle's theory of man.

ARISTOTLE'S THEORY OF SOCIETY

Aristotle's conception of society and the state are so intertwined that it is better to use his own term, 'polis', to denote the civic community which he believes to be man's natural social setting (*Politics*, Book I). The small city-state, with its face-to-face relationships and the mingling of personal friendship with the obligations of citizenship, is quite unlike the modern nation-state, or the ancient imperial kingdoms of Aristotle's own time, although the polis does incorporate a well developed and institutionalised idea of the rule of law, that is of government through general rules and not by the arbitrary decisions of individuals.

Aristotle's most general term for a social group is 'koinonia', which covers all sorts of community or association in which there is any degree of sharing or partnership. The simplest group is the family or household ('oikos') which arises from the sexual or pairing instinct which man shares with the animals and is supported by the mutual love of parents and children. These implanted or innate affections are the forms of friendship that sustain the familial koinonia which provides the context for the life of all individuals in the early stages of social development and remains the centre of existence for women and children even in the polis.

The family or household is, however, more than a sexual, reproductive and rearing institution. Originally it serves a defensive role, and it remains the basic economic unit. Aristotle believes that farming is the most natural form of economic activity so that the extended family of the household (father, wife, children, other blood relations and slaves who perform both domestic and agricultural labour), is the proper means for the provision of material needs as well as an essential part of the educational process in even the most fully developed society.

The friendship of the household is not one of equality. The father's love for wife and children is the love of a natural superior. It creates obligations of care towards them but it also gives the father a dominant role in the family unit, particularly with regard to the children. In this patriarchal set-up the master of the house, because of his superior strength and wisdom, rules the wife as if he were a limited monarch, the children he rules as if he were an absolute monarch and towards his slaves he is a despot, these graduations reflecting the extent to which the master defers to the views of those whom he rules. Wife and children are treated as ends in themselves although deficient in rationality. Slaves have no reason beyond the capacity to understand what is required of them, they therefore require total direction from the master. Thus differences in natural capacity are used as a basis for a simple division of labour and a quasi-political familial organisation.

The household is the most basic type of community but it is limited in the scope which it affords for the development of human nature. Because of the need to make better provision for material requirements and self-defence, natural social development is towards the village. Villages are associations of families based largely on considerations of utility. The friendship bond to which they give rise is limited to that which feeds on the recognition of mutual need, the friendship of utility.

The same considerations that lead to the growth of the village result in the emergence of the polis as an association of villages around a central town. Not only does the polis increase security against external attack and facilitate the trading which is necessary for economic development, it also provides the setting for genuine friendship between equals. A polis consists of a community which is self-sufficient materially, militarily and ethically, having enough people in sufficient variety to support the material basis for the good life but not so many that they cannot get to know each other and form personal relationships based on frequent face-to-face contacts.

Although the polis arises historically after the household and the village, it is prior to these in the sense that it is the telos or end which gives point and place to the lesser forms of community. The polis perfects human life and is thus much more than an association based on the pre-existing desires of the individual.

Although the advantages of the polis include the economic progress made possible by the development of the division of labour and the military security provided by the larger unit, the economic and military purposes of the polis are limited, and require to be justified and controlled according to their usefulness in making possible a form of life which is neither militaristic (like Sparta) nor materialistic (as Athenian traders wished). The desires for power and wealth are not in themselves natural and are to be curbed once they lead beyond the satisfaction of those needs which must be met before men can enter into fully fraternal relationships and pursue the intellectual pleasures of theoretical wisdom.

Aristotle is not wildly unrealistic here. He accepts that human nature is such that total community of property and people is impractical (*Politics*, Book II, Chapter 5). No one can feel the same affection for everyone as he feels for his own family and none will work for the community as a whole as he will work for the benefit of himself and his family. Aristotle does advocate the common ownership of sufficient lands to support the communal meals and religious ceremonies he thought necessary to stimulate community feeling and loyalty. However the polis is in essence a union of small, relatively independent, farmers, together with a diversity of traders and artisans who provide the services required by agricultural activities and a certain limited degree of urban living.

Where Aristotle is utopian is in his insistence that the purpose of all this co-operation is the development of the virtue of each type of person within the polis which is in turn directed towards the attainment of the highest forms of human excellence by those few wealthier farmers and business men with the leisure and virtue to develop their faculties to the full.

Aristotle does not devote all his attention to these lofty ideals. He acknowledges that, while the friendship of equals is sufficient basis for the unity of the privileged elite, for most inhabitants of the polis friendship can flourish only if there are adequately enforced laws to regulate their interactions, particularly as regards the distribution of rewards and honours. This is why justice is the principle of order in political society.

'Justice' Aristotle tells us in Books V of *Nicomachean Ethics* is sometimes taken to mean all the demands of reason as they affect human relationships, but the more particular form of justice which is basic to the civic community has to do with the allocation of benefits in proportion to the deserts of those involved. What counts as desert varies from polis to polis, virtue and excellence being the criteria of distribution in an aristocracy, wealth in an oligarchy, and so on. In addition there is a need for rectificatory justice to make the necessary readjustments where injustices have arisen.

The principles of distributive and rectificatory justice are both moral and legal, for Aristotle makes no distinction between the two means of social control. In the polis the rules of justice are inculcated through a politically controlled educational system and administered by magistrates and juries selected from among the citizens and also, in important cases, by the whole assembly of citizens (*Politics*, Book VIII, Chapter 1). As their source is in human reason they are, in their most general form, part of natural law and so fundamentally the same in all places; thus in every polis equals are to be treated as equals. There is however a conventional element which varies from polis to polis, but even this variable element is not decided from day to day by the assembly of citizens but is a relatively fixed body of rules established by a legislator and generally only *applied* by the assembly, or its officers. The main public functions in which citizens participate are therefore judicial and executive rather than legislative, so that Aristotle is able to hold that even the rulers in a polis are subject to the law, and can argue that reason rather than corruptible men determines the normative framework of the civic community.

Aristotle does not accept complete democracy. His belief in the natural superiority of some men leads him to favour a privileged governing position for the best men and even for the wealthier sections of the community, but he is aware of the need for some sort of balance of interests in the polis between rich and poor and of the tendency of even good men to be corrupted by office. He therefore allows that all citizens might, in principle, be elected to the offices of magistrates and serve on juries, thus preserving a degree of equality among citizens and giving some basis for his assertion that the ideal polis is 'a community of equals, aiming at the best life possible' (*Politics*, Book VII, Chapter 8).

PRACTICAL IMPLICATIONS

The natural life for man is in a polis, but Aristotle is aware that there are different types of polis and that not all of these are equally suited to the development of human potential.

A polis is a community or koinonia whose members are citizens, a citizen being a person who has some sort of right to hold office in the city-state, even if only as a member of the assembly. (In Athens this was an inherited right and most inhabitants were non-citizens). The exact political function of the citizen is determined by the constitution of the polis. This lays down not only how the offices of power are to be distributed but also 'the end at which the community aims' (*Politics*, Book III, Chapter 6). Constitutions are thus both institutional and ethical, setting out not just who is to rule but the purpose of that rule. Since this purpose is the realization of a particular form of the good life, the virtue of the citizen is to carry out his citizenly duties to that specific end. And so, Aristotle concludes, the virtue of the good man is the same as that of the good citizen. This tight connection between the legal and the moral, and the fusion of social and political organization in the city-state, suggest the almost total absorption of the individual in the life and goals of the polis. In the polis there is no significant division between public and private. All aspects of the individual's life, from his tightly controlled education to the manner in which he carries out his particular part in the organic structure of the city-state, including the organization of the household in which he lives, are evaluated and governed by the purposes and institutions of the polis. Individual well-being is thus inseparable from the organization and ethos of the polis.

Aristotle's classification of types of polis is based on the make-up of the civic body which carries out the chief functions of government, namely making war and peace, modifying and interpreting laws, trying important criminal cases and electing magistrates to carry out day to day executive functions. This supreme or 'sovereign' body (which is not sovereign in the modern sense since it must govern within unchangeable laws) may consist of one person, a few, or many people, and in each case it may rule either in the interest of the polis as a whole or in the interests of the ruling group. In consequence there are six main types of polis. The three good forms are (1) kingship, when one man rules in the interests of the polis (2) aristocracy, when a few rule in the same manner and (3) polity, the rule of the many to the same end. The equivalent defective forms of rule are (1) tyranny (2) oligarchy and (3) democracy, the rule of one, few and many when directed towards the interests of the rulers themselves. Each ruling individual or group has certain characteristics and aims. The king pursues honour, the tyrant pleasure, aristocrats seek to perfect the virtue which is their qualification for office. Oligarchies consist of wealthy men pursuing yet more wealth; democracy, as the rule of the poor, favours complete liberty, while a polity is directed to moderate or consensual goals.

Aristotle's assessment of these different types of polis is obviously to some extent written into their definition since those forms which are not directed to the interests of the polis as a whole are clearly perverted. It might seem that his preference is for aristocracy since this best exemplifies the pursuit of excellence, and he does indeed regard aristocracy as an ideal form of government. But in the end he favours a mixed form of government, which is nearest to polity, as a compromise between what is best and what is practicable. He therefore admits an element of oligarchy into the constitution, making wealth a qualification for magisterial office in order to protect the interest of the rich against the liberty-loving poor who are nevertheless the dominant force in the assembly or civic body. He argues that with this constitution the influence of the moderate middle groups who are neither rich nor poor will be beneficially influential.

Aristotle does however have some arguments in favour of the democratic participation of all in government. He acknowledges that when each individual adds his wisdom to the deliberative group the total outcome of 'collective wisdom' is likely to be superior to that of a select group, and that, since the aim of government is the well-being of the polis as a whole, the judges of whether or not this is being achieved must be those whose interests are meant to be served by it. The main reason he has against total democracy is that the mass of people are too poor to be able to share in the time-consuming practice of ruling and develop the qualities of true friendship. Given the possibility of a polis in which there were no extremes of wealth or poverty a polity seems well suited to realizing his ethical objectives (*Politics* Book IV, Chapter 11).

It is possible, therefore, to extract from Aristotle a model of a community of equals united by ties of friendship jointly conducting their common business according to rationally justified impersonal laws. That he does not adopt this pure position reflects, to an extent, his realism. He sees himself as describing actualities rather than erecting speculative utopian schemes. He is aware that, given the facts of economic political life, only a relatively small number of people can have the leisure and prosperity to cultivate the style of virtuous friendship and wise ruling which represent the highest excellence of community existence and develop the intellectual pursuits in which the greatest human satisfactions are to be found. The necessities of the division of labour in the polis dictate that what should be for all is reserved for a few; consequently some form of oligarchy must operate in practice and the social bond must be rooted in mutual economic interest more than in the friendship of the virtuous.

But there is more to Aristotle's coolness towards democratic society than these practical considerations. He has more fundamental reasons for favouring a relatively aristocratic or meritocratic system: he simply does not believe in human equality. Not only does he regard women as inferior to men in reason and so in moral leadership, but among men there are natural divisions of intellect and birth. This is most obvious in the case of natural slaves who have only sufficient reason to follow the directions of their mental superiors, but it applies also within the class of citizens, some of whom are fit only for relatively menial tasks and what he regards as degrading activities such as trade and commerce. Only those of high natural ability and good birth are fit to rule and capable of attaining the cultivated life-style which Aristotle admires. The rest of the community are of lesser importance and their lower way of life is of significance largely because of the contribution it makes to maintaining the conditions necessary for the material security of the gifted few.

And so, paradoxically, having given us the materials to envisage a community of equals, Aristotle ends up with a hierarchical system: at the top are those well-born and relatively wealthy persons who are also virtuous. These are followed by the wealthy but non-virtuous sections of the community, the masters of agricultural households, all of whom have some place in the civic life of the polis. Beneath them are the mass of the towndwellers at work in trade, shops and manual labour and, at the bottom of the hierarchy, natural slaves and foreigners.

CRITICISM AND ASSESSMENT

The most devastating and direct criticism of Aristotle's theory of society is that he commits the naturalistic fallacy (see p. 35) by moving without justificatory arguments from factual observations about actual societies to normative conclusions about the ideal or best forms of social organization. His apparently empiricist regard for what is 'natural' turns out, it is said, to be a thinly disguised way of claiming some sort of objectivity or rationality for a particular style of life which he happens to regard as excellent. If by 'natural' we mean what occurs in nature then, although he may be correct in saying that some form of social organization is natural in that it is the universal condition of mankind and even in his view that there is a common core of human needs, this does not in itself show that any one type of society is superior to any other. Aristotle's use of the term 'nature' is therefore ambiguous and unclear. His confusion of 'ought' and 'is' under the terminology of 'nature' makes it difficult to know when Aristotle is describing and explaining social phenomena and when he is making value judgements about them.

Once we do separate out the empirical and the normative aspects each can be separately criticized. Thus historians have pointed out that, although much of the material he gathers on political constitutions provides valuable information about the ancient world, Aristotle does not give us an accurate picture of the Athenian system in that the emergence of the civic ideals Aristotle admires was in fact the work of the producing classes, the small traders, manufacturers, shopkeepers and wage-earners and not the landed and leisured class.

Even if he had correctly described something approaching an actual city-state his theory of society must be regarded as parochial even for his own time in that he fails to see the instability and weakness of a system which depended on a particular form of small farm economy that proved unable to protect itself against the rise of imperialistic kingdoms, such as Alexander's Macedonian empire.

More obviously still Aristotle's theory of natural slavery, although it does not justify slavery as he observed it in Athens, makes unwarranted empirical claims about the inferior abilities of particular biological groups. These can be inter-preted as purely ideological assertions which served the function of defending the privileged position of Aristotle's own race and class.

No doubt some of the empirical inadequacies of Aristotle's work are to be accounted for by his wish to describe the best and not merely the existing forms of society. And yet Aristotle's realism does bring him back again and again to the realities of social life so that his ideals are never far removed from some aspects of the social phenomena he observed around him. His rejection of extensive communal ownership, his examination of such a wide variety of constitutions and his concern for social stability, particularly his appreciation of its necessary economic basis in the satisfaction of a variety of competing material interests, leads him to make many acute points about the basis of social stability and the causes of social disintegration. Moreover his dualistic portrait of man as both naturally sociable and yet a prey to selfish acquisitiveness remains a starting point for most contemporary social theory, as does his realization that the balance of these two elements in practice depends to a large extent on the economic and institutional arrangements operative in each society.

Turning to the normative adequacy of Aristotle's social theory we can level criticism both at the philosophical basis of his ethical theory and at the content of his moral ideals.

His ethical theory depends on the combination of the

naturalistic idea that there is an end or 'telos' to human life whose content is to be gleaned from a study of man's behaviour, and a more rationalistic and idealistic element according to which the correct balance of human feeling and action is to be discovered by processes of thought or intellectual intuition. However, Aristotle fails to demonstrate that, either by an appeal to natural process or by the use of intellectual insight, we can gain knowledge of anything more than the most appropriate means for obtaining that which we happen to desire. Practical reason may enable us to get what we want but it does not give us standards by which to assess our wants and decide which desires are best. For all that Aristotle is aware that a great deal in ethics comes down to the judgement of the individual person his claim that the judgements of wise men will divine some sort of 'mean' to give us correct beliefs about the proper ends of conduct is unconvincing, for whatever type of conduct we care to designate as morally right can always be described as some sort of balance between extremes.

As for the specific content of Aristotle's ideas, we have here to recognize a clear inconsistency between his partial espousal of democratic ideals, such as the participation of equals in the common pursuit of the good of the whole society, and the aristocratic qualities which dominate in his list of virtues (magnanimity, temperateness etc) and feature in his practical recommendations for the hierarchical organization of the polis. Once we have ceased to regard Aristotle's virtues and values as 'natural' it is easy to see that his evaluations are parochial and perhaps ideological. He tends to favour the aristocratic values of the economically independent man of leisure who has an important role to play in social life. A prime example of this is his disdain for purely commercial activities, which he regards as 'unnatural', and his tendency to see not only slaves but also wage-earners and small tradesmen as inferior creatures whose existence is justified only by their contribution to the polis as a whole. No wonder that Marx saw Aristotle's polis as an association against a subjected producing class.

Nevertheless there is to be found in Aristotle the elements of a rather different view: a form of human society based on the twin ideas of friendship and citizenship, brought together in the concept of a self-sufficient civic community. The ideas of equal citizenship, the rule of law, the rejection of purely commercial relationships, the stress on participation in political process and the provision of an organizational basis which enables the various forms of human sociability to flourish—these still present what many find an attractive and not necessarily impractical social goal. But the problem of size remains to haunt the modern Aristotelian. Today the requirements of self-sufficiency patently demand a large impersonal political organization which splits off man's personal relations from his political life and generates division of labour in social functions to an extent which makes Aristotle's fusions of morality and law, private and public, society and polity, seem both utopian and oppressive.

FURTHER READING

The most accessible and relevant works of Aristotle are the *Nicomachean Ethics* and the *Politics*. A good general introduction is D. J. Allan, *The Philosophy of Aristotle* (Oxford University Press: London 1952). On Aristotle's theory of man see Stephen R. Clark, *Aristotle's Man* (Clarendon Press: Oxford, 1975). His social and political theory is discussed in John B. Morrall, *Aristotle* (George Allen and Unwin: London 1977). See also R. G. Mulgan, *Aristotle's Political Theory* (Clarendon Press: Oxford, 1977). For Aristotle's concept of friendship see W. W. Fortenbaugh, 'Aristotle's Analysis of Friendship', *Phronesis*, Vol. XX, 1975, pp. 51–62. An interesting study of Aristotle's analysis of economic relationships is to be found in Scott Meikle, 'Aristotle and the Political Economy of the Polis', *Journal of Hellenic Studies*, Vol. XCIX, 1979, pp. 57–73.

CHAPTER 4

Thomas Hobbes: Instrumental Individualism

In the first chapter we took Hobbes as our example of an individualistic theorist who regarded society as a type of association in contrast to Durkheim's more holistic model. In this chapter we will look in more detail at Hobbes's ideas, making comparisons this time with Aristotle, and concentrating on the weaknesses in Hobbes's theory which mark the starting point for later, less atomistic, thinkers.

Like Aristotle, Hobbes has a political conception of society, but the politics of Hobbes has little in common with Aristotle's ideal of civic community. Hobbes's man is more thoroughly selfish than Aristotle's and although both point to human reason as that which makes man fit for society, reason, for Hobbes, is no more than an instrument for enabling the individual to work out how to get and keep what he wants. Hobbes regards society and the political order on which it depends as intrinsically unwelcome but nevertheless necessary conditions of survival, the desperate devices of panic-stricken egoists who can find no other way to avoid mutual destruction.

Hobbes's vivid awareness of the dark side of human nature and his experience of the havoc and dangers of civil war in seventeenth-century England gave him a deeply rooted fear of anarchy and a belief that social life is an inherently fragile enterprise. In the second half of an extremely long life (he died in 1679 at the age of ninety-one), during which he spent many years at the Court of James I, and some time in exile, Hobbes sought a solution to this unhappy human condition by undertaking the gigantic intellectual task of producing a precise, comprehensive and certain theory of nature, man and society, which he set out in his three major works *De Corpore*, *De Homine* and *De Cive*. We will use his more famous work, *Leviathan* (1651) as our main source; page references are to the Penguin edition, edited by C. B. Macpherson (Harmondsworth, 1968).

Hobbes's defence of political absolutism in *Leviathan* has attracted constant hostile criticism, as have the moral and psychological theories on which he bases his social theory. But the immediate plausibility of his assumptions and the apparent rigour of his arguments have led many to doubt the Aristotelian contention that society is natural to man. Hobbes, in facing the problems of the break down of the centralized feudalism of his day, set what many sociologists still see as *the* theoretical problem of social theory: how is social order possible? His answer is that society is an artificial erection held together by a combination of rational self-interest, violence, intimidation and deceit.

HOBBES'S APPROACH

As with Aristotle, Hobbes's approach is both descriptive and prescriptive, but his explanatory models are radically different and his prescriptions are more sweeping and dogmatic.

In the Middle Ages Aristotle's idea of a rational natural order which is the same at all times and in all places was developed by Christian theologians, such as Thomas Aquinas, into a concept of natural law by which was meant the divinely ordained standard of right and wrong. Hobbes, whom his contemporaries mistakenly regarded as an atheist, adopts the terminology of natural law but uses it to denote the dictates of intelligent selfishness. To work out the content of these dictates he conducts what he believes to be a scientific study of human desires and how to satisfy them. He then assumes that it is rational for each individual to act so as to satisfy his desires maximally.

Hobbes was, for a time, secretary to Francis Bacon, an early advocate of the inductive method of reasoning (that is using the accumulation of many observations of similar events as the basis for making generalizations about regularities in our experience of phenomena). But Hobbes rejected such narrow empiricism on the grounds that 'experience concludeth nothing universally' (*Human Nature (De Homine)* Chapter 4, Section 10). In his view, however many times we may have observed that particular things of type A have characteristic B, we can never be absolutely sure that all A's are B, for we have not observed, and we cannot ever observe, all of them. Hobbes seeks absolute certainty as the only intellectually satisfying goal and the only adequate basis for establishing a stable form of society. He therefore distrusts inductive reasoning.

Hobbes thinks that he has discovered the path to certainty in the method of geometry. He became entranced by the way in which Euclid, on the basis of a few self-evident truths about lines, points and angles, could prove beyond all doubt a vast range of unobvious conclusions about triangles, squares and circles, which appear to have immediate application to the observable world. This is achieved by the method of deduction (that is the demonstration that, given certain axioms, it is impossible to deny certain conclusions without contradicting oneself.)

The belief that knowledge is to be found by deducing complex truths from simple axioms leads Hobbes in two directions. Sometimes he starts by stating his axioms or definitions and then puts them together to derive novel truths about the world. This 'synthetic' process of thought he describes as 'knowing the consequences of names'. At other times he starts with the observation of phenomena and works back to the primary propositions from which these phenomena can be deduced by the synthetic process. This is called the 'analytic' mode of thought. Putting together the two procedures of analysis and synthesis we get what was called the Paduan methodology employed by many early scientists, such as the astronomer Galileo, and the physiologist Harvey (who discovered the circulation of the blood). Hobbes seeks to emulate these pioneering scientists by analytically resolving social experience into its basic elements and then synthetically recomposing them in a strict deductive manner. In this way he hopes to discover the basic elements of human nature which are the causes of social phenomena.

Hobbes combines his ideas about geometrical method with the materialistic assumption that everything can be reduced to matter in motion. What Galileo had done to explain the movements of the planets by the laws of motion Hobbes sets out to do in the study of human behaviour. He approaches man as part of physical nature and assumes that human movements are subject to the same laws of cause and effect as the rest of the natural world. It is clear that Hobbes, despite his concentration on human psychology, is not seeking an interpretative understanding of behaviour. He is a positivist. And he aims to explain the mental and spiritual life of man in purely physical terms. These materialistic assumptions go along with his deterministic view that human behaviour is subject to causal necessity. He thus exhibits the characteristic positivistic programme of theorizing about society along the lines of the most successful scientific method of the time.

Hobbes's investigations of the ultimate causes of human society are not without practical point. He strives to use the knowledge gained by his sociological application of the Paduan methodology to prescribe for the proper ordering of social relationships. Once we know what it is that all men desire we are then able to say what they must do if they are to satisfy their desires. And so, for Hobbes, no less than for Aristotle, there is no gap between 'is' and 'ought'. Once we know that men fear violence and death it is possible to determine the most desirable form of society, namely that which minimizes these evils; indeed that is the whole point of the enterprise.

HOBBES'S THEORY OF MAN

Parodying Aristotle's definition of man as a social animal, we can say that, for Hobbes, man is an anti-social machine. Into this machine pass inputs from the environment through the five senses. These inputs produce internal physical reactions (a type of 'vital motion' which correlate with desires). If the internal motions are towards the cause of the sensation then they are called 'appetites'. If they are movements away from the stimulus then they are called 'aversions'. Both sorts of reaction may result in overt physical activity ('voluntary motion'), the observable output of the human machine. Where there are competing stimuli a process of decision making occurs in which an oscillation of appetite and aversion takes place in the brain until one or other appetite or aversion proves strong enough to produce or prevent action. 'Will' is therefore defined as the last appetite or aversion immediately prior to the action or inaction (Part I, Chapter 6, p. 128). Choice is thus a causally determined process since it follows from the strongest desire.

To this theory of psychological determinism (set out in Part I of *Leviathan* and in *Human Nature*), Hobbes adds a naturalistic theory of ethics according to which 'good' is the object of desire and 'bad' the object of aversion (*Leviathan* Part I, Chapter 6, p. 120). Moreover, the individual's desires all relate to his own well being. Morality is thus reduced to the individual's rational calculation of what satisfies his desires. This makes Hobbes an ethical egoistic for he holds that each individual, as a rational being, ought to maximize his desire satisfaction. To be moral is to be prudent.

In accordance with his view that everything is matter in motion Hobbes argues that all desires are connected with the need to keep the human body in motion and so avoid death. Each passion is analysed to show that it is an egoistic appetite or aversion. The most important passions for his social theory are hope or 'appetite with an opinion of attaining' (Part I, Chapter 6, p. 122) and fear, or 'aversion with opinion of hurt from the object'; the former drives men towards society, the latter drives him away from it. All apparently unselfish motives are interpreted as indirect ways of furthering our own interests. For instance men, it is alleged, are kind to each other only so that they may receive kindness in return.

Human life is a constant struggle to satisfy desire. To aid him in this process man is endowed with reason whereby he is able to learn from experience what are the most effective ways of gaining satisfaction and avoiding disappointment. Here induction does come into the picture. These cognitive activities are all explained, like human actions, in physical terms (see Part I, Chapter 2, pp. 88 ff). They are the result of the physiological movements of sense perception retained in the mind as ideas or 'conceptions'. These conceptions are vivid immediately after perception but eventually fade to nothing. Consciousness is thus an 'appearance' in the mind of bodily movements; imagination is decaying and fading sense; memory is no more than attending to the fading images of sense. Putting all this together, thinking is simply a matter of adding words to this basically physiological process. More specifically inductive thinking operates by strengthening fading images through frequent perceptions of the same conjunction of events, for men take more note of what they perceive more often. The details of this account of reasoning may be dated and highly speculative but it is very much in line with the modern concept of human reason as a sophisticated computer composed of a network of neurological pathways.

All human action, according to Hobbes, involves the coming together of reason and desire in the form of appetite and aversion. Desire provides the ends of human action, reason intimates the means to these ends. The means to achieve one's ends Hobbes calls 'power', or the 'present means to obtain some future apparent good' (Part I, Chapter 10, pp. 150 ff). Human life is a 'perpetuall and restlesse desire of power after power, that ceaseth only in death' (Part I, Chapter 11, p. 161). But power cannot be obtained without conflict. First men must struggle for scarce resources (Hobbes calls this 'competition'); second they must defend themselves and prevent others taking away the power they have accumulated ('diffidence'); and third, even when resources are not scarce and men are secure in their possessions, they seek the feeling of superiority which comes from having power over others ('glory') (Part I, Chapter 13, p. 185). These three 'causes of quarrell' set men against each other and entail that, in the absence of external controls, they are in a constant 'state of war' with each other. Hobbes, therefore, contends, against

Aristotle, that man's nature makes him totally unsuited for social life. In the state of nature (which, we noted on p. 8, means the absence of social and political institutions) men's approximate physical equality ensures that the consequence of constant warfare is a life which, in Hobbes's characteristically punchy phrase, is 'solitary, poore, nasty, brutish and short' (Part I, Chapter 13, p. 186). Life in accordance with the nature of man is not just a race, it is a battle, and a battle without any rules or restraints in which all are, in the end, losers.

HOBBES'S THEORY OF SOCIETY

Hobbes's analysis of human nature appears to make peaceful and co-operative human relationships impossible. But man needs society; as a child he cannot live alone, and all through his life he requires the help of others to survive and to provide for himself in an adequate manner. And so, although he has no natural delight in company, he does need and wish for its benefits. Consequently 'we do not by nature seek society for its own sake, but that we may receive some honour or profit from it: these we desire primarily, that secondarily' (*Philosophical Elements of A True Citizen*, Chapter 1).

However, while men may hope for an ordered social life for the reason that this would be instrumental to their own selfish interests this is an insufficient basis for any but the most transient of co-operative relationships. Self-interest divides men as quickly as it unites them. If people join together only for gain or glory then they separate as soon as they can obtain more of these desired objectives in other ways. This means that even for the protection of their most prized possession—their lives—men are debarred from establishing effective relationships with each other. No one can be trusted to refrain from harming others when it is to their benefit to do so. And yet if just a few people threaten the lives and livelihood of a peaceful majority, this is enough to generate fear and suspicion to an extent which inhibits any lasting co-operation. No rational person will enter into even a mutually beneficial agreement if he fears that others will take the advantage of him which he knows he would take of them should the opportunity arise. It is therefore irrational to co-operate with another person whom one cannot control. Fear drives out hope.

The Hobbesian solution to this paradox is that men in the state of nature, before they make any other agreements, must first contract with each other to set up a power that will force them to keep to their bargains. This 'social contract' by which civil society is established is a device whereby it becomes rational for men to act on their instrumental desire for peaceful relationships because they then have the assurance that they will receive the benefits they wish for as long as they themselves refrain from harming others.

The social contract consists of 'Articles of Peace' which Hobbes deduces from the 'laws of nature'. In his scheme a law of nature is not a moral imperative but simply a 'precept, or general rule, found out by reason, by which a man is forbidden to do, that, which is destructive of his life' (Part I, Chapter 14, pp. 189 f). The first law of nature is 'to endeavour peace, as farre as he [man] has hope of obtaining it'. This law does not in itself take men out of the predicament of desiring peace but waging war. But the second law is a step towards a solution since it requires that 'a man be willing, when others are so too, as farre-forth, as for peace and defence of himselfe he shall think it necessary, to lay down this right to all things: and be contented with so much liberty against other men as he would allow other men against himselfe' (Part I, Chapter 14, pp. 104 f). (Here we must note that the natural 'rights' men have in the state of nature and give up in the social contract are merely 'liberties' or absences of obligations. Such liberties are not to be confused with the rights discussed in Chapter 1 which correlate with the obligations of others towards the right-holder; these rights and duties could not exist outside society.)

It is the mutuality of the social contract that is the basis of social life. If all men give up their natural right to defend themselves and entrust that task to a single man or assembly of men, then everyone is protected against the 'free-rider' who takes the advantages of social co-operation without fulfilling the obligation that makes these advantages possible. This single person or group (the 'sovereign') can call on the collective strength of all other members of society to act against the free-rider or contract-breaker, thus ensuring conformity to the third law of nature that 'men performe their Covenants made' (Part I, Chapter 15, p. 201).

Hobbes notes that 'Covenants without swords are but words', but after the social contract the collective power of all is the sword which enforces that contract. Once civil society is set up it becomes rational for men to enter into all sorts of other agreements to their mutual advantage. In particular it becomes possible to acquire property. In the state of nature there could be no 'mine' and 'thine' since there were no rules laying down who was entitled to what, thus while men could have things in their possession they could have no right to anything, (in the sense defined in Chapter 1). Hence there could be no theft or tresspass. But once property is instituted industry and cultivation becomes viable and mutually beneficial trading can begin in the market place. So men begin to make life comfortable as well as safe for themselves, thus escaping from the evils of the state of nature in which there are 'no Arts, no Letters, no Society; and which is worst of all, continuall feare, and danger of violent death' (Part I, Chapter 13, p. 186).

Hobbes's view, then, is that all social relationships are artificial in that they are the product of calculation and agreement rather than affection or impulse. Society is based entirely on instrumental rationality and not at all on love or altruistic friendship. This is an extreme form of conflict theory since the causes of human conflict are ineradicable, being rooted in human nature, and will always require to be held in check by a power sufficient to overawe men's selfish passions and compel obedience to norms that they would otherwise break. Social relationships are therefore 'external' to the individual rather than part of a shared moral consenses.

Even the family is not sustained by natural affection but holds together because of the superior power of the father whose relative dominion over the wife and absolute dominion over the children is based on force. Here, unless the sovereign intervenes with his superior power, might is the basis of right, although it is in the interests of parents to bring their children up to be their friends—something equivalent to Aristotle's friendship of utility. And although Hobbes contends that all men are equal in power, so that there is no basis for Aristotle's idea of natural slavery, he permits a master-slave relationship founded on consent rather than natural differences, the consent being given as an alternative to accepting death at the hands of a conqueror (Part I, Chapter XV, pp. 201 ff).

It should be noted that Hobbes's sovereign is not just the central repository of the force which is necessary to underpin the agreements on which the institutional rules of society are based; he also has the task determining what is right and wrong for the purposes of social interactions. Since there is no moral authority higher than self-interest, no objective good and evil beyond human desires, and no concept of justice prior to the existence of positive law, the rules of social life must be created by the sovereign. What matters for social organization is less that the norms of that society are 'correct' than that they are authoritatively determined. The sovereign must therefore play a role in creating as well as enforcing social norms. Nor is he constrained in this task by any religious considerations other than his own fear of God as the most powerful of all beings (for Hobbes did believe in God as an omnipotent creator). Indeed the sovereign uses religious belief as a means for obtaining conformity to his commands.

Hobbes is clear that religion is a means of social control, involving, if not deceit, then something like Marx's false-consciousness (see p. 124): 'Fear of power invisible, feigned by the mind, or imagined by tales publicly allowed [is] religion; not allowed Superstition' (*Leviathan*, Part I, Chapter 6, p. 124). It is a crime to teach an unorthodox religion not because it is false but because it undermines the credibility of rulers who claim to be more than human in order to sustain their authority by playing on men's irrational fear of the gods. (See

Part III, Chapter 42, p. 567). Complete liberty in these matters is incompatible with social existence.

PRACTICAL IMPLICATIONS

Hobbes couches his social and political theory in terms of a story about the distant past and focuses our attention on the idea of a single historical contract, but in fact his use of this notion is as much prescriptive as descriptive. He does not push the claim that all societies originate in a social contract but suggests that, because it would be rational for men in a state of nature to enter into civil society, this justifies the sort of absolute political authority set up by the social contract. The clear implication of his theory is that, whatever the actual origin of despotic government men have good reason to support it now.

The powers which Hobbes says that individuals must hand over to the sovereign are extensive (see Part II, Chapters 17 & 18). The sovereign, as we have seen, must have the right to decide what is good and evil in the 'official' moral and legal sense as distinct from the natural idea of good as that which satisfies individuals' desires. Men give up the right of private judgement as they give up the right to defend themselves. Anything less will result in chaos and anarchy. Only if the sovereign can no longer defend the individual citizen may the latter revert to the state of nature, disobey the sovereign's commands and see to his own defence. Within these limits the individual has no choice but to obey. Indeed the contract makes him the 'author' of the sovereign's acts since he appointed the sovereign to this role so that in obeying the sovereign he is in effect obeying himself.

The sovereign on the other hand has no duties to the citizen since he himself is not a party to the contract which is concluded between all other men who transfer to him their natural rights. This rules out the possibility of justified rebellion which for Hobbes would simply be another way back to the dissolution of the state and so to the collapse of all society. Given the known inclinations of men a sovereign authority must be perpetual, unlimited and indivisible. Anything less will bring about a reversion to 'perpetuale warre of every man against his neighbour' (Part I, Chapter 20, p. 312). There can be no safeguards against the sovereign because, if we set up another power to defend ourselves against the dangers of the sovereign abusing his powers, we are undermining the basis of his effectiveness. The hope must be that, however much the sovereign neglects his projected role or looks to his own self-interest, this cannot produce results worse that the state of nature and is likely to be a considerable improvement.

In this way Hobbes derives from his premises about human nature and the human condition a prudential prescription: men must give their consent to absolute government. This follows from the descriptive sociological point that anything less than this makes government, and hence its benefits, impossible.

ASSESSMENT

Can we accept Hobbes's axiomatic propositions about human nature? And, if we do, are we forced to accept the conclusions he deduces from them? Is man a self-preserving and anti-social machine? And, if so, is political absolutism the precondition of social existence?

If we take his geometrical model seriously then it is tempting to interpret Hobbes's theory in the light of modern ideas about the theoretical basis of geometry, the axioms of which are no more than stipulative (or arbitrary) definitions of spatial concepts (such as that a straight line is the shortest distance between two points) which need have no exact instantiation in the real world (no actual line is completely straight). It therefore remains an open question whether or not the conclusions of Euclidean geometry apply to actual phenomena. Hobbes may have assumed that they do, but we now know that, according to Einstein's Theory of Relativity, this is not always the case. Thinking along these lines we could take Hobbes's psychological terminology to be a set of stipulative definitions, admire the deductive system he builds upon them, reject his assumption that definitions in themselves prove what the world is like, and then look to see whether the conclusions of his theorems have any application to the actual social world.

But it seems clear that Hobbes did not regard his analyses of psychological terms as mere stipulative definitions, for he supports them with various appeals to experience. He sees himself as presenting truths 'known by the experience of every man who takes care to observe the motions in himself'. In the introduction to *Leviathan* he asks each of his readers to consider 'what he doth, when he does think, opine, reason, hope, feare etc, and upon what grounds . . . [and] he shall thereby read and know, what are the thoughts, and passions of all other men, upon the like occasions' (p. 82).

This sort of appeal to introspection can hardly be an effective method for proving the existence of the insensible physical motions which he believes to be the causes of observable motions, but it may have some force in relation to his analysis of emotions and thoughts. Many people have accepted his challenge, examined as honestly as they can their own psychological processes, and decided that he is basically correct, at least as regards the dominance of self-interest and the importance of fear and anxiety in determining their actions.

Nevertheless introspection is an unreliable scientific method and it is a risky inductive procedure to generalize from the analysis of one's own experience to that of all other men, particularly those living in different types of social environment. Why should we assume that Hobbes's introspections are more typical than those of Aristotle, or our own? And it may be that his arguments lead us to misinterpret our own experience for it is part of his technique to take apparently disinterested attitudes and emotions and reinterpret them so that they are shown to be 'really' selfish after all. Critics have alleged that Hobbes is too ready to lead us from the admission that our behaviour is less than fully altruistic to the conclusion that there is no such thing as altruism in any degree. More particularly, it is urged that he confuses us by gaining our assent to the thesis that satisfying a desire is always pleasant and then treating this as equivalent to saying that the object of our desire is always the pleasure of satisfying it. This overlooks the possibility, accepted by Aristotle and used against Hobbes by eighteenth-century critics such as Francis Hutcheson and Bishop Butler, that a person may get pleasure from being benevolent to others without being benevolent in order to get pleasure for himself. Indeed it can be argued that unless we already have a desire to help others for their own sake we will get no pleasure from benefiting them.

A similar sort of confusion seems to underlie Hobbes's assumption that a mechanistic view of human nature entails than man is necessarily selfish, in the sense of always preferring his own happiness to that of others. Even if we assume that internal physiological movements are necessary causes or accompaniments of all feeling, thought and action—although this is highly speculative—and that all human behaviour and experience is caused by the physical condition of the agent, this does not in itself prove that the focus of that experience and the objective of action is inevitably directed towards the movements of the person in question. Because an act is self-caused does not mean that it must be directed towards some future condition of the self: being self-determined is not the same thing as being self-interested. We need not, therefore, be led by the attractiveness of Hobbes's mechanistic model of man into adopting his egoistic psychology.

Perhaps the most that can be said at this stage is that Hobbes's psychological postulates are over simplified and inadequately supported by empirical evidence, particularly if they are claimed as universal truths about all men. And even if his axioms are thought to be acceptable—perhaps in a modified form—they cannot be said to have the certainty and universality with which he sought to endow them. It may be that his account of man is more accurate of human behaviour in early capitalist societies than in early feudal or classical ones, and more applicable to the relations of large scale impersonal politics than to the intimacies of domestic and personal life. These are empirical issues which cannot be settled by slick definition, individual introspection or limited observation of a particular society.

Does the guarded and provisional concession that there may be some truth in Hobbes's analysis of human nature land us with a similarly qualified acceptance of its implications for social theory? This question takes us to his account of the transition from the state of nature to civil society. Two types of criticism are made of this part of Hobbes's theory. The first relates to the precise content of the terms of the contract and the second to the whole idea of founding social relations on any sort of contractual relationship.

As regards the terms of the contract, a century later John Locke argued against Hobbes that the citizen's vulnerability to the whims of an all-powerful arbitrary sovereign placed him in a condition worse than the state of nature. As Locke put it in the *Second Treatise of Government* (1690, Section 93), a rational person would not enter a contract in order to escape from pole-cats and foxes if this placed him at the mercy of lions. Locke suggests instead that the contract between all potential citizens would entrust to the ruler limited powers to govern with their consent, allowing for the withdrawal of that consent if the ruler did not fulfil his trust. But then Locke did not accept that men were utterly selfish or without moral scruples so that he thought of the state of nature as being inconvenient rather than horrendous.

In fact it is hard to resist Hobbes's argument that, if men fear death above all else and if imminent death is a feature of the state of nature, then it is rational for them to accept whatever is necessary to preserve themselves. Whether or not this requires total commitment to an absolute sovereign right up to the point at which he threatens the contractees' lives must depend on just how despotic, malevolent and just plain inefficient the sovereign turns out to be, a topic to which Hobbes devotes insufficient attention. But it is a fair criticism of the consistency of Hobbes's position to say that, if the sovereign is a typical example of Hobbesian man, seeking only his own power, wealth and glory, then it must be extremely dangerous for everyone else to place unlimited power in his hands. The cure does seem to be at least as bad as the disease.

A modified Hobbesian position, which does not go as far as Aristotle's view that man has a natural affinity for social relationships, is that the social contract involves balancing the risks of the state of nature against those of life under an absolute sovereign (thus accepting that social relationships involve a loss of liberty for the sake of increased security) but allows that in those situations in which men do not reach the heights of Hobbesian selfishness social life may subsist largely on mutual interest and much less on external physical constraint and the manipulation of religious belief. The burdens which men may have to take on can thus vary inversely with the dangers they seek to avoid through making the contract. A Hobbesian is free to tinker with this balance to a considerable extent without abandoning the theory of instrumental individualism. There has recently been a return to such speculations, albeit in a more Lockeian vein, in the revival of social contract theory by John Rawls (*A Theory of Justice*, Oxford University Press, 1972) and Robert Nozick (*Anarchy, State and Utopia*, Basic Books Inc., 1974). In the work of Rawls particularly we are once again faced with the question of what rational egoists in a state of nature would agree to concerning the principles for setting up basic social institutions, although in Rawls's case the answer is sought more for moral guidance than for sociological insight and political prudence.

The second type of criticism made of Hobbes's social contract is more radical in that it cast doubt on the plausibility of the whole idea. One form of this critique simply points to its unhistorical nature. There never was such a contract because there never was a time when men lived outwith a society of some sort. Hobbes does make some attempt to defend the historicity of the contract, but on the whole he is happy to agree that most states and hence societies originate in conquest, and modern contract theorists are quick to point out that their purpose is to exhibit the reasons men have for making a commitment to political authority and not to establish any historical facts.

But if the state of nature is not historical then we have a further problem. Hobbes's account of human nature draws heavily on the idea of how men behave without government. If men have never been in a state of nature how can we know how they would behave in it? If Hobbes is really telling us how men behave when government breaks down, then this quite a different matter since the behaviour of men who have been members of a society is affected by their social experience. If the behaviour that makes the state of nature so bad is in fact the behaviour of men who have been brought up in societies then it makes less sense to say that we must enter society in order to escape from such behaviour. Indeed it can be argued that at least some of the causes of conflict mentioned by Hobbes, such as the desire for glory and reputation, are inconceivable outside a society.

This raises a more disturbing question, not this time about the empirical basis of Hobbes's contract theory, but about its intelligibility and coherence. Is Hobbes not inconsistent to assume that men in the state of nature have capacities which can only emerge in civil society? Language, for instance, is a rule-based activity requiring learning and authoritative standards, and yet men cannot make contracts without using language; therefore it must be nonsense to think of contracts being made in the state of nature.

Again, can we conceive of how the social contract gets under way given the situation Hobbes describes? He alleges that no contract is binding unless there is a superior power to enforce it, yet a contract is needed to set up that power; this means that the social contract presupposes the future existence of that which it is meant to institute. Enough people must keep the contract without being coerced before anyone can be counted upon to keep it. But this is not possible on Hobbes's scheme.

This is no mere logical conundrum but is a way of stating the obvious fact that no society can subsist if it requires the constant presence of an intimidating coercive power. In any society effective force requires the co-operation of numbers of men and this co-operation cannot itself be based on force, therefore some degree of consent or agreement is a prior requirement for the effective development of the sanctions of political power. Going further it can be argued that the external coercions of the state cannot operate except against a background of consent either to the existence of that authority or to the rules of behaviour which it lays down. In brief, sanctions can never be effective against the bulk of a population if citizens have only artificial prudential reasons for conformity. The Hobbesian contract model of society does not provide a complete account of social cohesion.

A final objection to the whole social contract mode of analysing social relationships is directed against its methodological individualism. The artificiality of the idea of a social contract points up the fallacy of thinking that human behaviour patterns exist independently of their social relationships. If not only language, and hence thinking, but all the emotional states and activities about which evaluative judgements are made, and to which rule-governed standards apply, are moulded by life in society, then the idea of a fixed and universal specific human nature abstracted from a particular social setting is a nonsense. Whatever disclaimers may be made about the hypothetical and unhistorical status of the social contract, thinking in these terms at all is a dangerous encouragement to the mistaken notion that man's nature is independent of his social existence.

In short Hobbes does not free himself from the Aristotlian assumption that it is possible to give a definition or description of man's essential nature and to build a social theory on this. Hobbes differs from Aristotle over what nature is like and makes a radical break with Aristotle when he denies that the reasonable man has insight into what is naturally right and wrong prior to the sovereign's dictates. But both are 'essentialists' (in that they base their theories on a thesis about the 'essential' properties of a thing) and both may be said to have committed the naturalistic fallacy by deducing normative standards from purely descriptive statements. However in Hobbes's case the normative conclusions are not *moral* ones. He regards so-called moral terminology as referring either to the object of individuals' desires or to the commands of the sovereign (and perhaps also to the will of an omnipotent creator), all of which is equivalent to saying that there is no such thing as morality. The 'oughts' he uses are maxims of prudence not the independent catagorical imperatives of ordinary moral experience. What he does provide is advice. If men wish to live then they should do as he says. He turns this hypothetical imperative into something like a categorical one by adding that everyone does in fact wish to live, therefore they must take his advice, at least if they are rational.

But are all men rational? And even if they are at least sometimes rational, can his mechanistic philosophy account for our conviction that some processes of reasoning are more valid than others? In a world of pure causation what place is there for rationality? But that is perhaps another and more complicated question.

A RECENT HOBBESIAN REVIVAL: SOCIOBIOLOGY

There is no doubt that Hobbesian assumptions still feature in a great deal of social theorizing, particularly since 'social order' is still widely regarded as the central problem requiring the attention of the social theorist. I have mentioned that the rationalistic side of Hobbes's contract model of social relationships has recently been revived in the influential work of John Rawls and others. It may be as well, however, to underline the continuing vitality of the less rationalistic aspect of the Hobbesian view of society according to which social organization is the product of the interactions of mechanistically determined individuals with innate competitive and aggressive drives. This is to be seen in the recent emergence of a type of theory called 'sociobiology' which draws on modern developments in the biological sciences to present what is in effect an updated version of Hobbesian individualism.

Sociobiology follows in the footsteps of the nineteenth-century theorist Herbert Spencer, who attributes the Hobbesian features of competitiveness and acquisitiveness to the nature of man as it has been formed by the processes of evolution. This 'Social Darwinism' was used in the nineteenth-century as a basis for criticizing any extension of state functions beyond establishing law and order, on the grounds that anything in the way of welfare provisions interferes with the natural evolutionary development in which the fittest survive and the weakest die off, to the ultimate benefit of the species.

Parallels between human and animal evolution are also used in twentieth-century biological versions of Hobbes's approach. Following the example of Konrad Lorenz (see Chapter 9 of Leslie Stevenson, *Seven Theories of Human Nature*, Oxford University Press, London, 1974) such popular writers as Robert Ardrey in *The Territorial Imperative* and Desmond Morris in *The Naked Ape* interpret animal behaviour in anthropomorphic terms and suggest that human behaviour is essentially similar and can therefore be explained in terms of biological drives, such as aggression and sexuality, manifested in patterns which are as much part of the evolved nature of man as they are of all animals. There is a certain plausibility in some of the parallels cited between men and other animals but the overwhelming anthropological evidence points against this approach as a basis for satisfactory accounts of human societies, which are culturally not biologically based. There is as yet no established close relationships between particular biologically based human drives and detailed patterns of social interactions.

Nevertheless we have in the 'sociobiology' of Edward O. Wilson another modern attempt to explain human societies in terms of the evolved drives of the human animal. In *Sociobiology: The New Synthesis*, (Belknap Press of Harvard University Press, Cambridge, 1955) Wilson propounds the theory that human social relationships are determined by the propensity of each individual to maximize the reproductive success of his genes, either by reproducing himself or by aiding the survival and reproduction of those carrying the same or similar genetic material. This means that individuals are inherently selfish except in relation to their biological kin.

This theory of genetic self-interest is essentially the same as Hobbes's model of competitive individualism in respect to the innate drives of the individual, but it improves on Hobbes in so far as it can explain examples of altruism, such as maternal behaviour, which don't readily fit into Hobbes's scheme. In place of the conscious contractual relationships in Hobbes Wilson appeals to the unconscious rationality of genetic self-interest which is said to produce social organizations geared to the biologically determined goals of the individual.

Unfortunately for the theory it goes no way towards explaining the endless variety of social codes which govern kinship as a social institution. In human society kinship rules are loosely based on biological ties of natural parentage or blood relationships. Their variations and ramifications have little discernable biological pattern. Efforts to explain the kinship institutions of different cultures in terms of genetic wisdom have so far been as unsuccessful as previous efforts to explain the variety of human warfare in terms of instinctual aggression, or to account for the details of human sexual behaviour as the expression of fixed and specific 'natural' sexual drives.

Human culture remains unamenable to all efforts at identifying as underlying its multiple forms a number of specific basic human propensities of sufficient precision to have any significant explanatory power. The plasticisty of human nature and the creativeness of human culture continue to defy all Hobbesian attempts to reduce society to the level of the detailed needs and instincts of the human organism whether or not these are the product of evolution. This does not mean that the Hobbesian approach to man as a pre-determined machine will not continue to emerge in one guise or another to exercise its perennial appeal.

FURTHER READING

In addition to *Leviathan* students of Hobbes's social theory might read *De Homine* (*Human Nature or the Fundamental Elements of Policy*). Among secondary works, an excellent introduction is D. D. Raphael, *Hobbes* (Allen & Unwin: London, 1977). See also J. W. N. Watkins, *Hobbes's System of Ideas* (Hutchinson: London, 1973) and R. S. Peters, *Hobbes* (Penguin Books: Harmondsworth, 1967). A book which stresses the ideological aspects of Hobbes's theory is C. B. Macpherson, *The Political Theory of Possessive Individualism* (Oxford University Press: London, 1962). Leo Strauss, *The Political Philosophy of Thomas Hobbes* (Oxford University Press: London, 1936) contains a discussion of Hobbes's reaction against Aristotle. For a critical discussion of Sociobiology see Marshall Sahlins, *The Use and Abuse of Biology* (Tavistock Publications: London, 1977). See also R. Dawkin, *The Selfish Gene* (Oxford University Press: London, 1976).

CHAPTER 5   Adam Smith:
              The Social System

ADAM SMITH (1723–90) is famous as an economist. His *Wealth of Nations* (1776) published when he was a customs officer in Edinburgh, marks the beginning of modern economics. He is also associated with the doctrines of liberal capitalism and the ideology of laissez-faire or minimal government. His more general theory of society is contained in his *Theory of Moral Sentiments* (1759) written when he was professor of Moral Philosophy at Glasgow University. Adam Smith's social theory is an interesting combination of Hobbesian and Aristotelian elements. Its most distinctive and original aspect is the idea that society as much as the individual is a system, or machine, whose operations are not the conscious product of human intentions.

Smith was a central figure of the Scottish Enlightenment, a close friend of the sceptic David Hume and an important influence on such early sociologists as David Millar and Adam Ferguson. He lived in a society which was heavily affected by Reformation theology and was still backward in commercial, although not in educational, terms. The capitalist system was just beginning to establish itself as the new world beyond Europe opened up the trade which was bringing prosperity to Glasgow. Intellectually Scotland's ties were with continental Europe as much as with England and Smith himself was immensely well-read in the literature of ancient Greece and Rome. Out of this milieu came several attempts to see the history of human society in scientific and yet human terms. For Smith this meant demonstrating how each society evolves a moral consensus as to what is proper, just and prudent which enables it to function as an 'immense machine whose regular and harmonious movements produce a thousand agreeable effects' (*Theory of Moral Sentiments*

VII.iii.1.1). References to Smith's works follow the form
adopted in the Glasgow edition of Smith's *Works and Correspondence* (Clarendon Press, Oxford, 1976–   ).

SMITH'S APPROACH

Adam Smith wished to become the Isaac Newton of the social
sciences and was acclaimed as such by his contemporaries.
Adapting the astronomical theory of Newton to the study of
human behaviour he regards society as a mechanism which
maintains its life and fulfils its purpose by establishing and re-
establishing certain natural balances or, in modern
terminology, equilibria. He was thus a pioneer of functionalism in the social sciences. But there is, for him, no conflict
between this attempt to explain social phenomena as part of
nature and his further philosophical tasks of justifying the
economic practices and moral sentiments which produce his
social equilibria and warning against the corruptions and
injustices which threaten to weaken systems which are by and
large productive of the general happiness. The happiness of all
sentiment creatures is, Smith believes, the objective which the
'Author of Nature' intends to achieve through the mechanisms
of social life. To understand Smith's approach we have
therefore to appreciate his Newtonian vision of science, his
concept of a social system and the way in which this fitted into
his theologically based utilitarian moral outlook.

One of Smith's many academic projects was to write an
explanatory history of science. This he never completed, but
he authorized the posthumous publication of a number of
essays on the subject, one of which—the 'History of
Astronomy' (in *Essays on Philosophical Subjects*, London,
1795)—tells us a good deal about his view of scientific theory.
In it he begins by discussing the speculations of primitive man
concerning the movements of the stars and planets and
concludes with an exposition of the attainments of Isaac
Newton, his own scientific hero.

Smith's primary purpose in the 'History of Astronomy' is to
provide psychological explanations for the growth of scientific

theories. They originate, he thinks, in man's wonder and surprise at what is new or unexpected, disturbing mental states from which they attempt to free themselves by relating in their minds strange and surprising objects and events to those which, because they are familiar and expected, cause no mental disquiet. Hence the universal human tendency to classify similar phenomena as being of the same kind and to generalize from observed sequences of events. Science goes beyond such straightforward procedures of classification and induction by attempting to fit all phenomena into a comprehensive scheme resting on a few simple familiar basic regularities or 'principles'. He illustrates this with the example of a piece of iron moving along a table towards a magnet. The first time we see this pheneomenon it surprises us and we therefore seek an explanation for such a novelty. Repeated observations of the phenomenon help to smooth the imagination by making it familiar to us, but only to an extent, for we are still not able to relate this particular phenomenon to yet more familiar experiences. At this point scientific creativity comes in and suggests a 'hypothesis' about possible unobserved connections of a type which we commonly see around us. In the case of the magnet and the iron Descartes's hypothesis that there is a flow of invisible particles between the two objects 'fills the gap' by suggesting that the operation of the magnet is an example of the familiar phenomenon of 'motion after impulse'. Similarly, in astronomy, the theory of 'concentric spheres' according to which the sun, the moon, the five planets and the stars each have a solid sphere, with the earth at their common centre, to which they are attached, was 'capable of connecting together, in the imagination, the grandest and the most seemingly disjointed appearances in the heavens' ('History of Astronomy', Glasgow Edition, 1980, p. 56). Science as a whole is the discovery of such 'connecting principles of nature'.

Smith concludes that a good scientific theory soothes the imagination by connecting the maximum number of observations by means of the fewest familiar principles. Simplicity is therefore a fundamental characteristic of a successful theory.

But simplicity takes second place to the requirement that a theory must account for *all* phenomena, particularly those which are 'irregular' in that they do not obviously fit into routine patterns. Science is therefore a constant dialectic between the pursuit of simplicity and the need for comprehensiveness. Thus the concentric sphere hypothesis could not account for the detailed movements of the sun and the moon and the necessary modifications which were intro-uduced to take account of these 'irregularities'—the postu-lation of 'eccentric spheres'—made it so complex that it lost its psychological appeal. At a later time the system of Copernicus, whereby the planets, including earth, were said to rotate around the sun, replaced that of Ptolemy because it is both more 'coherent' in connecting such a variety of apparently unrelated motions and better able to account for the observed 'irregular' movements of the planets. But above all it was Newton by his use of the 'simple and familiar fact of gravitation' in connecting in a precise and comprehensive way even the most detailed of astronomical observations, who could be said to have discovered 'the real chains which Nature makes use of to bind together her several operations' ('History of Astronomy', p. 105).

In his own work Smith uses this astronomical model to explain social systems as living mechanisms whose parts unwittingly contribute to the life and activity of the whole. The mechanism operates by maintaining certain natural balances, or equilibria, which it is able to re-establish when they are for some reason disrupted. One of these equilibria is represented by the moral sentiments felt by the 'impartial spectator' of human conduct in each society. Smith uses the concept of the impartial spectator to identify the consensus on attitudes of approval and disapproval in every society which is created and maintained by the psychological and sociological processes he describes in the *Theory of Moral Sentiments*. Another state of balance or equilibrium is the idea of the natural or normal price of a commodity in a free market economy; this is the price of each commodity to which actual prices 'gravitate' under the influence of the market mechanisms he outlines in the *Wealth of Nations*. This goes beyond Newton's idea of a purely physical system, in which the equilibrium is simply the point of rest or unchanging motion which establishes itself when all the forces are equal and opposite, to the more biological notion of a mechanism with the capacity to adapt itself to changes in its environment in such a way as to enable it to continue functioning in its normal or 'natural' way. Much of Smith's work is concerned with explaining these various hidden 'feed-back' mechanisms which contribute to the adaptive functioning of the social system.

Smith does not himself use the language of 'function' and 'equilibrium', instead he talks of the purposes of God and certain 'natural' conditions. Thus, when he is dealing with a social phenomenon such as man's tendency (in daily life and in law) to judge actions by their actual rather than their intended consequences – which he regards in terms which echo the 'History of Astronomy' as an 'irregularity' in that it does not seem to accord with common sense to blame people for what they did not intend to do – he sets out his objectives as follows:

This irregularity of sentiment. . . I proceed now to explain; and I shall consider, first, the cause which gives occasion to it, or the mechanism by which nature produces it; secondly the extent of its influence; and last of all, the end which it answers, or the purpose which the Author of nature seems to have intended by it. (*Theory of Moral Sentiments*, II. iii. Introd.).

His explanatory scheme thus culminates not in observed regularities, but in religious faith. Indeed he uses the metaphor of an 'invisible hand' to describe how the basically self-interested actions of individuals lead to the prosperity of all. This need not affect our acceptance of Smith as a social scientist for God is not invoked to explain how the unintended good effects for the system are brought about, but to account for the existence of such wonderfully adapted mechanisms. God created man and the world, hence the natural processes may be regarded as revealing God's intentions; but He is the maker and not the mechanism. The mechanism can therefore be analysed and described without reference to God.

Where God does come into Smith's scheme in a more fundamental way is as the guarantor of moral values. His religious belief provides Smith with the ultimate justification for accepting the natural moral sentiments as standards of moral right and wrong. It is by reference to God's universal benevolence that Smith underwrites the utilitarian outcome of the entire social process, namely 'the greatest happiness of the greatest number' – the phrase coined by Smith's teacher at Glasgow, Francis Hutcheson.

SMITH'S THEORY OF MAN

Adam Smith stands between the extreme atomistic and psychological individualism of Hobbes and the more holistic sociological theories of the nineteenth century. Although he has no time for the idea of a state of nature as a pre-social condition, his theory of human nature is Hobbesian to the extent that he posits certain fundamental and original passions, such as hunger and the propensity to barter, which 'though they may be warpt, cannot be entirely perverted', (*Theory of Moral Sentiments*, V.2.1). Among these is an 'original' or primary desire to gain the approval and avoid the disapproval of other men which gives rise to all sorts of 'secondary' social passions. This is what renders man naturally fit for society and marks Smith's radical break with Hobbes. (We should also note that, despite his causal model for social theory, Smith, unlike Hobbes, does not say that man *is* a machine. The psychological or mental realm has its own laws which, although they are like those of natural science, are not identical with them. He is not, therefore, a straight forward materialist.)

As we have seen from his account of scientific development, man also possesses certain psychologically based reasoning capacities. In practical life this manifests itself in his ability to learn by trial and error how to gain his overall objectives, although most actions are the result of the immediate promptings of the passions or sentiments. These passions are conceived of as being analogous but not equivalent to physical forces, impelling men to action according to their cumulative magnitude and direction. He follows Hobbes in allowing that 'every man . . . is much more deeply interested in whatever immediately concerns himself, than in what concerns another man'; the selfish passions, which are directed to the satisfaction of the individual's own interests, predominate in that they are usually stronger and more persistent than other passions. He also accepts that there are natural unsocial—or, as we would say, anti-social—passions, such as hatred, anger and envy which can be strong but are usually less persistent than selfish ones. But he argues, against Hobbes and with Aristotle, that there are also social passions, such as benevolence, which although they are weak in relation to all but a few friends and kinsmen do operate when they are not opposed by selfish or unsocial passions. But the major departure from the Hobbesian scheme comes with Smith's account of the moral sentiments. These give rise to social rules directing self-interest, restraining selfishness and reinforcing natural benevolence, thus making a consensus-based social life possible.

Smith's theory of social morality is based on the thesis that men approve of the actions and attitudes of others if, when they imagine themselves to be in the situation of that other person, their 'sympathetic' feelings accord with those that actually motivate that person; and, similarly, men disapprove of actions and attitudes which they cannot 'enter into' by such imaginative changes of position. Sympathetic feeling is not the same as pity or benevolence; rather it is any feeling which arises from any imagined change of situation with another person. At the beginning of the *Moral Sentiments* we are asked to consider what happens when we see a man on the rack:

By the imagination we place ourselves in his situation, we conceive ourselves enduring all the same torments, we enter as it were into his body, and become in some measure the same person with him, and thence form some idea of his sensations, and even feel something which, though weaker in degree, is not altogether unlike them. (*Theory of Moral Sentiments*, I.i.1)

This is the psychological phenomenon on which Smith bases his explanation of the genesis and operation of social norms. He accomplishes this by adding to his contention that men approve when they sympathize (that is share the sentiments of the agent) the assertion that men desire to achieve mutual sympathy because of its intrinsic pleasure; we like to share the opinions, attitudes and feelings of others and so feel 'at one' with them. Even more we enjoy approval and dislike disapproval. So a process of mutual accommodation takes place. To achieve the desired harmony of feelings the agent alters his own actions and attitudes so that the sentiments involved are closer to those felt by the spectator, and Smith notes that a spectator is never able to experience the full force of the agent's feelings in the moment of action; the spectator in turn makes an imaginative effort to enter into the agent's situation, thus stirring up his sympathetic feelings so that they approximate to those of the agent. There is thus a continuous process of adjustment between agents and spectators. Where the average sentiments of agents and spectators meet, the degree of feeling on which they compromise, or in Aristotle's terms, the 'mean' attitude, is the feeling which is characteristic of morally approved behaviour in a particular group or society, and by generalizing on the basis of these shared sentiments this 'norm' comes to be expressed in social rules by which men direct their actions so as to gain the pleasures of mutual sympathy.

The analysis is complicated by the fact that the spectator's judgements are affected by whether or not he can enter into the feelings of gratitude and/or resentment felt by those who have, or might have, enjoyed or suffered the consequences of the agent's actions. Sympathy or lack of it with these reactive sentiments of gratitude and resentment follows on the original judgement of the propriety or impropriety of the action, reinforcing approval of benevolence, which evokes gratitude, and supporting disapproval of harmful or unjust actions, which provoke resentment and retaliatory action. Thus the spectator tends to disapprove of acts which injure others and approves of restrained retaliation, so furnishing a natural basis for the criminal law. In similar ways all social standards are based on that species of 'immediate feeling or sensation' which is the product of the imaginative consideration of the causes and effects of specific actions, and which, through a process of mutual and multilateral accommodation between agents and spectators, results in agreed social norms of conduct. All this Smith ties together by reference to a social construct or ideal type which he calls the 'impartial spectator', whom he identifies with the average person in a society or group when he is in the position of observing the conduct of any person with whom he has no special connection.

When it comes to explaining the content of social norms Smith refers to the strength of the original passions, the extent to which they can be controlled by the agent, and the degree to which they are characteristically called into play in different environments (fear, for instance, will be most in evidence in dangerous situations; this accounts for the considerable divergencies between the norms of different societies). The level of approved feelings is also affected by the ease with which spectators can enter into different types of feeling. Here there are regularities in the operation of the imagination which influence on the impartial spectator's judgement. Thus it is easier to sympathize with or enter into pleasant sentiments such as benevolence than into painful ones such as anger, so the consensual level of approved benevolence is close to the feelings of the agent concerned, whereas agents have to curb their anger considerably in order to reduce it to the approved level. Similarly, Smith generalizes, it is easier to enter into emotional states such as jealousy than into physically caused pains like toothache so we are socially required to restrain at least the manifestations of the former less than those of the latter.

These 'laws' of sympathy each have their several effects on the average moral sentiments in a community and form part of the hidden mechanisms which Smith uses to explain even the 'irregularities' or inconsistencies in social norms. As each individual seeks 'to conform to the average or impartial spectator's attitudes these attitudes serve not simply as the source of social norms but as a point of equilibrium towards which the feelings of individuals tend. Thus the mechanisms of sympathy contribute to a moral system which brings an operative consensus to the otherwise unco-ordinated and conflicting attitudes of interacting individuals. The Hobbesian state of war is avoided not by contract, but as the unintended by-product of millions of acts of mutual accommodation between agents and spectators.

Smith extends this account of social morality to cover the internalization of the attitudes of the impartial spectator. As each individual grows up his desire for the pleasures of mutual sympathy prompt him to become the imaginative spectator of his own conduct so that he may anticipate the friendly or adverse responses of others. Once started, this process leads him to approve and disapprove of his own behaviour for he is able to divide himself into the self-as-agent and the self-as-spectator and to experience agreement or disagreement in the attitudes of both selves. Thus, looking back on his conduct he may not be able to enter into his unprovoked anger and he will therefore condemn himself. Hence the development of conscience as a guide to and supporter of socially approved conduct. Moral pressure is not therefore merely an external matter for the individual seeks to conform to the judgments of his own conscience. Man's nature is social not so much because of his rather limited benevolence but because every man desires the approval both of others (the love of praise) and of himself (the love of praiseworthiness).

Yet within the limits set by the impartial spectator either through public opinion or through 'the man within', the individual naturally pursues his own welfare. Indeed in so far as he does so with prudent foresight he gains the approval of the spectator who, as a detached observer unaffected by the urgency of the immediate present, is as much concerned for the agent's future as for his present happiness. And so the natural self-centredness of man is taken for granted and prudence is encouraged and approved so long as it does not conflict with proper benevolence and strict justice. Only to this extent is there truth in the standard caricature of Smith as the apostle of self-interest.

SMITH'S THEORY OF SOCIETY

To live in society means to live together in sufficient peace to avoid death, reproduce the species and carry on economic activities essential to survival. Its first prerequisits is therefore justice, that is some system to restrain man's natural tendency to injure others. Without justice a society will, says Smith, destroy itself, hence the sympathetic resentments of the impartial spectator, shared and reinforced by all who experience injury at the hands of others, is the basis of social life. By retaliating to the degree that the impartial spectator approves the individual does not intend the survival of society but his actions have this effect by deterring future potential wrongdoers. The institutionalized procedures of courts in trying and punishing offenders is simply an organized extension of this modified instinctive retaliation, and the content of the criminal law simply regularizes the different degrees of resentment felt or imagined to be felt by those who suffer different types of injury, highest in the case of death and serious bodily injury but covering also the loss of property and personal reputation. The connection between justice and resentment explains why justice is a purely negative virtue in that, because resentment is evoked only by positive actions which result in harm, it is possible to be just merely by doing nothing.

Smith therefore rejects the Hobbesian view that justice is artificial. Justice is firmly based on unreflective moral sentiments, but it does in fact serve the general interest and it does so not only by preserving the lives of individuals and so the possibility of life together, but also by establishing the necessary peacefulness for economic activity, particularly commercial activity. In this it is supported by institutionalized religion which originates in man's fearfulness at the uncertainties of human life and his metaphysical speculations as to the cause of the universe but, by invoking the terrors of eternal punishment, provides further motives to restrain men's tendency to injustice. Hence religion supports legal restraints and so benefits economic life. By pointing to such relationships

Smith builds up his case for viewing society as a whole as an integrated mechanism with an over-all purpose, a theme which is reflected in his account of the family as originating in the sexual instinct but being held together by the ease of sympathetic identification with those with whom we are in constant contact. This has the unplanned but socially necessary consequence of providing a setting in which children, through the long period of human maturation, can be cared for and brought to the point of internalizing the spectator attitudes of their society.

Given the rules of natural justice and some measure of organized enforcement of them, the core of social relationships outside the family are, for Smith, economic ones. Societies are distinguished according to their basic methods of production into hunting, pastoral, agricultural and commercial types (the latter being dominated by artificers and merchants) each with a distinctive property and class system. In line with his general theory the rules of property are not conscious creations but emerge naturally from the expectations of continued possession which are generated by the occupation of land or the use of objects in the normal course of domestic economic activity. Hunters, with no settled homes, have few such expectations except in relation to animals they have killed in the hunt; in pastoral society the constant care of flocks build up 'reasonable expectations' of continued possession of those animals, and with the development of agriculture it becomes natural for each to cultivate the land nearest to his fixed settlement thus building up an expectation of exclusive use and occupation of land. With the emergence of skilled crafts and extensive division of labour, different expectations are created concerning the possession of tools and products, and there emerge complex property rules giving expression to these expectations.

Closely allied to property is the factor of class divisions which are based primarily on wealth, something which is little in evidence in the almost propertyless society of hunters when men lived in bands of about two or three hundred. Pasturage and the ownership of herds produce great inequalities between the few wealthy and the remaining poor. This leads directly to authoritarian government such as that of the Tartar chiefs, for the wealthy need organized protection for their property and have the means to maintain numerous dependants to protect themselves and their animals. Similarly settled agriculture gives rise to the small peasant farmer's need for protection and so to the wealth and authority of feudal aristocracies, whose position is impregnable until the development of towns produce an alliance of a new class of tradesmen and mechanics with feudal monarchs, so making possible the existence of a trading class. This in turn facilitates the growth of manufacturing and a whole new economic system in which there are three 'great constituent orders', landlords, capitalists and wage labourers.

The details of this historical saga need not concern us, but we must note how much of the organization of society, on Smith's theory, follows from the fundamental economic relations of the method of production, so that man's desire to achieve material goods, first for survival and then to stand high in the estimation of his fellows, is the underlying cause of social structure and social change. Smith does not discount the significance of military power, particularly in determining who can protect their property and accumulate wealth by establishing themselves as governors (thereby obtaining the automatic respect that goes to the wealthy), but this cannot alter radically the basic organization of a society according to the prevailing method of production. Economic life needs to be understood in terms of each individual's natural propensity to exchange goods and the desire for the improvement of his material position with the expenditure of the least amount of work. This desire is not only for material benefits for their own sake, since man's physical needs are easily met, but is more for the attention and admiration, in a word the sympathy of others. Thus his account of economic motivation ties in with his theory of sympathy giving his social theory a unity which approximates to that which the idea of gravity confers on astronomy. Because of the imagined pleasures of wealth men readily sympathize with the sentiments of the wealthy who thereby enjoy the real benefits of wealth, namely the attention and veneration of the rest of mankind. This explains both the tendency of men to amass wealth beyond their physical needs, and the deference of the the poor to the wealthy which reinforces the distinction of ranks and the authority of government. Hence the mutual support of the economic and political structures of society, a prime illustration of the organic unity of the social mechanism.

This analysis of economic motivation carries the implication that much economic activity is irrational, for the actual pleasures of wealth are nowhere near what they are imagined to be. Smith also reflects that the preoccupation with wealth is a corruption of morals since wealth obtains admiration which is more properly given to the virtuous. But this is one of those 'irregularities' which he is pleased to explain causally by reference to sympathy and teleologically by the beneficial consequences it has for the stability and hence the prosperity of society.

Although Smith carefully traces the interlocking relationships between the economic, political, property, religious and other aspects of society in the total social system, much of his fame rests on his analysis of commercial economies as self-regulating systems. Smith's analyses of commercial systems involves the idea of a natural or 'real' price of all commodities, which is originally the amount of labour involved in the production of the commodity in question, but, as an economy develops, comes to include such returns on capital (profit) and on land (rent) as are necessary to ensure that sufficient capital and land are forthcoming for production purposes. In Book I of *The Wealth of Nations* Smith argues that in every society there is an average or natural level of wages, profit and rent which go to make up the natural price or that sum which it really costs to bring a commodity to market and which is therefore the lowest price at which anyone will sell his goods for any length of time. If the market price is below the natural price then the former will rise (or else the supply of the commodity will dry up), but if the market price is higher than the natural price then other potential producers, looking for a share in the inflated profits, will set themselves up in the production of the overpriced goods and enter the market by selling at less than the current market price, thus forcing other producers to reduce their prices, a process which continues until the natural price becomes the norm.

The natural price is thus a point of homeostatic equilibrium to which, in Smith's words, the market price is 'continually gravitating'. This point of equilibrium changes as an economy develops since it is affected by the cumulative effect of the causes of economic progress, such as an increase in the division of labour, an extension of markets, the improvement of communications, and so forth, but the natural price of a commodity always relates to the cost of production and the natural rates of return on capital, labour and land, which reflect the prevailing level of supply and demand for these factors. The general tendency of this system is the production of a steady flow of consumer goods at the lowest feasible prices. In this way, given the constraints of justice, the efforts of each individual to improve his own situation maximizes the prosperity of society as a whole, while the relative wealth of the successful minority adds to the political stability which economic progress requires. All this has the appearance of being the work of an 'invisible hand'.

PRACTICAL IMPLICATIONS

An efficient self-regulating system ought not to be tampered with, particularly if its inner workings are not fully understood. Smith's account of the operations of the commercial economy carries with it the clear implication that governments should leave well alone and so allow to emerge what he called 'the obvious and simple system of natural liberty'. This is the liberal idea of the minimal state, embodied in the policy of laissez-faire.

Natural liberty exists when

every man, as long as he does not violate the laws of justice, is left perfectly free to pursue his own interest in his own way, and bring both his industry and capital into competition with those of any other man.

This means that 'the sovereign is completely discharged from . . . the duty of superintending the industry of private people, and of directing it towards the employment most suitable to the interests of society.' (*Wealth of Nations*, Book IV, Chapter ix). Government must, of course, maintain the conditions for the operation of the economic system; it must administer justice, raise taxes to provide for national defence and even provide the capital for commercial infra-structure such as roads and bridges, but it should not attempt to intervene for other reasons in the forces of supply and demand or prevent any person seeking to maximize his own income by the use of his land, capital or labour. Thus nearly all restraints on trade (internal and external), monopoly rights and restrictive occupational regulations should be removed. This must inevitably lead to an improvement in national wealth not at the expense of but to the mutual enrichment of neighbouring countries since larger markets mean more developed division of labour and more efficient manufacturing processes. Moreover the internal distribution of wealth would be such as to benefit all citizens and not merely the wealthy. The system of natural liberty is therefore both just and expedient.

Similarly it is not the government's duty to intervene in social morality in so far as that this is a matter of beneficence, for no one should be compelled to help others; government must limit itself to the enforcement of the negative aspect of morality, the prohibitions on injuring others, that is, with justice. Here again government is not a creative agency but is an instrument for the effective administration of the natural moral sentiments of sympathetic resentment which develop their own specific content in each type of society in accordance with the type of injury to which men are most vulnerable in that society. Governments do not make law out of nothing or to serve their own purposes, they discover and apply what is already established by natural processes. Indeed they are powerless to enforce laws which run counter to strong sentiments of natural justice. Somewhat paradoxically for a customs officer, he illustrates this point by governmental failures to prevent smuggling because it is not naturally regarded as a criminal activity. Natural law is thus there to be discovered and applied and Smith warns against attempts to improve on it for these are liable to be undertaken in ignorance of the hidden mechanisms which make apparently 'irregular' moral sentiments useful for the system as a whole.

Smith is not, however, all optimism and complacency. He is sceptical of the capacity of politicians to act sensibly for the common good and fearful of the power of vested interests. All groups of men associate for their own benefit; politicians are 'insidious and crafty animals' who look only to their immediate political advantage, merchants join together to press trade restrictions on governments, and every industrialist seeks to protect himself against effective competition. Government can and should resist the pressures of these partial groups but Smith does not expect his ideal of a totally unfettered economy to be realized. Moreover he is aware of the harmful effects of the division of labour on the labouring class: constant repetition of a boring manipulation induces a 'torpor of mind', while life in cities removes men from the wholesome influence of the social pressures of village communities, so that commercial society brings a real loss to the 'intellectual, social and martial virtues' of the labouring class, which can only partially be relieved by the provision of elementary education, a function which Smith was, interestingly enough, happy to see subsidized by government.

ASSESSMENT

Smith's achievements are those of a pioneer. The effort to see commercial society as a system and trace the interconnections of the various aspects of social life contributed to the development of modern social science. But although he aspires to follow Newton's methodology he does not bring to the study of society the sort of mathematical precision that is possible in the study of the movements of physical bodies. Despite his search for proportional variations between economic factors such as the accumulation of capital and the extent of the division of labour he demonstrates few precise quantitative relationships in his attempted psychological and economic laws. Thus despite the detailed nature of his economic evidence there is inadequate empirical evidence for a determinate 'natural' price in each economic area. Although, in the large, he made a convincing case for the existence of economic and social systems and many of the particular pathways he charted, e.g. in the laws of supply and demand, still remain in contemporary theory, the empirical adequacy of much of his work has, not surprisingly, been called in question.

Also, much of what he pointed to in the economic sphere, particularly concerning the effects of unfettered competition, has more application to the early stages of capitalism when it was still dominated by small businesses, and has less relevance to the world of the joint stock company, trades unions and international corporations. His economic vision is to that extent parochial.

His theory of social norms is also problematic, perhaps more so, because of the empirical elusiveness of the phenomenon of the 'natural' sentiment, that is the theoretically pre-social attitudes of men from which actual social norms are built up through social interaction and individual experience. All actual impartial judgements are affected by the social norms of the observer so that the effort to enter into the sentiments of another is bound to be affected by the existing moral attitudes of the observer. That behind this, at the origins of a genetic process of personal and social development, there are universal 'original' or raw sentiments of sufficient precision to give rise to the whole galaxy of social norms, is a speculative hypothesis rather than an empirical observation for if these natural sentiments exist they are buried in the history of individuals and societies and cannot be recalled for observation. This might not matter if the hypothesis could be subjected to empirical testing by deducing detailed predictions from it, but the evidence Smith offers is too rough and ready for this purpose. The suspicion remains therefore that sympathy is a vehicle for moral attitudes not an explanation for them.

But while Smith may leave us questioning whether or not his theory can account for the detailed content of social norms, the analysis of the process of 'socialization' whereby the attitudes of peer groups, parents and teachers are internalized through psychological mechanisms involving the imagination is remarkable for its time and of continuing relevance today. His account of conscience is arguably more realistic because more sociological than that of Freud and its influence in sociology can be traced through the work of G. H. Mead whose notion of the 'generalized other' owes much to Smith (see p. 198), moreover David Reisman's distinction between 'inner-directed' and 'other-directed' societies is foreshadowed in Smith's distinction between the love of praise (from others) and the love of praiseworthiness (the approval of one's own conscience) (see David Reisman, *The Lonely Crowd*, Yale University Press, 1950).

Smith's views are, however, most dated, in the role which the Deity plays both in his explanatory scheme and in his normative ethics. The whole basis of his account of final causation is undermined if we drop the hypothesis of a benevolent creator, and one suspects that his confidence in the acceptableness of the results of laissez-faire would also be shaken by agnosticism.

Also the easy identification of what is 'natural' in the sense of normal and what is 'natural' in the sense of desirable does not readily outlast the demise of the theological assumption that what God has created must be good. Smith's evaluations eventually come down to the meta-ethical justification that those feelings of which we cannot rid ourselves after extensive reflection have a felt authority and indubitability which justifies our regarding them as the voice of God within us. So, although we cannot accuse Smith of having totally confused 'is' and 'ought', his assumption that in the end the two realms, that of fact and that of value, coincide is more an expression of religious faith than philosophical reason.

Whether Smith's theory of society is capable of being modified to meet these criticisms is hard to say. We shall later return to the issue of the modern equivalent of Smith's divine teleology, namely functionalism (see p. 193). However, there has been a resurgence of belief in an essential connection between human values and what is in some way 'naturally' good for man, and certainly utilitarianism has flourished in a post-theological age. Further the criticism that Smith's account of the economic system does not fit modern economies can be taken, with F. A. Hayek and Milton Friedman, as more of a criticism of these economies than of Adam Smith; it may be that a move in the direction of the 'system of natural liberty' is both feasible and desirable. However it is unlikely that there could be any straightforward application of Smith's ideas to the modern world and the simplicity of his vision of a system centring on the phenomenon of self-interest modified by sympathy would seem to have suffered death from the accretion of countless qualifications so that, on his own view of theoretical development, it is vulnerable to replacement by other sets of theoretical assumptions which may provide intellectually more satisfying accounts of social life and rather different practical implications.

FOR FURTHER READING

A good general introduction to Smith's work is E. G. West, *Adam Smith* (Arlington House: New York, 1969). For Smith's moral and social theory see T. D. Campbell, *Adam Smith's Science of Morals* (Allen and Unwin: London, 1971) and D. A. Riesman, *Adam Smith's Sociological Economics* (Croom Helm: London, 1961).

For a comprehensive study of Smith's work the new Glasgow Edition of the *Works and Correspondence* of Adam Smith (Clarendon Press:

Oxford, 1976–   ) is invaluable. Of the many other editions of the *Wealth of Nations* which are available the abbreviated version edited by A. S. Skinner (Penguin Books: Harmondsworth 1970) has the best introduction. Excerpts from *The Moral Sentiments* are contained in D. D. Raphael (ed.) *The British Moralists*, Vol. II (Oxford University Press: London, 1969).

CHAPTER 6

Karl Marx:
A Conflict Theory

KARL MARX sees human society as a process of development that will end conflict through conflict. He anticipates that peace and harmony will be the eventual result of a history of war and violent revolution. With the exception of the earliest period of society, before the emergence of private property, the major feature of social relationships has been and is class struggle. Yet these clashes of economic interests will terminate in a classless, conflict-free and creative form of society called communism. Marx's attention is not, however, concentrated on the nature of the co-operative social relationships of the promised communist utopia. His theoretical writings deal much more with the explanation of existing social realities, and his central contribution to our understanding of society lies in his analysis of the economic causes of social conflict and the ways in which it is contained and suppressed by the ruling class in each society before breaking forth into new forms of social life.

Marx's emphasis on the role of conflict in social relationships is reminiscent of Hobbes, but Marx sees social conflict as between groups or classes rather than between individuals, and, although there is a similarity in their views of the social significance of power and on the topic of what Marx called false-consciousness, Marx has an optimistic belief in the possibility of humanly satisfying community life which is more characteristic of Aristotle than of Hobbes.

Marx lived in various European countries in the mid-nineteenth-century, a time of rapid industrial development, political upheaval and major social change. Born into a Jewish family which had converted to Christianity to avoid discriminatory laws, Marx must have become aware at an early age of the tensions which exist between social groups, an awareness which was heightened by the obvious contrast between the liberal ideals in which he was educated and the policies of the reactionary feudal Prussian state of which his home town of Trier, in the Rhineland, was a part. Later, as a student in Berlin, and then as an impoverished exile in Paris, Brussels and London, he was confronted with the misery and deprivations of the industrial workers in the expanding cities of the time, and he could contrast this inhuman poverty with the massive enrichment of those who owned the new machinery and factories.

These experiences led Marx to take a much more pessimistic view of capitalism than did eighteenth-century philosophers such as Adam Smith and to work out in less individualistic and more aggressive terms the implications for social theory and political action of the apparently irreconcilable conflicts of interest which emerged in this period of capitalist expansion. He concludes that once the internal conflicts or 'contradictions' of the capitalist system were fully developed to the point of self-destruction the violent seizure of the privately-owned means of production would open the way to a genuinely free, satisfying and sociable life for all men, a vision which has much in common with Aristotle's ideal of civic community.

The theoretical framework in which Marx presents this prognosis of the cataclysmic demise of capitalism owes much to the philosophical ideas of G. W. F. Hegel whose thought dominated the intellectual life of Berlin where Marx became a student, first of law and then of philosophy. Marx accepts the historical perspective of Hegel but adapts and transforms Hegel's method and concepts to suit his own rather different approach to historical understanding. Thus, while the Hegelian notions of the dialectical development of history and the alienation of the creator from his creation are the inspiration for Marx's explanations of social conflict and eventual social harmony, from the start Marx rejected Hegel's nationalist, authoritarian and conservative political opinions. Instead he associated himself with the 'Young Hegelians', a group of intellectuals critical of repressive government and laissez-faire capitalism. Marx's connection with this group cost him the chance of an academic position. He turned instead to political journalism. When his attacks on the censorship laws of the German government led to his expulsion, he went to Paris where he came into contact with French socialists and industrial workers. There he became familiar with the works of the French 'utopian' socialists Saint-Simon and Fourier, and met many intellectual radicals such as Proudhon. These experiences helped him to see the political weakness of socialist movements led by paternalistic members of the middle class and led him into the organization of working class political movements.

Involvement in the unrest which swept Europe in 1848 forced Marx to find sanctuary in Britain where he continued working to organize and articulate the ideas of the growing socialist movements of the time. This led to the writing of the highly influential *Communist Manifesto* (1848). It was in London that Marx, living in great poverty but with the support of his collaborator Frederick Engels, spent many years working on his major work, *Capital*, which was still unfinished when he died in 1883.

Some of Marx's writings, like the *Communist Manifesto* (written jointly with Engels) are journalistic political pamphlets. Others, like the *The Class Struggle in France* (1850) are analyses of economically determined historical change. His later works, such as the *Critique of Political Economy* (1859) and *Capital* itself are more purely economic in content. There is also a contrast, now thought by most commentators to have been exaggerated, between the earlier philosophical works such as *The German Ideology* (1846) which use the Hegelian language of 'alienation' and the later, more positivistic, economic writings in which he speaks instead of 'exploitation'. The recent discovery of a transitional work, the *Grundrisse*, a draft for *Capital*, has led to a new appreciation of the unity of his work as a development and adaption of German Hegelianism, French liberal socialism and British Political Economy, particularly the work of Adam Smith on whose analysis of capitalism Marx drew heavily.

No single work of Marx's provides a comprehensive introduction to his thought. There are however, many excellent selections available. Page references here are to *Karl Marx: Selected Writings in Sociology and Social Philosophy*, edited by T. B. Bottomore and Maximilien Rubel (Penguin Books: Harmondsworth, 2nd edition, 1961).

MARX'S APPROACH

When we come to consider Marx's theory of man, it will become clear that there is a strong 'humanist' element in his thought: he looks to the full development of man's creative capacities as the goal of historical progress. But genuine creative freedom is a feature only of the future communist society when man will at last be in control of his own destiny. In the meantime the individual is forced into particular moulds and patterns of behaviour by the economic realities of his society. Marx believes he has acquired a knowledge of the forces operative in society which is sufficiently scientific in nature to provide causal explanations of past history and generalized predictions of the future course of events. As regards his major analyses of feudal and capitalist societies Marx is therefore a positivist, although he believes that positivism would cease to apply when men were no longer in the grip of impersonal economic forces, and were thus able to make their own history, and so, on his theory, their own natures.

Marx's particular version of positivism has been called 'historical materialism' (pp. 67–72). It is historical in that the scientific generalizations he seeks to establish are about the course of human history. History he believes to be a process of evolution in which societies pass through various stages, each stage destroying and yet building on the previous one. In this respect his ideas on social development are to be compared with those of Darwin's on the evolution of species—and it is interesting to note that Marx was a great admirer of Darwin (p. 78). Marx considers it possible to identify these evolutionary steps and to explain why societies pass through their various stages by exhibiting what he refers to in the 1st Preface to *Capital* as 'tendencies working with iron necessity towards inevitable results'. On the basis of this scientific analysis he predicts the imminent revolutionary downfall of the capitalist system and the state after what Engels called a Darwinian struggle for survival between the classes (p. 207).

In his commitment to discovering an ordered pattern of historical development, Marx is being true to his Hegelian heritage. He also follows Hegel in using the idea of the dialectic to account for the dynamics of historical change. Hegel started from the Platonic idea of dialectic as a process of argument leading up to the disproof of a proposition by way of drawing out its inherent inconsistencies or contradictions. He recast this process of argument into a feature of general historical change in which ideas work themselves out in historical events until they are superseded in the new situation they have helped to create. In this way Hegel sought to overcome the ancient tension between thought on the one hand and material existence on the other, the dualism between mind and matter. History is to be seen as a process in which the gap between the external world and the experiencing mind, which involves the 'alienation' of the experiencing subject from external reality, is overcome by progressively more successful attempts to understand and so change the world through the exercise of reason. In the life of each individual and even more so in the development of each society, thought comes to master the material world by reducing it to a comprehensible form and changing it to conform with its own order. Alienation, the experience of the 'otherness' or hostility of the external world, is transcended by this recurrent embodiment of thought in material things, for example, by treating them as property. This 'dialectic' is a reciprocal procedure in which matter is changed by the operations of mind while at the same time mind is altered by its embodiment in material things, an ongoing interaction in which periods of tension between human thought and its material embodiments are followed by a reunification of mind and matter in an integrated whole. The ultimate outcome of all this is presented in religious and metaphysical terms as the realization in human history of God as the 'Absolute Idea'.

Hegel's philosophy is thus a form of philosophical 'idealism' in that the underlying reality which fuels historical change and in which all things are eventually united is mental rather than physical. Marx follows Feuerbach in transforming Hegel's theological idealism by putting man rather than God at the centre of the process. For Hegel God created the world by an act of self-alienation and eventually gathered it back into himself. Feuerbach in his interpretation of religion (see *The Essence of Christianity*, 1841) put this the other way round and argued that man created the idea of God, endowed Him with the highest human characteristics and then worshipped this 'alienated' conception of himself.

Marx adapts this to the economic sphere by thinking of the activity of working as the embodiment of human qualities in the material things produced. These material products come to dominate man's life as for Feuerbach men's religious ideas came to control their creators. This results in alienation, which is, for Marx, the condition of being the slave of one's own products. Man is dominated by the material things he makes for his own use, a domination from which he is freed only by the development of new production processes over which he can assume full control. And so we get Marx's version of history as a dialectical process according to which the real contradictions, which manifest themselves in social conflict and a sense of alienation between man and the world in which he lives and between men, and are to be traced to the material circumstances of each particular stage of social development (pp. 177 ff).

Marx is thus a materialist, not because he values material goods above all else, or because he rejects the reality of mental phenomena, but because he held that the laws of tendencies which describe, explain and, to an extent, predict how societies work, are laws of economics. The forces which conflict and synthesize in society are economic or material ones; history is therefore a movement of the contradiction and resolution of economic factors. This inverts the Hegelian notion of history as the progressive embodiment of ever more rational thought. In contrast, Marx believes that ideas are only pictures of things and hence the effects rather than causes of the historical process. This does not prevent him from saying that political and social ideas (or 'ideologies') are instruments in the struggle between classes, but he always holds to the view that these ideological weapons are manifestations of the underlying economic interests of the dominant social classes.

The essence of Marx's approach to social study is thus the claim that the nature of any society and its pattern of development are a function of the way in which the material requirements of human life—food, clothing, housing and so forth—are obtained through labour. The production of the means to support life is the basis of all social structure, social conflict and hence social change. Much of Marx's work is taken up with the detailed composition of this thesis.

Marx's historical theory of society has a positivistic ring. He sets as his goal the strict causal interpretation of social change which presupposes that history is a tightly determined and inevitable process. Certainly, from the point of view of individual behaviour, Marx's analyses allow for only slight departure from a path mapped out for the individual by his class position and the stage of historical development in which he finds himself. But the materialist basis of the process does not render history purely mechanical since the struggle between classes is waged through ideological means as well as physical conflict, and the dialectical nature of the process allows for an interplay between material factors and social and political ideas which Marx does not in practice attempt to fit into a rigid pattern. Moreover the goal of historical development involves the emancipation of mankind from the shackles of materially determined interactions and Marx is certainly prepared to claim that his own social theory is not simply an expression of the class interests of the proletariat;

it is also objectively true and its universal acceptance is part of the movement towards the freedom of communist society.

The contrast between the determinism of previous history in which moral and political ideas are simply a reflection of particular class interests and the emerging freedom of communist society of which Marx's own ideas are a prognosis, allows us to argue that Marx could claim universality and objectivity for his own ideals without contradicting his scientific assumptions. The passionate tone of his descriptions of the inhumanities of capitalism and his evident preference for the free, spontaneous and creative communal activity of unalienated man amply demonstrate his commitment to the goals of material prosperity and the development of human powers within a harmonious social context. There is therefore, in the end, something of a happy coincidence between the predicted outcome of historical development and the social values which Marx endorses.

MARX'S THEORY OF MAN

It is part of Marx's holistic approach to social explanation that man has no precise and fixed nature. The individual's actions, attitudes and beliefs depend on his social relationships and his social relationships depend on his class situation and the economic structure of his society. Man's nature is therefore social in the sense that he has no nature apart from that with which he is endowed by his social position. There is therefore no place for Hobbes's universal truths about human motivation, or even for Adam Smith's belief that there are certain aspects of man's make-up which can never be 'entirely perverted' (see p. 97). In so far as man's nature is equated with his behaviour it is 'the totality of his social relations' (p. 83) and these vary from society to society.

Marx's rather extreme view of the social determination of individual behaviour is designed to counter the assumption of the classical economists that man is inherently self-interested. He declines to accept that social conflict is the result of the intrinsic competitiveness, aggression and selfishness of man. The Hobbesian picture he accepts as applying only in certain stages of capitalist development when alienated men are forced to act and feel in a self-centred and hostile manner, but such behaviour and emotions are the result not the cause of capitalism and will be superseded by new forms of behaviour and motivation once capitalism has been transcended and new economic relationships established.

On the Hobbesian analysis the most that can be done towards controlling social conflict is via the agreement to apply sanctions against anti-social behaviour. Marx saw that this approach presupposed that there were at least some unselfish and enlightened men in control of the coercive apparatus, whereas in reality the economically most powerful section of the population was generally able to use sanctions for their own benefit (p. 231). For the same reason he does not anticipate successful social engineering through the deployment of the more subtle educational devices of the utilitarian 'materialists' like Jeremy Bentham who 'forget that circumstances are changed by men and that the educator must himself be educated' (pp. 82 f).

On the other hand Marx does believe that, in the fullness of historical development, the 'capitalist' nature of man will be transformed into a genuinely benevolent and spontaneously co-operative disposition which will require no coercive manipulation. After the proletarian revolution men will willingly play their part in the communal life and distribution could therefore be in accordance with the principle 'from each according to his ability, to each according to his needs' (p. 263). It is not so much that Marx believes man to be inherently unselfish although temporarily corrupted by social factors, but rather that man has the potential to be either selfish or unselfish according to the nature of the relationships into which he is born or has to enter.

Indeed it is somewhat misleading to think of Marx's man in communist society as *un*selfish since this suggests a tension between the interests of competing individuals, whereas it is part of Marx's prediction that in such a society the spontaneous co-operation between men destroys the alienation between men which leads them to perceive their interests as opposed. This is because when there is communal ownership of industrialized means of production it will in fact be the case that objective clashes of economic interest will be a thing of the past. Further the type of fulfilment which is available to men in this society is a communal not an individual achievement for it must be achieved together or not at all. Communist society is 'the real appropriation of human nature, through and for man. It is therefore the return of man to himself as a social, that is, really human, being' (pp. 249 f).

This truly human existence is one in which man's productive capacities are developed in a balanced and satisfying manner. Although man is always a producer there are some systems in which he is more genuinely a producer than others. These are the systems in which he is in command of his actions and can choose to make what he wants in the way he wants. Man affirms himself in his labour but not all forms of labour enable him to make this affirmation in its fullness. Work may be forced, dehumanized, and meaningless: the condition of alienation. It may also be free, human, satisfying and creative: the condition of unalienated man in communist society. How labour has become the former and will become the latter is the framework within which Marx sets out his view of human history.

Marx's ideal of creative productivity as the end-result of history carries the implicit assumption that there is a potential in all men which can be brought to fruition only in certain social conditions. Despite his more historical and scientific approach Marx presents an essentially Aristotelian combination of empirical observations concerning the activities men find satisfying and evaluative appraisal of what is most worthwhile in human life. He even speaks in his early writings of the 'species character' of man. In this respect Marx does, therefore, have a view as to what is essentially human amidst the diversity of actual human behaviour.

MARX'S THEORY OF SOCIETY

Marx identifies the causal basis of society with the 'forces of production' that is with 'what is produced and how it is produced' (p. 69). These forces of production include the raw materials, the end-products and the entire method of work used in the productive processes, including the tools and skills of those involved. This economic basis of society, from which everything else follows, incorporates all those factors which lead to the production of a certain type of thing in a certain manner.

The most important and immediate effects of the forces of production are the 'relations of production' into which men enter in order to carry out their productive tasks. The relations of production are the roles men occupy in the work process: they involve the division of labour, the chain of command, and, most fundamentally, the relationship of the owner of the means of production to the non-owners. These are relationships into which, outside communist society, men are forced to enter in order to earn a living. They include the relationship of plantation-owner to slave, of feudal lord to peasant, and of factory owner (capitalist) to proletarian (industrial wage labourer). Thus a feudal lord owns the land and the mill, so that the serf is forced to work for him in order to survive, and the industrial capitalist who owns the means of production can buy the labour of the proletarian who must sell his labour if he is to acquire the means of subsistence:

In the social production which men carry out they enter into definite relations independent of their will; these relations of production correspond to a definite stage of development of their material powers of production. The totality of these relations of production constitutes the economic structure of society (p. 67).

From these relations of production class divisions arise along the line of ownership and non-ownership of the means of production. All societies (except communist ones) are thus divided into classes or orders, whose members, because of their different relationship to the means of production, have conflicting economic interests; what benefits one class tends to harm another (pp. 186 f). Class divisions are therefore economic divisions. But these divisions are not simply a matter of different income levels since the nature of the distinction and so of the conflict between classes depends on the sources from which their income derives, not on its amount. It is because the proletarian earns wages and the capitalist lives off profits, and not because the former is poor and the latter wealthy, that their economic interests are antagonistic.

The nature and intensity of the struggle between economic classes determines the characteristics of the rest of the 'superstructure' as Marx calls the institutions and cultural arrangements of which the economic basis is the cause. The morality and religion of a society are means whereby the ruling class maintains its position by having its own 'ideology' accepted as being in the interests of all classes, a phenomenon Marx describes as 'false-consciousness' since all classes erroneously believe in the objectivity and universality of rules and ideals which are simply the expression of class interests. Similarly, the legal institutions of a society are mere instruments of the state. Here Marx sides with Hobbes against Aristotle and Smith: there is no natural justice. Marx goes beyond Hobbes in asserting that the function of the state is nothing more than the violent protection of the interests of the dominant economic class. Government is a manifestation and defence of economic power.

Like Adam Smith before him, Marx distinguishes types of society on the basis of their modes of production. On Marx's scheme history is a progression from tribal to slave-owning society and thence into feudalism, capitalism and eventually to communism. His most detailed analyses concern the transition from feudalism to capitalism and the development of capitalism through its various steps towards its ultimate self-destruction. By looking at this in a little detail we will see how he relates the structure of a society to the type of division of labour involved in its system of production.

In tribal society, sometimes called primitive communism because it involves the communal ownership of land, the central economic activities are hunting, fishing, cattle breeding and, at a later stage, settled agriculture. Tools are primitive, and there is little specialism of labour, so that the fundamental social unit is the family, the tribe consisting of a number of such families with their own patriarchal chief. At this stage there are no classes because there is no private ownership of the means of production; hence there is no need for a state, all social relations being kinship relations and such division of labour as exists occurring spontaneously within the family group.

With the move to agricultural production, increases in population and the beginnings of trade, large tribal societies gradually develop a system of slavery as a more effective way of organizing the more specialized system of production, resulting in a growth of output which makes possible the creation of cities by the voluntary or coerced union of tribes. This slave-owning society represents the beginnings of classes and hence class conflict for the slaves are part of the means of production, although initially at least they are communally owned by the whole body of citizens. Slavery is thus the consequence of developments in productive methods and is not attributable simply to the human tendency to plunder and fight wars.

Feudal society emerges more out of country than out of urban life. The basic productive process was small-scale peasant farming carried out by serfs. At this stage production is an individual or family activity in that each peasant farmer or handicraft worker gathered his own raw materials and worked on them through to the finished product. This means that the means of production, particularly the tools, were such as could be used by individuals. Each peasant had his own piece of land and his own plough, while in the towns craftsmen worked in their own homes on hand tools such as the spinning wheel and the handloom, which were themselves owned by the worker.

The natural division of labour occurring within the family and depending on age, sex and the changing seasons, becomes extended to cover a certain degree of specialism, but it is always possible for the individual worker to identify his own product and since, in the early stages, production is largely for immediate consumption the individual worker normally appropriates what he makes for his own needs and those of his family, handing over a certain proportion to his feudal superior whose military power enables him to live on the surplus of the subject productive class.

As the source of wealth in such a productive method is the land the natural resulting social structure is a hierarchical territorially based feudal aristocracy in which the peasant exchanges some of his products for the protection of his immediate superior and the use of those means of production, like the flour-mill, which the feudal superior owns, the latter retaining his place in the hierarchy by contributing to the maintenance of a yet superior feudal lord who controls the use of military power over a wider area. Such relationships were clearly defined and fairly personal in that the feudal superior retains something of the patriarchal qualities of the head of a family and does not seek to extract the maximum profit from his control of the land. In the towns there is something equivalent to this in the structure of guildmasters, master-craftsmen, journeymen and apprentices, all centred around the individual productive unit, the guildmasters controlling and protecting the activities of the master-craftsmen and journeymen, each with their own tools, the apprentice undergoing a period of training before becoming a journeyman.

The change from feudalism to capitalism is initiated by the excess of production over consumption, leading more and more individuals to produce for the purposes of exchange and sale rather than for their immediate wants, and so prompting the rise of a new class of merchants. The crucial change comes with the introduction of new methods of production which involve the gathering together of numbers of workers in the same establishment in order to co-operate in the operation of larger and more complex tools and machinery. As these new means of production have to be provided there emerges a totally new class, the bourgeoisie, to supply the raw materials, tools and premises that are required, who then pay wages to those that work together on the materials and machines provided. The new classes are thus the direct consequence of new tools.

The whole process of change is boosted by the enlargement of markets and the discovery of new raw materials made possible by the exploration and colonization of hitherto unknown parts of the world, but it is held back by the entrenched power of the feudal classes who, through their control of the state and the restrictive devices of closed guilds, are able to thwart the free competition between bourgeois manufacturers which is an essential part of a system devoted to the production of 'commodities', that is goods for sale rather than consumption by the producers themselves.

The struggle between the feudal aristocracy and the bourgeois capitalists is a classic example of social conflict. Its outcome is determined by the economic realities of the situation. These are that the greater efficiency of the manufacturing system gives more wealth and hence eventually political power to the bourgeois class which is then able to control the state and usher in the fullness of capitalist production, although individual capitalists are forced to compete to the point of mutual extinction.

In the capitalist system the means of production are social because they are no longer workable by one man working alone. The spinning-machine and the power-loom make production a series of social acts. This requires a highly organized division of labour and carefully planned and closely supervized relations of production. In this situation men are treated merely according to their usefulness to those who own the means of production who have no ties to the wage labourers other than a monetary one. In feudal society wage-labour had been characteristic only of the temporary stage of apprenticeship. Under capitalism it becomes the standard relationship of men in society.

The tight organization of labour in the production of commodities in the factory is in contrast to the disorder or anarchy of the market. The capitalist has to produce as much as the market will absorb as cheaply as possible in relative ignorance of what other producers are doing and what the market can be expected to support. This results in a cycle of under-production followed by over-production and hence of full employment and then high unemployment.

It is obvious that this economic system destroys the relationship of the individual producer to his individual product, for the commodities produced in factories are social products. And yet, Marx points out, the capitalist who has provided the means of production himself appropriates what is made as if it were his own creation. This is the essence of capitalism and is the source of the major conflicts between proletarians (the wage-labourers in industrial concerns) and the bourgeoisie (who own the socialized means of production and appropriate its products). Marx expresses this inherent 'contradiction' between social production and individual appropriation in terms of the idea of surplus value and exploitation. Taking over Adam Smith's view that the value of a product is to be equated with the labour which goes into its production, he uses this labour theory of value to argue that the capitalist does not give the worker the full value of what is produced. The capitalist pays only a subsistence wage and keeps the 'surplus' (the difference between the full value of the goods produced and what he pays out in wages) for himself. This 'profit' enables him to build up his capital and so provide more machinery and factories to make yet more profits. Since this capital is in fact a social product the capitalist is exploiting the worker by treating it as a personal possession. Moreover it is a possession which gives him vast economic and hence political power and so makes it possible for the capitalist class as a whole to control the state and protect the private property on which the system depends.

The result of fierce competition and recurrent economic crisis is a simplification and polarization of the class system so that fewer and fewer but wealthier and wealthier capitalists confront an ever increasing number of poorer and poorer industrial workers. The end result is 'an accumulation of misery corresponding with accumulation of capital' and 'an agony of toil, slavery, ignorance, brutality and mutual degeneration' in which the bourgeois class cannot even provide for the basic needs of its slaves and 'Society as a whole is more and more splitting up into two great hostile camps, into two great classes directly facing each other—bourgeoisie and proletariat' (p. 207).

These laws of capitalist development illustrate very well Marx's idea of the social determination of individual behaviour. The individual proletarian *has* to sell his labour in order to survive just as the individual capitalist has to modernize his machinery to remain a capitalist. Further, members of both classes are forced through the sanctions of law or through false-consciousness to abide by the laws of property, which are the product of the economic system. Capitalism makes property relations the central feature of political order so as to protect the economic powers without which it could not survive. Further the rules and attitudes concerning all aspects of life come to take on the same characteristics as the economic aspects so that even sexual relations in capitalist society come to reflect bourgeois values, marriage being regarded as a commercial contract in which material support is exchanged for sexual and domestic services while children are treated as commodities over which paternal rights are absolute.

Similarly religious belief and practices are not an external source of values and social organization, but are part and parcel of the same economic conflicts and tensions. Thus all religion, especially the highly emotional millenarian type of cult which promises the believer divinely initiated and imminent heavenly rewards, is to be seen as an expression of the alienation of the proletarian from his present existence and a means whereby the ruling class can divert the energies of the suffering classes from political activity to relatively harmless religiosity.

PRACTICAL IMPLICATIONS

The implications of Marx's theory of society are primarily causal. By uncovering the mechanisms at work in the capitalist economy Marx feels able to foretell its imminent collapse. For even if individual capitalists become aware that the anarchy of the market place coupled with constant innovations in manufacturing processes must eventually undermine the stability of the system, they are powerless to do anything about it. If any individual capitalist attempts to hold back change another will take his place and any agreements to restrict modernization of the means of production will be undercut by those who stand to gain from breaking the agreement or remaining outside it from the start.

The inevitable consequences of the rationally calculated acts of individual members of the bourgeois class are recurrent economic crises, increasing impoverishment of the proletariat and a gradually increasing awareness on the part of the proletariat of the now manifest contradictions between social production and individual appropriation. Socialism is, for Marx, the reflection in thought of this very real suffering on the part of the industrial masses in the final period of capitalist development. In particular his own doctrines mark the end of the false-consciousness which hid the underlying realities of class conflict behind the rhetoric of equality of opportunity, individual freedom and justice under the law. In the graphic imagery of the *Communist Manifesto* the advanced member of the proletariat begins to see through the bourgeois state and its commitment to the protection of bourgeois property: 'law, morality and religion are to him so many bourgeois prejudices' masking bourgeois interests. Eventually the bulk of the proletariat see that they have no security and no benefit from capitalism, they become aware that they are not in competition with each other and have 'nothing to lose but their chains' and that together they have the power to defy the system. And so the proletarian revolution takes place.

The essence of the revolution is the abolition of private ownership of the means of production. This is no more than the logical consequence of the social nature of the forces of production but from it immense changes follow in all aspects of social life. With the abolition of private property in the means of production the entire bourgeois class is eliminated, since there is no longer individual ownership of the productive forces. For the same reason there is no longer a proletarian class as all are equally owners and therefore free from exploitation and external control.

With no classes there can be no class conflict, and with no property to defend there is no need for the state or for laws to establish who owns what. With the means of production under communal control there is no basis for conflict between groups and so the coercive mechanism of the state can simply 'die out' as Engels put it in *Socialism: Utopian and Scientific*. As production is no longer under the control of the bourgeoisie decisions about what to make and how much to produce can be made on the basis of the satisfaction of the real needs of individuals rather than the requirements of profit and the artificial demands created to serve the interests of the manufacturers, and so the alienation of the worker from his product ceases.

Since the techniques of the industrial processes remain collective those involved in this social production, now that the causes of economic conflict are removed, co-operate naturally and spontaneously with each other so that the relations of production are harmonious. This extends to all other social relationships. Once men are no longer alienated from their product they are no longer alienated from each other. At this stage of social development, in complete contrast to Hobbes's state of nature, there is a peaceful society without the existence of any state: social relations have lost their political character.

The changed basis of economic life alters the very nature of individual men and women. The selfish greed of capitalist man gives way to an effective sense of solidarity and mutual interest. Together men are able to control their productive acts and to organize their working life in such a way as to realize their full potential as creative social beings.

Marx's vision of communist society is one of material plenty for he believes that modern scientific production is well able to provide more than adequate means of subsistence. It is also an approximately egalitarian society, although he puts little stress on strict equality, an ideal which has no significance when each person cares for the welfare of others and is aware that his development as a human being can be fully accomplished only with the freely given help of others. The transformation of human relationships is exemplified in the ending of the cash-nexus as the basic form of co-operation. Money symbolizes the self-interested exchanges of Hobbesian men and its accumulation is the foundation of inequality and of capitalist production; it has no place in communist society. Similarly the divisive and dehumanizing effects of the division of labour will also cease because men will specialize only to the extent that they wish to do so.

But the prime value which Marx sees embodied in communist social existence is that of freedom, by which he means the capacity to control the human environment and make it serve human needs. Society can now be organized on a definite plan to serve real human requirements. The result is a realization of the productive essence of man in a way which frees him from the deterministic control of economic forces and makes him master of his own destiny. In this final stage of social development conflict has no place.

ASSESSMENT AND DEVELOPMENTS

Marxian theory is sometimes said to be internally inconsistent. For instance it can be argued that a determinist (see pp. 234 ff) who claims to be able to predict the future is thereby debarred from urging us to act in one way rather than another since our actions are, on his own theory, the inevitable results of causal factors which are beyond our control. Knowledge only gives power when we are free to use that knowledge to obtain the objects of our own choices. And, in any case, if the future is the inevitable outcome of present social realities it seems unnecessary to urge us to help bring that future about by our own efforts. Yet Marx appears to urge the workers to unite and rise in revolution.

It is true that Marx does not think that the material causes of social behaviour bypass human consciousness and he is clear, for instance, that it is part of the necessary conditions of the downfall of capitalism that the proletarians become aware of the economic and political realities of their exploited and oppressed position. But this is only to say that men will become conscious of their historic situation and that this will be part of the process leading to revolution. It does not help us understand the rationality of exhortation in a deterministic world. This criticism is best countered by pointing out that much of what Marx says is not strictly determinist and that, at least as regards the timing of historical changes, he concedes that individuals can have an influence in retarding or hastening the processes in which they are caught up. This fits with Marx's claim that after the revolution men enter a period of increasing freedom to use the natural environment and the manufacturing powers according to their own assessment of human need. Such a picture implies that the limited scope afforded in pre-communist societies for effective causally-independent human choice is widened to become a central feature of the unalienated condition of communist man. In this way the consistency of Marx's theory and practice can be maintained, although this more flexible position makes it appropriate to raise the question of whether Marx may not have under-estimated the extent to which men in non-communist societies are able to modify their social institutions in the light of their long-term self-interest or even in the light of their moral convictions.

A similar inconsistency is said to occur in Marx's critique of morality as an expression of class interests disguised as standards of universal right and adopted by other classes as a result of false-consciousness. How can he hold to this interpretation of morality while evidently condemning the immoralities of capitalism and extolling the virtues of communism? However, it is not the case that Marx indulges in direct moral criticism of capitalists as individuals or as a class. He accepts that capitalists are playing a necessary part in historical change and that they are not morally culpable for acting according to the norms of their class for these are not of their own making. Similarly progressive proletarians are not morally better people, they are simply representatives of the next stage of society. Marx does believe that capitalism is evil in that it degrades and harms human beings and that communism is to be preferred because it is the condition which makes possible the full realization of what is most worth while in human life. It is perfectly consistent for him to make such valuations while maintaining that men are not free to choose which form of society to create for themselves or others. Necessary facts can be either welcome or un-welcome.

Marx does still have a philosophical problem on his hands as regards the justification of such value judgements since he appears to have no room for this in his essentially positivistic approach. The most that we can glean from his writings on this score is the claim that communism is preferable to capitalism because it comes later in the historical chain. But unless we simply assume the Hegelian view that what comes later is thereby more progressive in some evaluative sense, an as-sertion which requires the support of independent moral judgements, Marx's confidence that the final stage of society is the best stage commits the naturalistic fallacy in a form typical of the nineteenth-century, by assuming that what is more evolved is more desirable.

Marx's weaknesses as a moral philosopher may be of relatively slight significance given the extent of evaluative agreement concerning the moral priority of peace, prosperity, social harmony and creative work over against war, poverty, competitiveness and the boredom of monotonous work under-taken for purely economic reasons. His significance as a socialist theorist depends far more on the alleged scientific status of his social analyses. Indeed his insistence on the importance of the economic foundations of a society for all its other aspects, including those features which are traditionally thought of as being due to 'human nature', has become almost the reigning orthodoxy of social science. Ahistorical, non-economic and purely individualistic accounts of social pheno-mena do not nowadays gain much credence. But there is still immense scope for disagreement about both the content of

Marx's particular scientific claims and the scientific status of his theory as a whole.

Hostile critics fasten on a number of Marx's specific predictions that have been falsified in the course of history. In developed countries capitalism has adapted and changed rather than collapsed, and even if modern economies, with their vast range of state controls, are scarcely capitalist in Marx's sense and may yet fail to maintain their prosperity, they cannot be said to be following the path which Marx foretold. And while there are, of course, countries like the Soviet Union and the Peoples Republic of China that claim to embody the Marxian idea this did not come about after the full development of the 'contradictions' of capitalism in these countries and so does not match the theories he propounded.

More radical is the sweeping rejection of Marx's 'historicism', as Karl Popper calls the claim that the proper method of understanding human history is to discover the sort of scientific laws which enable us to predict its future course. Popper, himself a powerful advocate of scientific method as the process of putting forward empirical hypotheses which can be disproved or falsified by experience, rejects the use of this method to predict human history on several grounds; Popper argues in *The Logic of Scientific Discovery*, revised edn (Hutchinson: London, 1968) that, since human history is a unitary and unique phenomenon, it is impossible to make the observations which would test historical predictions for to do this adequately we would have to observe very many examples of human history. He also points out that the course of economic change is affected by developments in knowledge and that this cannot (logically) be predicted since to predict future knowledge is to possess it at the moment of prediction.

Such arguments lend weight to the impression that Marx's method is often more deductive than empirical, depending too much on inherited dogmas about historical stages and the use of abstract or logical 'inconsistencies', like the 'incoherence' of social production and individual appropriation. Too often he seems to confuse the logical necessity of non-contradiction with empirical claims about the clash of interests.

In the face of such criticism it is natural for the scientifically minded Marxist to retreat, as Marx sometimes appears to do, into limited claims about short term predictions based on the observation of a variety of advanced capitalist countries which provide a range of examples on which to base tentative inductive conjectures. This more limited approach has led to a great deal of interesting and significant social science but it inevitably treats the detailed findings of Marx as open to revision, and involves the abandonment of the broad and sweeping claims about the inevitable demise of capitalism which gave Marxism its political attractions.

What we are then left with is a general methodology of seeking in the economic basis of each society the explanation for its other social arrangements. This leaves as relatively open questions whether or not there is something more fixed in human nature than Marx himself allowed and whether men individually or collectively can use their rationality and moral beliefs to affect the economic basis on which everything else is said to depend.

Whether at the end of the day the accumulation of studies made on this methodological basis confirm or cast doubt on the fruitfulness of Marxian assumptions it is difficult to say. But one recurrent problem which arises from a certain lack of clarity in Marx's own position is the determination of which factors are to be counted as part of the economic basis of a society and which are part of the superstructure. Many writers have noted the ambiguous position of the relations of production in this respect. But there are also formidable problems in describing any economic bases without reference to their legal and political backgrounds. This is particularly the case with the institution of property, a legally defined and politically central concept which is inseparable from the description of the economic base of capitalism, for without a law of private property there could be no private ownership of the means of production. How then can the latter create the former?

One response to the Popperian criticism of Marxist historicism or scientism is to reassert the significance of the early philosophical Marx and to develop Marx's theory of ideology to encompass the whole corpus of modern science as being simply another example of bourgeois thinking which reduces human thought to the instrumental function of serving to increase commodity production. Thus in the 'Critical theory' of the 'Frankfurt School' (the label given to a group of neo-Marxist philosophers including Max Horkheimer, Herbert Marcuse and Jurgen Habermas) much science, especially social science, is an ideological weapon whereby the bourgeoisie manipulates the proletariat by making out that their descriptions of existing social relationships have to do with inevitable and necessary processes. This 'reification' or 'hypostatization' of events as if they are what inevitably must and ought to be the case is supported by a bureaucratic organization that approaches social problems solely from the point of view of technical control. Science is thus used to gain power over the workforce and this power is reinforced by the palliatives of the welfare state. On this view Marx mistakenly extends the application of science from the material to the social world whereas human freedom and fulfilment depend on men taking control of the apparatus, which at present makes them slaves to productive 'necessities'. Science should be used, if at all, only in a very limited way as a means of incorporating technology into a way of life aimed at freeing men from phoney 'scientific' truths, such as those of economic theory.

The weakness of this school of thought lies in its inability to justify its hopes for a more liberated form of society in such a way as to vindicate the call, made by some members of the school, for the destructive overthrow of existing social systems. But the force of their critique may be better appreciated after we have examined the theories of Max Weber, whose model of a rational, bureaucratic form of society is a main target for the attacks of the Frankfurt School.

FOR FURTHER READING

We have used as our text the selection edited by Bottomore and Rubel, (see p. 116). The best initiation to Marx and Engels is the

famous *Communist Manifesto*. For an early authoritative exposition of
Marxian ideas see Engels, *Socialism, Utopian and Scientific*. Both are to
be found in Lewis S. Feuer *Marx and Engels* (Fontana Library,
Collins: Glasgow, 1969) Marx's most important works have been
published in the Pelican Marx Library edited by Quintin Hoare
(Penguin Books, England).

The secondary literature on Marx and Engels is vast. The reader
might start with David McLellan, *Marx* (Collins: Glasgow, 1975)
which is part of the useful Fontana Modern Masters series. More
taxing are Michael Evans *Karl Marx* (Allen and Unwin: London,
1975) and Angus Walker, *Marx*, (Longman: London, 1978). S.
Avineri, *The Social and Political Thought of Karl Marx* (Cambridge
University Press: Cambridge, 1968) is particularly relevant to
Marx's theory of society.

For examples of the work of the Frankfurt School see Jurgen
Habermas, *Knowledge and Human Interests* (Heinemann: London,
1972), Herbert Marcuse, *One Dimensional Man* (Boston: 1964; Sphere
Books: London, 1968). For commentary read Alistair MacIntyre,
Marcuse (Fontana Modern Masters, Collins: London, 1970). See also
Paul Connerton (ed.) *Critical Sociology* (Penguin Books:
Harmondsworth, 1976) and David Held, *Introduction to Critical
Theory* (Hutchinson: London, 1980).

CHAPTER 7

Emile Durkheim:
A Consensus Theory

THE life and work of Emile Durkheim (1858–1917) mark the acceptance of sociology as an autonomous academic discipline. In his proselytizing writings and through his exceptional gifts as a teacher, Durkheim won recognition for the idea of a science of society which could contribute to the solution of the moral and intellectual problems of modern society.

He sought to make this vision a reality in major studies of the nature of social solidarity (*The Division of Labour*, 1893), the social causes of suicide (*Suicide*, 1897) and the function of primitive religion (*The Elementary Forms of the Religious Life*, 1912). His eventual success may be gauged from the fact that despite the considerable controversy that his ideas provoked, a professorship of social science was created for him in 1887 at the University of Bordeaux, where he taught for many years before going to the Sorbonne in Paris as Professor of Sociology. There he founded and edited the famous journal *L'Année sociologique* and gathered round him a group of scholars who became highly influential in academic and political affairs. In his later years he became increasingly preoccupied with the difficulties of the Third Republic, concerning himself with patriotic educational activities designed to bolster the unity and progressiveness of the French nation as it approached the world war which was to claim the life of his intellectually gifted son André and of which he himself did not live to see the end.

Durkheim's work remains of considerable intellectual significance as a powerful empirically based exemplification of organic functionalist theories of society. His influence has been particularly strong in the United States of America and is evident in the structuralism of Levi-Strauss and the functionalism of anthropologists such as Radcliffe Brown.

DURKHEIM'S APPROACH

Following in a tradition marked out by Saint-Simon (1760–1825), Durkheim is the hesitant but loyal disciple of Auguste Comte (1798–1857) the French pioneer of positivism who coined the word 'sociology'.

Comte's 'positive-philosophy' is rooted in an intense admiration for the quantitative precision of the natural sciences, particularly mathematics, physics and biology. In his *Cours de philosophie positive* he sets out to apply these methods to discover the principles of order and change in society, so providing a new body of knowledge which could be used to reorganize society for the betterment of mankind. This scientific and rationalist approach, combined with a historical perspective, is embodied in his 'Law of Human Progress' according to which all societies pass through three stages: the Theological or fictitious, the Metaphysical or abstract, and the Scientific or positive. Each stage involves a different intellectual attitude: in the Theological stage men seek 'absolute' knowledge of the 'essential nature of things' and the 'first and final causes of events', culminating in the explanation of everything as the product of God's will. This basically emotional mental set gives way to the Metaphysical attitude in which abstract forces take the place of supernatural ones but explanations are still couched in terms of essential natures as, for instance, when economic value is explained by the 'intrinsic value' of things. This largely destructive stage makes way in its turn for the Scientific or positivist style whereby the mind, putting aside the quest for ultimate explanations, applies itself to the observation of phenomena for the purpose of establishing laws of invariant succession and resemblance. According to positivism, knowledge is confined to what appears to the senses and as such it can deal only with relations of antecedence and consequence between observed phenomena (see p. 40).

Although Comte's three stages are characterized in intellectual terms each goes with necessary social arrangements: the Theological attitude dominates the period of human history up to the Middle Ages, the Metaphysical stage in the sixteenth, seventeenth and eighteenth centuries brought the decline of monarchy, the power of the military and the emergence of secular political ideas such as natural right, the sovereignty of the people and private property. The scientific age is industrial and elitist, controlled not by priests or soldiers but by bankers and technocrats. It will see the end of class and economic divisions, the establishment of urban living, the overall planning of economic activity, and will mark the summit of man's moral achievement in the full flowering of altruism and love.

Presiding over intellectual life in the positive stage is the science of sociology. This dominating position is justified by the claim that sociology is not only a distinct analytic discipline but also a synthetic study whose aim is to relate social phenomena to the organic whole of which they are a part, that is to the whole history of mankind, hence its overarching Law of Three Stages.

Comte's work is speculative and programmatic. Durkheim seeks to remedy these defects whilst retaining Comte's general objectives. He holds to Comte's belief in the possibility of showing that society is subject to natural causes although he lacks his master's total rationalistic confidence in the potentiality of the scientific organization of society. He therefore rejects a strict interpretation of Comte's Law of Human Progress which he regards as highly dogmatic and imprecise, but he approves of the Comteian mix of science and social reform. Specifically Social Science is to be applied to the problem of re-establishing social order in the wake of the revolutionary upheavals of the eighteenth century and the socially dislocating effects of industrialization. Durkheim hopes to show how a new social consensus could recreate the values of community and social order without sacrificing the human emancipation which followed from the demise of feudalism.

It is also to Comte that we can trace Durkheim's organic view of society and the important distinction between 'social statics' which deals with the anatomy and order of human societies and the interaction of its parts, and 'social dynamics' which describes the processes of social change and discovers the laws of social evolution which relate social developments to such factors as climate, race and population size. But while Durkheim adopts Comte's general organic approach he is less concerned to crown sociology as the queen of the sciences than to establish the existence of distinct 'social facts' as the subject matter of the new science. In the *Rules of Sociological Method* (1895) he urges that social theorists adopt the presupposition-less detachment of the observing scientist faced with an unknown social reality. This means rejecting the methods of introspective, individualistic psychology used by Hobbes and Adam Smith. Durkheim regards introspection as inherently deceptive and in any case believes that social reality is to be found not in individual consciousness but in the realm of social facts.

In the first chapter of the *Rules* Durkheim defines social facts as 'ways of acting, thinking and feeling, external to the individual and endowed with a power of coercion, by reason of which they control him' (8th edn, ed. George E. G. Catlin, The Free Press: Illinois, 1938, p. 3). What he has in mind are people's habits, customs and general way of life as embodied in institutions, laws, morals and political ideologies. These may be at work in individual consciousness but they are distinguishable phenomena to be discovered by observing behaviour in the large, not by examining the contents of our own minds. Social facts, he argues, are 'external' to the individual in the important sense that they come to him from outside himself and dominate his behaviour. Social scientists must, therefore, treat social facts 'as things' in the same way as natural scientists treat the physical objects whose reality they must accept and explain.

Despite the acknowledged idealistic or 'moral' nature of social phenomena Durkheim seeks to find ways of rendering social facts observable and measurable. Thus he equates 'social density' with population concentration, uses statistics (e.g. of divorce rates) to make general factual statements about societies as a whole and takes the observed operations of different types of legal sanction as external indices of underlying social realities.

Although social facts are in these ways rendered open to observation, society is, for Durkheim, essentially a moral or normative phenomenon, having to do with the regulation of individual behaviour through an imposed or external system of constraining values and rules; as a moral system its typical manifestations are the obligations which the individual, however willingly, must perform in accordance with the language, laws and customs of his society, all of which are social facts he did not create and to which he must conform or suffer the consequences of social disapproval and punishment. There is thus a large element of sociological idealism in his theory.

Durkheim sees the social scientist's task as the mapping of these patterns of behaviour, including departures from them and the modes of correction employed to re-establish them. As a positivist his aim is to capture these phenomena in laws summarizing the constant repetition of observed sequences. Thus he suggests, for instance, that the division of labour is the result of increases in population density and argues that religious belief and emotions follow from the gathering together of group members in the close proximity of ritual gatherings. He establishes more precise regularities by using statistical material as a tool for comparative analysis.

Although, like Smith, Durkheim seeks causal regularities of a type familiar in the natural sciences, his positivism differs from Smith's in being more purely sociological. He aims to find the cause of all social phenomena entirely in *other* social phenomena to the exclusion of any reference to pre-social elements of human nature. He regards it as necessary to genuine sociology that its facts cannot be reduced to any lower degree of reality such as those studied in psychology or biology. He is thus very much a methodological holist (see p. 38) and is therefore in total opposition to individualistic methodologies, like that of Hobbes, which he attacked in the guise of Herbert Spencer's fashionable utilitarian theory of society.

Again like Adam Smith, Durkheim is as interested in functions as in causes: 'When . . . the explanation of a social phenomenon is undertaken we must seek separately the efficient cause which produces it and the function it fulfils' (*Rules*, Chapter 5, p. 95). But by 'function' he, unlike Smith, never means what serves the needs of individuals; Durkheim's functionalism is sociological or holistic in that the needs he considers relevant to sociological explanation are needs of the social organism as a whole. Thus the function of the division of labour is identified as the production of a new form of community (organic solidarity) while religion is said to contribute to social cohesion by giving the individual a sense of the sacredness and authority of social reality.

The characteristic feature of Durkheim's positivism is thus the single-minded attempt to approach society as an independent organic reality with its own laws, its own development and its own life. As in the case of Marx, Durkheim's methodological holism goes with a highly deterministic position according to which individuals are powerless before the constraints of the social forces which produce conformity to social norms or cause deviance from them. And yet Durkheim manages to combine the assertion of scientific detachment and causal determinism with the belief that his science of society provides some sort of answer to the normative ethical problems of traditional philosophy.

Having insisted that morality is a social phenomenon and that moral facts are to be explained like any other type of social facts by reference to historical causes and functional considerations, he nevertheless goes on to claim that his science, besides providing knowledge of the best means to social goals, also indicates what the best social goals are. He claims that there are objective criteria, inherent in the facts themselves, which the social scientist can adopt as his moral guide. How this can be is not made very clear. Sometimes he simply appeals to the truism that men wish to live saying that this is sufficient to transform the laws of science into imperatives of conduct by making them laws of survival. But even if we accept this line of thought it does not enable us to decide which of the many forms of viable society is preferable.

In fact what lies behind Durkheim's confidence in the ability of the sociologist to determine moral goals is the organic frame of reference embodied in his functionalist explanations. This way of thinking permits him to draw naturally on the idea of the 'health' of the social organism as the appropriate moral standard for his subject. His normative position is thus very like that of Aristotle in that the normal functioning of a particular type of society is standardly assumed to be its morally desirable state. Generally speaking anything which is normal or average for a particular social organism is held to be healthy and therefore acceptable, while the abnormal or unusual is 'pathological'.

Accordingly Durkheim sets himself the task of discovering what, for instance, is the usual extent and type of the division of labour in different types of society. But, interestingly enough, he is also concerned to argue that some normal (in the sense of common) forms of the division of labour in industrial societies are nevertheless abnormal (in the pathological sense). This enables him to condemn 'forced' divisions of labour and commend only such specialization as is based on natural differences between men. He reaches this conclusion by assuming that the division of labour is healthy when it contributes to social solidarity. A similar line is taken in *Suicide* where to an extent he accepts the average level of suicide rates as part and parcel of the normal and therefore desirable operation of a society, and yet commends attempts to reduce it on the grounds that self-destruction conflicts with the value which is placed on human life in modern society. No doubt he would justify these normative views in functionalist terms by saying that consensus, particularly consensus on the value of human life, is necessary for the very survival of society, but it is hard to miss the personal moral and political commitment to community and autonomy which underlie these allegedly purely scientific normative positions.

DURKHEIM'S THEORY OF MAN

Durkheim is an extreme example of a holistic theorist. It might, therefore, appear misguided to attempt to dissociate his theory of human nature from his theory of society. But the fact that Durkheim holds that everything which is distinctively human—such as language, morality, religion and economic activity—is attributable to and dependent upon society, no more precludes him from having a theory of man than Hobbes's individualistic postulates prevent him from having a theory of society (see p. 11). Indeed it is precisely because of Durkheim's emphasis on how little the individual brings to society beyond the raw material to be shaped by the transforming influence of group life, that he is able to attribute so much to social as distinct from individual factors in his explanations of human behaviour.

In practice Durkheim is very much taken up with the place of the individual in modern society. The polarity of individualism and collectivism is a recurrent theme in his work. It arises from his concern for social order and human self-fulfilment. He is hostile to the anarchistic, undisciplined 'individualisme' which many saw in the chaos precipitated in France by the Revolution of 1789. But he stands equally strongly against the absorption of the individual into the collectivity of the modern state, with the consequent loss of that independence and variety of human experience which has been achieved through the breakup of feudalism and the development of industrial life.

In his posthumous essay *Socialism* and elsewhere, Durkheim argues that genuine individualism—the flourishing of individual differences and personal autonomy—can be attained only through what is in effect a syndicalist version of non-revolutionary socialism, in which the individual is protected from the state by his membership in an economic or occupational group and is in turn protected from the smothering influence of group life by the countervailing rights which he has as a citizen under the protection of the state. In this way the distinctive characteristics of modern life—autonomy and inter-dependence—can be fused in an ideal which was both realistic and humanly satisfying.

Somewhat paradoxically this normative individualism is based on a methodology which is rampantly anti-individualistic. As we have seen he holds that no explanations of social phenomena are to be found in the psychology of the individual. This is because there is no individual nature of man either in the Hobbesian sense of a collection of human traits present in all men at all times, or in the Smithian sense of a universal set of original desires and capacities on the basis of which the social nature of man develops in different directions according to his social experience. Nor does Durkheim have an Aristotelian concept of man's natural potentiality of the sort which underlies many of Marx's ideas. Rather man is, in himself, no more than an undifferentiated malleable indeterminate substance which social forces determine and transform.

Perhaps the best way to envisage Durkheim's theory of human nature is along Hobbesian lines as a bundle of sensations, reflexes and instincts, but with two important modifications: firstly, the individual is in himself without reason and, secondly, man has no fixed patterns of appetites inevitably and necessarily directed towards such specific goals as self-preservation and glory. There is thus nothing within the individual by way of reason or instinct to limit the range and extent of his appetites. Hobbes's imagined universal propensities of human nature are in fact transient and local. Some of those propensities may be entirely lacking in certain societies and none is sufficiently pervasive and powerful to determine social conditions in any detail.

Durkheim views human nature as an almost total abstraction from the behaviour of actual people in real situations. Methodologically the 'individual' is, for Durkheim, a residual category in which he places only what is left after he has taken away all that is contributed to human life by society. This remnant is no more than an undifferentiated substratum. His interest is in showing how the group controls and moulds this pliable material and turns the abstract individual into a group member with distinguishable characteristics typical of his group. What we normally take to be the universal features of human nature, including the powers of choice and reasoning, are actually the product of the environmental situation that all men have in common—life in some sort of social group.

Durkheim applies this to the processes of human thought by taking over Kant's idea of the *a priori* categories of the human mind which we bring to our experience of the world (the capacities to order our perceptions in the framework of space and time and to relate them to each other in a causal succession) and attributing these capacities to the operations of society. It is thus society that leads us to think of the world in certain ways. For instance, men do not start out with the capacity to classify things, and then come to regard themselves as divided up into different classes or tribes. Rather it is because men live in clans or other groups that they come to classify things in general. Similarly, Durkheim argues in *The Elementary Forms*, that the territorial nature of the clan underlies men's concept of space. This explains why there are societies in Australia and North America where space is conceived in the form of an immense circle; they believe this because they live in a camp which is circular in form.

This—from the individualistic point of view—topsy-turvy vision of the relationship between the individual and society is very typical of Durkheim's theories. Men do not come to have religious beliefs by reasoning that there must be hidden causes for observed events, rather their religious experience gives rise to the very ideas of cause and effect. Again, it is not that we disapprove of that which is immoral, but rather that acts are immoral because we disapprove of them. So, in general, he argues that the observable qualities of human beings are not the explanation for or origin of social organization but that social life is both the cause and the 'end' of these apparently individual attributes.

The paradigm example of this inverted vision is the view that social existence precedes the human capacity to communicate by speech, a process in which each individual participates only by learning the social rules which give meaning to symbols; on this premise Durkheim builds the theory that the form and content of these and all other social rules reflect the requirements of social life in general and the specific requirements of the societies whose rules they are. Just as the words men use to classify objects originate in the ways in which they classify themselves within their group, so their idea of the universe in its entirety is an image of their conception of the overall unity of their society. Similarly in the sphere of moral choice, the individual does not generate moral standards and develop moral commitments on the basis of which he then enters into, sustains and criticizes his social situation, rather his values and moral allegiances are the expression in him of collective forces which have not only a social origin but also a social function, namely to sustain the ongoing social group in which the individual is located. This is a sociological version of Kant's philosophical idealism.

It is Durkheim's view of the shapeless, non-rational perhaps sub-human form of unsocialized human nature that explains his conception of 'anomie', a human condition marked by the absence of social regulation. Anomie is Durkheim's most distinctive conceptual innovation in social theory. In his analysis of social order he assumes that when the moral forces of social life disintegrate the individual is completely at sea, with no idea of what to aim for or how to live a satisfactory life. Anomie is thus both a condition of society in which religion, government and morality have lost their effectiveness (something like Hobbes's state of nature) and the resulting psychological state of disenchanted individuals with no purpose in life and hence no permanent fulfilment, something like Marx's state of alienation. When people lose their sense of belonging to a group and become out of touch with the form that the group gives to their lives, they lose their own identity, their sense of place, their commitment to what they believe to be worthwhile activities and so any realistic hope of a meaningful existence. This is the condition of anomie expressed in the disorders and unhappiness of modern industrial cities.

Durkheim's explanation of the psychological consequences

of the social disintegration which occurs in the transition to modern industrial society presupposes that there are no natural limitations to human needs and desires. Animals, governed by instinct, have relatively fixed and determinate appetites and normally available means to satisfy them. But man has no such inner regulation, so that, without the control of the social group, his life is one of unabated desire resulting in 'the malady of infinite aspiration':

Greed is aroused without knowing where to find ultimate foothold. . . . Reality seems valueless by comparison with the dreams of fevered imagination. . . . A thirst arises for novelties, unfamiliar pleasures, nameless sensations, all of which lose their savour once known. (*Suicide*, Chapter 5, p. 250 in the translation edited by George Simpson, Routledge and Kegen Paul: London, 1952).

The result is weariness, disillusionment and futility. Again the comparison with Hobbes is apt to the extent that anomic man seems to resemble the hedonistic, competitive individual whom Hobbes considers representative of universal human nature. In the phenomenon of urban living in an industrial society, where men have some capacity to get what they happen to want, but little capacity to keep their desires within manageable bounds, we have an updated image of Hobbes's state of nature. The crucial difference here between Hobbes and Durkheim is that the remnants of rationality in the life of modern man are not the input of human nature but come from the residual effectiveness of such social forces as remain operative. Durkheim looks to the reconstruction of society to reconstitute the human individual and so resolve the problem of anomie. This reconstituted individual will not be a Hobbesian man with purely external and self-interested social relationships, but a socially integrated person whose relative autonomy and individuality is inseparable from a social presence in all his thoughts, feelings and actions. Given the disordered sensationalist raw material of human nature, society alone can provide the discipline which gives form and meaning to human life.

DURKHEIM'S THEORY OF SOCIETY

How does Durkheim characterize the independent reality which is the cause of all that is distinctive and most valuable in human life? What is the god-like entity that gives so much to the individual and requires so much of him? We have noted that a society, for Durkheim, is a moral order, that is a set of normative requirements with an ideal rather than a material reality, which is present to individual consciousness and yet in some way external to it. But how is this ideal reality to be identified among the purely individual elements of consciousness and what gives it the independence and influence it requires to play its part in Durkheim's scheme of things?

These are questions with which Durkheim wrestled throughout his life. Partly as a result of developments in his thinking, no clear and consistent answer can be given to them. Sometimes it appears that 'Society' is nothing more specific than a mysterious supra-personal entity introduced to fill the void created by his criticisms of individualistic explanations. If men cannot create a moral order out of their own resources, and if God does not exist to do the job for them, then, Durkheim rather too readily concludes, the origin and authority of morality must be traced to that rather nebulous something which he calls 'Society'. He does, however, bring two associated concepts to bear on his explication of social reality. These are *'conscience collective'* (translated 'collective consciousness' or 'collective conscience'), and *'représentations collective'* (translated 'collective representations').

Collective representations are symbols which have a common meaning for all members of a group and enable them to feel identified with each other as group members. They exhibit the ways in which the group members see themselves in their joint relations with the objects which affect them. National flags, tribal totems and sacred books are examples. Collective representations are part of the content of the collective consciousness, an entity which is something between a metaphysical group mind and the more prosaic reality of public opinion. The collective consciousness contains all those ideas which individual members of societies have in common and which stand for collective ends or purposes. Thus the general belief, say, that parents ought to care for their children, if widely believed and normally followed, is part of the collective consciousness. But it does not count as a content of collective consciousness should all these individuals just happen to be fond of children.

Durkheim's claim is that the totality of such commonly held normative beliefs with implications for social relationships form a determinate system with the function of regulating life in society and hence constituting its unity. The collective consciousness, which varies from society to society in its intensity, rigidity and extent, is that part of the conscious life of individuals which they have in common regarding their common life: it is a normative consensus inclusive of supporting religious or other beliefs which underpin it, something akin to Marx's concept of ideology without its class associations.

In *The Division of Labour* Durkheim has frequent recourse to the idea of the collective consciousness. He argues, for instance, in Chapter 2, that crime is not an offence against any particular individual but offends the collective consciousness—indeed this is what makes it crime. Moreover, the importance of crime for social life is not the harm done to individuals but the danger to the integrity of the shared normative order if it goes unpunished. It is difficult to know how literally this type of statement is intended. For while Durkheim is prepared to admit that the idea of crime as an offence against something above and beyond the individual is an illusion, albeit a necessary one, he also says that talk of a collective consciousness is a metaphor 'not without truth'. (In *Suicide* he denies that there is anything metaphorical in saying that each social group has an inclination towards suicide which is tied up with the nature of the collective consciousness in each type of society (pp. 307ff)). And in his later study of primitive religion he seems to move even nearer to the idea of society as a reality on a different level from that of individual consciousness which may operate without manifesting itself in the awareness of individuals: the conscious life of individuals is said to be in the same relationship to group consciousness as the subconscious states of individual egos are to their conscious ones.

Durkheim's concept of the collective consciousness has to be seen against the background of his rejection of all accounts of society which treat the interplay of individual self-interest as an adequate basis for social explanation. Durkheim is at his clearest and most convincing in his criticism of the idea that permanent social relationships could be founded on interest. In this he goes far beyond Adam Smith's position for Smith still believed that, given certain underlying notions of justice, a society could be held together in large part by mercenary exchanges. But for Durkheim 'where interest is the only ruling force each individual finds himself in a state of war with every other since nothing comes to modify the egos and any truce in this eternal antagonism would not be of long duration'. Interest-based alliances are as unstable as the interests on which they are postulated: 'there is nothing less constant than interest. Today it unites me to you: tomorrow it will make me your enemy' (*Division of Labour*, Chapter 7, p. 203 translated by George Simpson, Free Press; Illinois, 1933). He moves from this critique of unrestricted utilitarian explanations to a position in which any reference to the self-interested calculations of individuals is rejected as anything more than a surface social phenomenon. Thus it is crucial to the argument of the *Division of Labour* that divided labour did not originate in rational foresight and is not sustained by an appreciation of its alleged benefits for human happiness. He goes to some lengths to argue that happiness, measured by such social indices as suicide and divorce rates, declines as civilization advances, the implication being that men could not have introduced and sustained the division of labour to increase their happiness, as the utilitarians assumed.

Durkheim's alternative explanation of the division of labour is a characteristic combination of causal and functional analysis expressed in purely holistic terms. Its causes are positivistically identified as material or population density. Its function is the provision of a novel form of social cohesion suited to the complexities of industrial life.

To develop this thesis Durkheim deploys his famous distinction between two types of society (the simple and the complex) and their two associated forms of social solidarity (the mechanical and the organic). In simple societies the population is small and spread out within its limited territory. Their members are similar in their characteristics and activities and belong to small largely isolated groups between which there is little interaction. A simple society is a 'system of segments homogenous and similar to each other' (*The Division of Labour*, Chapter 6, p. 181), so that any of them can be added to or subtracted from a society without affecting the others.

Institutionally simple societies are tightly integrated in that there is no sharp distinction between the rules and requirements of family, religious, political, moral and legal life. All are highly traditional and closely controlled so that the individual is born into clearly defined social situations in which his obligations are precise, clear and inescapable. There is thus little scope for individual achievement, or private property and most importantly, there is little room for economic and other division of labour.

Durkheim's thesis is that the cohesiveness of such simple societies is based on the similarity and interchangeability of their parts; this 'mechanical solidarity' arises from the essential sameness of the individuals who share a powerful and definitive collective consciousness. In simple societies the overwhelming majority of ideas, sentiments or representations present in one person's consciousness are also present in that of others, for most mental or, as Durkheim calls them 'moral' phenomena, are part of the collective consciousness. Consequently there is little to mark off one person's thoughts and feelings from those of another and there is no serious tension between individual desires and group constraints. Durkheim draws on the details of religious tradition and tribal practices to illustrate the specific and comprehensive forms of life embodied in the collective consciousness of simple societies and the automatic and yet emotionally intense commitment of its members to their shared social norms.

As external and observable evidence for the existence in simple societies of a strong and efficacious collective consciousness Durkheim points to the nature of the sanctions used against those who transgress its norms. In simple societies sanctions are purely repressive or penal, in that their aim is simply to inflict punishment, 'a passionate reaction of graduated intensity' (*Division of Labour*, Chapter 2, p. 96). Punishment is an expression of the collective consciousness against which the criminal has offended. It is vengeance, but not personal vengeance for it demonstrates the natural reaction of the collective consciousness in defending its health, vitality and integrity.

From this analysis Durkheim concludes that crime and the associated repressive sanctions are functional for simple societies, not because, as Smith believed, retaliation leads (unintentionally) to the deterrence of other potential offenders, but because the act of punishment, by allowing the collective consciousness to express itself, reinforces that consciousness. Thus 'its true function is to maintain social cohesion intact, while maintaining all its vitality in the common conscience' (*Division of Labour*, Chapter 2, p. 108).

The basic characteristics of complex societies are the obverse of those which apply to simple societies. Complex societies have large territories densely populated, with a multiplicity of differently structured groups. Instead of being segmented complex societies are internally integrated in that their parts depend on each other for mutual support, they are thus 'organic' rather than 'mechanical'.

In complex societies institutional arrangements are specialized so that each type of institution—familial, religious, educational, political and economic—become more clearly distinct and correspondingly each type of institution becomes less central to the lives of the members of the society. Individuals no longer come under the tight control of the collectivity of closely knit institutions which dominate simple societies. Internally also each institution allows for specialism of roles and hence for the emergence of significant differences between the individuals who occupy them. This specialism of interdependent activities is a feature not just of economic process but of all aspects of society. For instance an organic society requires a specialized political organ, the state, to deliberate and decide on behalf of the whole society, and within this distinct organ of society there is a variety of interdependent political roles, those of legislating, adjudicating and administering being only the most obvious ones.

In the specialized legal sphere there is a shift from the repressive sanctions characteristic of simple societies, to restitutive sanctions which have the function of restoring situations which obtained prior to the occurrence of the legal wrong. The private law of contract and tort replace criminal law as the dominant feature of legal codes and in the diminished province of criminal law more emphasis is placed on the harm done to individuals and less on the idea of offending against society as such. Restitutive law has the negative purpose of demarcating the boundaries between individuals, a mark of the development of the personal autonomy which requires a measure of private property to express and defend itself. Restitutive law thus serves as a framework for the co-operative activities of individuals which is a prime feature of complex societies.

The organic solidarity which develops in complex societies arises from interdependence rather than from similarity of parts. The differences on which this new form of bonding is based must be complementary not antagonistic ones, for each specialized role depends for its performance on the activities of inter-related types of people in a variety of occupations and activities, none of which is self-subsistent. Organic solidarity is thus a unity of a whole whose parts are different but related in such a way that each helps to serve the ends of the whole. The function of the division of labour is not, as might be expected, and as Adam Smith contends, to increase productivity, but to make possible an integrated social existence which does not depend on a rigid homogeneity in the parts of the system. This is the point at which he parts company with Marx and Comte, both of whom think that the division of labour is uncompromisingly disruptive of social order.

There has been a great deal of controversy over the precise nature of organic solidarity, particularly as some of the things that Durkheim says about it sound similar to the utilitarianism he elsewhere so firmly rejects. The making of contracts between autonomous individuals seems to be just the sort of thing he says could not produce stable social cohesion. And if, in complex societies, there is a dropping away of the intensity and extent of the collective consciousness does this not undermine the very foundations which he had argued were necessary even for contractual relationships?

However it is clear that Durkheim never thought that complex societies could dispense with an underpinning from the collective consciousness, even if this is less extensive and forceful than that of simple societies. Organic solidarity is not a straightforward alternative to mechanistic solidarity; the latter can exist without the former but the former cannot exist without a measure of the latter. But, more importantly, Durkheim's acquiescence in individual differences does not commit him to the acceptance of the thesis that the individual is free to adopt just any goals; in a properly organized organic society the disparate ends of society are not chosen at random but assigned by that society. Moreover these ends are not characteristically self-interested but are to a degree directed towards societal goals. Further the consciousnesses of the individuals involved includes the awareness of complex collective representations embodying the idea of interdependence and co-operation. Theirs is no blind artificial harmony of interests for it involves an actual and conscious mutual dependence of interests which are not in themselves antagonistic to each other.

This sophisticated form of social cohesion is not the universal result of specialism or social organization. Durkheim allows that there can be abnormal forms of the division of labour in which differences give rise not to mutual attraction but to conflict and hostility. This, he thinks, is not due to the decrease in the power of the collective conscience, since this is normal in industrial society. It happens particularly in periods of transition before organic solidarity has fully developed to fill the void created by the decline of the collective consciousness, a theme he develops in his later work, *Suicide*. In such periods the individual, cut off from the simple certainties of mechanical solidarity, is more prone to inner miseries, 'anomic' suicide and socially disruptive behaviour in general. This he regards as forced division of labour and its evils are not to be overcome, as Adam Smith suggests, by education, or, as Marx believes, by the almost total abolition of specialization, but by the gradual emergence of more normal and less coercive forms of complex co-operation.

Before passing to the implications of Durkheim's theory of society we should note two points. Firstly, Durkheim, even if he is eventually concerned to point up the differences between two types of 'moral' or conscious life, does so on the basis of a good deal of empirically accessible data, such as population size and density, the division of labour, criminal statistics and types of legal sanctions. This is supplemented in his later work by detailed studies of primitive religions and professional groups.

Second, we should note that the cause of the social changes which lead from simple to complex societies are, at base, material factors, viz the ratio of population to territory (what he calls 'material density') which leads in turn to self-conscious interaction (what he calls 'moral density') and hence to the division of labour. From this we get a deterministic law, reminiscent of Book I of Adam Smith's *Wealth of Nations*, according to which the division of labour varies in direct ratio to the volume and density of societies, with the material conditions providing the essential preconditions of the psychic aspects of the process. It is the growth and concentration of societies that necessitates the division of labour. However his limited materialism is not so narrowly economic as that of Marx for whom production was the sole important factor in social causation (see p. 118).

PRACTICAL IMPLICATIONS

Durkheim's preoccupation with social order and in particular with the disintegration of societies characterized by forced division of labour is illustrated by his account in *Suicide* of what happens when the regulative power of society breaks down.

In this classic work, which is as important for its development of statistical method in sociological study as for its particular conclusions about suicide, he relates different types of suicide to the social forces present in different types of society.

Taking a suicide to be any death resulting 'directly or indirectly from a positive or negative act of the victim himself, which he knows will produce this result' (*Suicide*, p. 44), Durkheim distinguishes 'egoistic', 'altruistic', and 'anomic' suicide. Egoistic suicide is that which arises from the excessive individuation which occurs when the individual is detached from the collective consciousness which gives his life direction and meaning. This type of self-destruction, he points out, is more typical among Protestants than Catholics and affects Catholics more than Jews. This is because egoistic suicide is caused by lack of social integration. The collective consciousness is weaker in Protestant than in Catholic communities and is stronger in Jewish groups. Egoistic suicide is an increasing phenomenon in modern society because of the development of individual autonomy.

In contrast altruistic suicide is the product of insufficient individuation and is therefore more common in primitive societies where the individual has no clear sense of his own distinctive existence and is therefore ready to sacrifice himself for the group. For the same reason this form of suicide is a feature of military life, particularly in élite regiments with strong *esprit de corps*.

It is, however, anomic suicide which is most distinctive to societies in the process of modernization. Anomic suicide is due to the breakdown of the collective order when individuals lack the backing of the primitive collective consciousness and have not yet been taken up into the new organic solidarity.

Such suicides do not, he demonstrates, correlate with poverty but arise from the frustration and despair which follows from unregulated and hence unrealizable desires.

Anomic suicide provides a pointer to Durkheim's diagnosis of the strengths and weaknesses of modern society. Given that anomic suicide is to an extent normal in industrial society Durkheim cannot regard it as an unequivocal evil. It is simply an extreme form of individual autonomy. But he attempts to argue that, since modern civilization stresses the importance of human personality and since suicide negates this ideal, this means that suicide is not 'normal' in the sense of being expressive of the true nature of modern society. Thus we ought to seek to reduce the suicide rate by increasing the pace of certain underlying social changes which would reimpose solidarity. The changes he considers desirable involve the emergence of occupational groups or corporations as a source of moral discipline. Through this medium it is possible to limit the extent of legitimate needs and so increase the general happiness of society and thereby reduce, among other ills, the incidence of suicide.

The practical implications of *Suicide* are in line with those of the *Division of Labour* where he reaches precisely the same conclusion about the need for organic regulation to counteract anomie. There he proposes the development of industrial corporations from which would evolve effectively enforced norms to meet the new forms of social life. Such groups will have more than economic functions. They are to provide the individual with a complete social setting within which to fulfil his specialized existence—for specialism would be one of the duties inculcated by the corporations—and at the same time these occupational groups would enable people to enjoy the fraternity that their nature requires but is lacking in the society Durkheim sees around him.

Out of the interaction of such groups would develop enforceable standards on which to base harmonious industrial production. Government by itself is incapable of regulating economic life. The state is too remote from the individual and cannot comprehend the details of economic life. Nor can the family be sufficiently strengthened to provide the cohesion lacking in an individualistic society. Further, religion has lost its credibility and can no longer provide social solidarity. The model which does provide hope, however, is that of the professional groups of lawyers, judges, soldiers and priests. Durkheim's idea is to encourage the development of similar associations in industrial life made up of 'all the agents of the same industry, united and organized in a single body' (*Division of Labour*, Preface to 2nd edn, p. 5). Such corporate groups are not intended primarily for the defence of their members' interests but function rather like religious organizations which incorporate a welfare function internal to the group but also enable their members to fit into the wider society. Their institutions are therefore of quasi-religious sort; the common cult, the common banquet, the common cemetery. They resemble an extended family or a medieval guild. Corporate groups subordinate private utility to the common interest, develop standards of honesty in relation to the industrial activities concerned and so control as well as serve the individual.

Durkheim realizes that occupational groups require a legal framework. They must be supervised by the state while remaining distinct and relatively autonomous in their own sphere. Internally they should be encouraged to develop collective activities to stimulate their members into providing mutual material assistance, and organize cultural facilities and promote other ways of generating group solidarity. Each is to have its own agencies and regulations suited to its particular function in the economy. An organized corporate body would meet regularly, with day to day control being in the hands of an elected council to see to the internal enforcement of the group's norms. Once this sort of institutional arrangement emerges in business and industrial as well as in other professional groups the disorder which gives rise to the amoral character of economic life would cease, for the worker would then have a precise idea of his rights and duties and an immediately effective organization to protect these rights and require the fulfilment of the appropriate duties.

If occupational groups are to perform these major tasks they have to be given a central place in a new political structure. They would therefore become the basic electoral unit in place of regional constituencies. This would produce well-informed and responsible delegates fitted to deal with inter-professional and inter-industrial relations. There would then exist important secondary organs between the individual and the state preventing, on the one hand, the control of the state passing to an agglomeration of self-interested individuals and at the same time protecting ordinary individuals against the power of the state. This would also preserve a balance between the egalitarianism to which state democracy gives rise and the necessary hierarchy of group organization.

All this is to the benefit of the individual members who require the sustaining and controlling power of the group and some protection against its claustrophobic omnipresence. For, although individual fulfilment is possible only in a group, a degree of personal autonomy is necessary for the flourishing of the highest human qualities. Protection for the individual against the group is provided by the state whose task it is to see that individual rights are not sacrificed to group expediency.

There is a socialist element in all this to the extent that Durkheim assumes that there would be an overall plan into which the individual fits via his occupational group, and a measure of central control of the economy provided by the mediating role of the state. But it is not the sort of anarchistic socialism which dispenses with the need for rules, nor the state socialism which involves government ownership of the means of production. He favours the abolition of inheritance and the gradual transfer of ownership of productive property to the occupational groups. But this does not imply a proletarian take over of the means of production.

Durkheim prefers in the end to present himself as an individualist for once the correct balance of power is set and people live within the ambit of occupational groups under the general oversight of a state charged with the protection of individual rights, then the conditions will exist for the emancipation of the individual which is the central ideal of modern society.

CRITICISM AND ASSESSMENT

Points which can be made against Adam Smith's theological version of functionalist explanations (see p. 96) and will be mentioned again when we consider Talcott Parsons's contribution to social theory (see p. 189), also count against Durkheim's theoretical approach. However Durkheim invites critical assessment not simply as a philosopher recommending a particular methodological approach to social study but also in terms of the empirical standards on which he himself insists. As a practising empiricist he cannot avoid his material being subjected to scientific testing procedures, and there are many areas in which his data has been questioned. It is clear, for instance, that he generalizes unwarrantably about primitive religion from limited material concerning some forms of Australian totemism. And modern statisticians are much less confident that official data on suicide rates are sufficiently reliable for research purposes, particularly where comparisons are being made between countries with different methods of collecting such statistics and different views of what suicide is. This fact diminishes the empirical basis of *Suicide*.

More serious scientific charges may however be laid against him in relation to the selection of his material. In his enthusiasm to exhibit the comprehensiveness of his purely social explanations of social phenomena he has a tendency to select just those examples of the phenomena in question which could be fitted into his project. Thus in his study of religion the insistence that religion has the function of providing the symbols for society's consciousness of itself in order to express the superiority of social reality over the individual leads him to select those examples of religion in which the coming together in ritual gatherings does lead to a heightening of group consciousness and a sense of the sacred. He ignores those more individualistic forms of religious experience typified by the lone prophet separating himself from the corruption of his society. Indeed his definition of religion incorporates the idea that it is a set of beliefs and practices which unite into one single moral community. There is thus a certain confusion of definition and description (see p. 48).

Similarly, in looking for instances of altruistic suicide, Durkheim classifies as examples of suicide the self-sacrificing deaths of soldiers in battle and martyrs who allow themselves to be killed by others. This amounts to redefining 'suicide' to fit his theory. Moreover, the statistics on which he relies must have involved, in their compilation, the assumption that the individual's reasoned intention to kill himself is a necessary element in suicide although this runs counter to his own attempt to get away from such subjective factors by defining suicide without reference to the reasons why a person sacrifices his life or permits himself to be killed.

It is however an advance in social science if its theories are capable of being empirically tested and Durkheim's many admirers stress his place in the development of sociology in this respect. But even at this level of assessment some doubts must be expressed about the scientific nature of his practice and the conceptual scheme which lies behind it.

The concepts of human nature on the one hand and of 'society' as an independent psychic realm on the other both lack empirical foundation in that they are highly theoretical postulates with relatively tenuous connections to empirical observations. Durkheim's plastic raw material of undifferentiated pre-social human characteristics is every bit as speculative as earlier attempts by philosophers like Hobbes to describe man's behaviour in the prehistorical state of nature, and no amount of criticism of the Hobbesian approach, however justified that criticism may be, can establish the scientific credentials of Durkheim's alternative scheme as anything more than a tentative starting point.

So also his idealist concept of society—particularly in the most sociologistic versions of his analysis when he speaks of an autonomous psychic reality with its own life and laws—sits rather too loosely on the empirical data to which he points.

Thus to maintain that society is 'external' to the individual he cites the felt coerciveness of social norms, but when it is pointed out that many social norms are internalized and are therefore not felt to be imposed on the individual, instead of accepting that this counts against his hypothesis he simply assumes that we are dealing with an example of the collective consciousness's presence in that individual. 'Externality' is thus redefined in terms of the alleged social origin of the norms in question.

The weakness of the positive side of Durkheim's sociological explanations is seen in his fallacious method of argument by the elimination of counter hypotheses. His typical mode of argumentation in, for instance, the *Division of Labour*, is to take each 'individualistic' or psychological explanation in turn, find some reason to dismiss it, and then rapidly conclude that his social explanation must be the correct one. Thus, if the division of labour is not caused by the foresight of self-interested individuals then, he reasons, it must be the result of an increase in material density. This manner of proceeding simply ignores the fact that disproof of hypothesis A does not establish the truth of hypothesis B, if only because there may be other alternatives that have not been considered.

Moreover the whole attempt to prove that categories of thought such as space and causality are entirely socially grounded seems vitiated by the fact that the very notion of a clan territory presupposes the use of the categories of thought to which it is said to give rise.

Moving more to the substance of his social theory it is generally agreed that Durkheim has greatly increased our awareness of society as a normative phenomenon which cannot be understood without an appreciation of the role of social consensus in providing a framework for social action, and that, perhaps more than anyone else, he identifies the crucial differences between traditional and modern societies. However as a total theory it seems defective in underplaying the elements of conflict and power in social relationships. He neglects both the ineradicable nature of disagreements between individuals and social groups and the way in which these are settled by the deployment of superior power, that is by the capacity to inflict physical, economic or other disadvantages on competitors. It may be the case that no society can hold together entirely on the basis of such coerciveness but it is equally clear that actual social norms are not unrelated to the capacity of those in positions of power to mould their content and see to their enforcement in the absence of consensus. Nor does Durkheim seem sufficiently aware of the possibilities of manufacturing consensus and hence controlling social behaviour without recourse to overt coercion. He does not, for instance, take adequate account of the use of religion to support political domination. This is the substance of the criticism levelled by those conflict theorists who see in Durkheim an ideologically motivated defender of a capitalist system which rests much more on power and repression than on a consensus of approximately equal interdependent groups.

The ideological criticism of Durkheim can also fasten on the helpfully frank and open way in which he sometimes sets out his assumption that natural processes reveal moral values. This lays him open to the charge of committing the naturalistic fallacy by illicitly drawing an 'ought' from what should be, on positivist assumptions, a morally neutral 'is'. Of course he does not always accept the *status quo*, for we have seen that he dubs social phenomena which he does not like as 'abnormal' or unhealthy. This is functionalist talk. But where his sociological theory goes beyond saying what level of consensus is necessary to the survival of a social group as a viable unit (although not necessarily in its existing form) and commends the development of a certain type of social organization to facilitate the 'normal' working of a certain type of society, then this must be seen as an unwarranted introduction of Durkheim's own semi-collectivist ideals into a theory which should have no place for such a mode of discourse.

Even if he is correct that values are social in origin and are unimaginable outside a social context this does not prove that these values must always support the maximization of some type of sociability. He seems to make the assumption that

'Society' is like an egoistic human individual who, if he creates something, can only do so for his own good or greater glory. In fact it is far from clear that Durkheim can establish that individuals cannot transcend the social origin of their moral experience and adopt values which reflect socially undetermined preferences. Even if values are socially caused this does not prove that social cohesion must be the highest value. There can be no values without society, but given a viable form of social organization there could be plenty of scope for choice between different types of social arrangement which are not themselves dictated by the need to preserve a degree of social order.

These possibilities are excluded by Durkheim's excessively empiricist approach which neglects the role of choice in human actions and hence in social organization. For this reason many of his critics have turned against what they see as Durkheim's obsessive attachment to the methods of the natural sciences (what his critics call 'scientism'). An alternative approach is provided by that other giant of modern social theory, Max Weber, whose theory of social action we will consider in the next chapter.

FOR FURTHER READING

Instead of tackling the main works of Durkheim which are cited in the text of this chapter the reader may find it easier to consult *Emile Durkheim: Selected Writings*, ed. and trans. with an introduction by Anthony Giddens (Cambridge University Press: Cambridge 1972). See also the same author's *Durkheim* (Fontana, Collins: Glasgow, 1978) for an excellent brief study of Durkheim's thought; also Giddens's *Capitalism and Modern Social Theory* (Cambridge University Press: Cambridge, 1971)

There is a substantial intellectual biography by Stephen Lukes, (*Emile Durkheim, His Life and Work*, Allen Lane: London, 1973), who has also written an excellent article on Marx and Durkheim 'Alienation and Anomie', which is to be found in *Philosophy, Politics and Society*, 3rd series, ed. by Peter Laslett and W. G. Runciman (Blackwell: Oxford, 1967).

Perhaps the most influential exposition and critique of Durkheim's work is contained in Talcott Parsons, *The Structure of Social Action* (Free Press: Glencoe, 1949). See also Robert A. Nisbet, *Emile Durkheim* (Prentice-Hall: Englewood Cliffs, 1965).

CHAPTER 8

Max Weber:
An Action Theory

WITHOUT repudiating the positivistic search for causal explanations, Max Weber (1864–1920) places the concept of meaningful individual action at the centre of his theory of society. For Weber the distinctive feature of social relationships is the fact that they make sense to those who participate in them. He believes that the complex of social relationships which make up a society can be rendered intelligible only by reaching an understanding of the subjective aspects of the interpersonal activities of members of that society. It is, therefore, through the analysis of different types of human *action* that we gain knowledge of the nature and variety of human societies.

Weber is best known for his study of the affinity between the world-view of Protestantism and the motivation of the capitalistic entrepreneur (see *The Protestant Ethic and the Spirit of Capitalism*, 1906) but he also wrote influential works on the methodology of social science (see *Methodology of the Social Sciences*, 1905) and produced encyclopaedic studies of Chinese, Indian and Jewish cultures. He never completed his most systematic sociological work—*Wirtschaft und Gesellschaft*. Part I of this work, translated as *Social and Economic Organization* (Free Press, Glencoe, paperback 1964) serves as the basis for our exposition of Weber's action theory of society; my page references are to this edition.

Weber's account of the rational organization of modern bureaucratic society betrays a tentative admiration for the achievements of the modern state—particularly in the disciplined and hierarchical form exemplified in Bismarck's Germany, for which he felt strong patriotic sentiments and concern. But as a sociologist he was able to appreciate the qualities of cultures very different from his own and was critical of the more aggressive and regressive aspects of the Kaiser's political ambitions and methods.

This ambivalence towards his own country and times reflected his theoretical awareness of the complexity of human action in which emotion and values play as central a part as rational calculation. It also related to his own personal difficulty in reconciling his penchant for practical involvement in military, administrative and political affairs with his academic commitment to the pursuit of a value-free social science. Overall, despite his participation in study groups such as the Social-Political Union, and a brief spell as a hospital administrator during the First World War, it was the life of scholarly detachment which won out until towards the end of his life when he became deeply involved in the origins of the Weimar Republic. This may have been due in some measure to his psychological incapacity to cope with the pressures of public life. He suffered a nervous breakdown after the death of his father, and he never resumed the teaching duties of the professorship of economics to which he had been appointed in 1897 at the University of Heidelberg.

In view of Weber's emphasis on the importance of interpreting society in terms of the meaningful action patterns of its members, it is perhaps worth noting his own ambivalent attitudes towards the stark political and organizational realities of modern society and his intermittent efforts to further the cultural and ethical ideals of the liberal middle classes of his day. These conflicting tendencies in his personality can be related to the problems he had in coming to terms with the contrasting characters of his father and mother. The former, a lawyer member of a wealthy linen manufacturing family, was a successful National-Liberal politician, smoothly effective in public and brusquely authoritarian in private. His mother, on the other hand, was a cultured and prudishly pious lady whose charitable activities were despised by her husband. The young Weber, in pursuing an intellectual career, took his mother's side against his father without being able to endorse what he regarded as her ineffectual religiosity. Although Weber followed in his father's path to the extent that he qualified as a lawyer and remained fascinated by the world of public affairs, it was the more cultured and spiritual values to which he in the main adhered. The internal conflicts to which this clash of outlooks gave rise undoubtedly helped Weber to analyse the varying types of meaningfulness which characterize different styles of human action and hence determine the fundamental features of each type of society.

WEBER'S APPROACH

Weber defines sociology as 'a science which attempts the interpretative understanding of social action in order thereby to arrive at a causal explanation of its course and effects' (p. 88). This represents a compromise between the strict positivist's preoccupation with causal generalizations and the humanistic historian's total rejection of the relevance of causal analysis to human behaviour.

As a science, sociology must be, in Weber's terms, 'value-free', by which he means in the first place that those in academic positions should separate their personal evaluations from their scientific pronouncements, for such value judgements cannot be logically deduced from empirically observable facts.

Weber did not see the scientific neutrality he advocates as a compromise between the conflicting opinions of the time, for he regards such compromises as themselves being evaluations. Nor does he require the social scientist to eschew moral and political commitment outside his academic work. But the student of society must aspire to strict evaluative neutrality in the interpretation and explanation of social phenomena.

Weber concedes that this value-freedom is difficult to achieve in sociology. He gives three reasons for this. In the first place, values are among the objects of study so that to describe, as he does, the affinity between Protestantism and Capitalism readily spills over into an evaluation of these value-laden systems of belief and action. However, he thinks that this difficulty can be overcome if care is taken to resist such temptations to scientific sinfulness.

It is less easy to nullify the second obstacle which faces the sociologist on the path of scientific neutrality. Because of the endless variety of facts to be studied the theorist must use his own value judgements to select the social phenomena he thinks worthy of his research. The phenomena to be studied are bound to be chosen for their 'value-relevance', that is for the significance which they have in the light of the value judgements of the observing scientist. Weber, for instance, is interested in the nature of the rationality he thinks to be the important feature of modern capitalism; he also wishes to discover how the stability of modern society could be maintained. He recognizes that value judgements are involved in the decision to concentrate on these social phenomena rather than other ones. However Weber believes that there is no real problem here since such evaluations have to be made before the start of the scientific investigation and are therefore quite separate from that investigation. But it is important, he thinks, that these prior evaluations be brought out into the open and clearly separated from the study itself.

A third difficulty in the idea of a value-free social science is that, according to Weber, explaining behaviour involves understanding it, and understanding requires entering into the mind and feelings of the social actors. This means that to explain society we have to empathize with the conduct of others. Empathy can be achieved by the method of imaginative sympathy analysed by Adam Smith in his account of moral judgement. To do this it is necessary 'to put one's self imaginatively in the place of the actor and thus sympathetically to participate in his experiences' (p. 90). The problem with this method is that it appears to result in sharing the values of the person whose actions are to be sympathized with and hence understood.

Again Weber regards this as a danger to the value-neutrality of sociology rather than an assertion of the impossibility of it being value-free. It is possible, he argues, to enter into the thoughts and feelings of another without endorsing them. In any case it is not always strictly necessary to go so far along the line of imaginative identification as to genuinely enter into the actual motives and intentions of the other. The social scientist is able, therefore, to stick to demonstrating the means rather than recommending ends of of social reform.

What, then, does understanding the actions of others involve if it may not require full imaginative sympathy? To answer this question we must first see what he means by 'social action'. Weber distinguishes action from behaviour in general by saying that a movement is not an action unless it has subjective meaning for the person(s) involved. This requires that the actor has an awareness of what he or she is doing which can be analysed in terms of intentions, motives and feelings as they are experienced. Action is thus contrasted with the purely mechanical aspects of bodily functioning, such as the digestive process, which have no 'intentional reference'.

Building on this distinction between action and mere movement, Weber stipulates that 'action is social insofar as, by virtue of the subjective meaning attached to it by the acting individual (or individuals), it takes account of the behaviour of others and is thereby oriented in its course' (p. 88). This excludes acts directed towards things rather than persons, unless these things happen to have some significance for the actions of other people, as it does in the case of solitary manufacturing work where the intention is to sell the product. Social action is, therefore, something more than mere similarity between the behaviour of lots of people (mass behaviour) although it need not involve mutual awareness since one person can behave intentionally towards another without the latter being aware of this fact. But social action does require that at least one participant gives meaning to his behaviour in terms of the subjective experiences of another person, that is with regard to the intentions, motives or feelings of other people.

To understand (*Verstehen*) social action it is necessary to have evidence covering the particular subjective meaning (*Sinn*) of the actors, and this requires a capacity to grasp the total complex of meaning which the actor uses to formulate his reasons for acting in the way he does. This cannot be done without knowing the symbols (mainly language) which the actor would use to describe his own behaviour.

Such understanding may consist in a direct intellectual grasp of what is going on (as in the case of a logical process such as arithmetical addition), by conjuring up within, through empathy, the feelings of the actor, or by drawing on our own assumptions about what motivates people in that sort of situation.

Weber accepts that there is a difference between 'understanding' behaviour and explaining it in causal terms. But he points out that sociological understanding of actions involves seeing them in the light of the standard meanings which crop up in typical social actions and can be expressed in common symbols. From the point of view of social science, to understand a particular action is to regard it as an instance of a type of activity characteristic of that society. This is possible because the actor himself sees his behaviour as of a certain socially recognized type. But since the investigator cannot directly perceive the meaningfulness of another person's behaviour, he has to frame a hypothesis about the nature of the social action in question on the basis of the type of conduct common to persons in such situations.

If to understand an action is to see it as typical, then we are moving in the direction of causal generalization for it assumes that there are ascertainable patterns of action. And Weber does maintain that social relationships are amenable to scientific laws despite the fact that the German historical school which influenced his early work taught that history is a unique sequence of particular events. Weber's compromise position in the debate between hard-line positivism and the extreme particularism of the narrative historian is to accept that the study of society is a study of history and that elements in the historical process, especially in the sphere of ideas, cannot be fully captured in the confines of invariable causal generalizations. But Weber believes that many social phenomena can be subsumed under scientific laws and he sees his task as a sociologist to pursue this path to its limits.

In his commitment to the discovery of social causes, particularly economic causes, Weber can be both compared and contrasted to Marx. Like Marx, of whose work he is constantly and critically conscious, Weber looks to economic factors for many of his major social analyses and explanations. But to a greater extent than Marx, Weber is prepared to attribute causal efficacy to a variety of interacting factors. Political, moral, environmental, religious and artistic factors —all these have a distinct and relatively independent input to the pattern of social action. Moreover his belief in the partial autonomy of ideas in all these spheres brings him into sharp conflict with the more doctrinaire version of Marxian thought according to which ideas are always effects and never causes.

The split between the pursuit of understanding and the objectives of causal explanation is evident in his concept of 'ideal types'. These are simplified models of social activities which are used in interpreting human behaviour. The adjective 'ideal' here draws attention to the fact that ideal types are mental entities—they are ideas of action—but the word has no moral or evaluative connotations; ideal types do not represent good or bad types of action. Rather they are extrapolations of selected aspects of action which form an intelligible complex in terms of which we can understand actual behaviour. Ideal types are meaningful stereotypes which exaggerate some aspects of social reality which somehow go together at the level of meaning. Thus the ideal type of capitalism contains selected features of actual capitalist behaviour isolated and extended to form a simplified and meaningful model of conduct in capitalist systems. As extrapolations from actual behaviour patterns ideal types are not themselves causal generalizations, but Weber suggests that they can be used to classify social phenomena and to formulate probable causal connections which can be tested empirically.

And yet ideal types are not used only to suggest causal hypotheses; they also provide explanations of empirical correlations. Ideal types enable us, for instance, to see a meaningful connection between certain beliefs and values on the one hand and other observable sociological facts on the other. Thus Weber invites us to see that there is an 'elective affinity' between the outlook of Puritan religious groups and the activities of capitalist entrepreneurs: the worldly success combined with frugal living (which make for an effective capitalist), are, on this religious view, manifestations of grace and divine favour. Weber does not claim, however, that his ideal type of Protestantism is a complete representation of the outlook of the average Protestant denomination. However its selective oversimplifications promote understanding of the nature of Protestantism.

In summary, Weber sees social studies as lacking the empirical rigour of the natural sciences but enjoying the additional benefit of generating empathic understanding of statistical regularities in the social sphere, something which is not possible in the case of non-human phenomena. It should be emphasized again that the ideal types which perform this central role in Weber's approach, while they may be selected because of their relevance to the researcher's personal values and are constructed so as to encapsulate a meaningful complex of values and beliefs, are not intended to be vehicles for the personal value judgements of the social scientist.

WEBER'S THEORY OF MAN

Weber's theory of man is best approached through his characterization of four types of human action.

Using his notion of ideal types, Weber starts his analysis by picking out from the vast range of human behaviour the ideal of rational conduct which he calls *zweckrational* or goal-rational.

This mode of orientation involves the accurate calculation and adoption of the most effective means to the chosen and clearly envisaged end, or goal, of the actor in the light of the particular circumstances of his action and the estimated side-effects of the means followed in relation to other purposes which the actor may have. This is very much a utilitarian or instrumentalist frame of mind. It is logical, scientific and economical.

Weber's analysis of this type of rational action carries no implication that human beings always act rationally. In so far as actual behaviour approximates to the rational ideal type it is immediately intelligible (and, given knowledge of the ends and available means, predictable) but actual behaviour deviates, often widely, from the rational model.

Moreover the extent to which human behaviour is goal-rational varies according to the type of society in question, means-end rationality being most characteristic of bureaucratically organized groups.

The second of Weber's four types of social action is *wertrational* or value-rational conduct. On this model the actor is committed to the unconditional importance or value of the activity in question. He is pursuing values rather than calculating means in an evaluatively neutral way. Here calculative rationality comes in only in the choice of the most effective means to the valued objectives, and typically the values determine the choice of means as well as the end, so that a morally good objective must be attained only by a morally good means. The man who tells the truth through thick and thin is obviously acting in a value-rational manner, but it is also the case that all rational human conduct involves an element of value-rationality since the logical pursuit of ends in any form assumes that those ends are valued by the agent.

Thirdly, Weber has an ideal type for affective or emotional action, that is behaviour which is under the direct domination of feelings. Here there is no conscious formulation of values or rational calculation of appropriate means. It is purely emotional conduct and hence non-rational.

Weber has a fourth category of human action which he labels 'traditionalist' to cover habitual conduct arising out of established practices and respect for existing authority. This type of behaviour may not be considered sufficiently conscious to count as 'intended' and hence as genuine 'action', but Weber allows for intentionality to be implicit and so relatively sub-conscious, and in this regard traditionalist action is not dissimilar to affective action.

These four types of action are more than sociologists' tools: they are ways in which individuals give meaning to their actions and, for Weber, it is fundamental to man's nature that he seeks to give some sort of sense to his life. Man is therefore a religious creature in that even his economic activities presuppose some general world-view which he uses to make his life intelligible.

Using his ideal types of action, Weber can construct a composite picture of individual persons according to the combination of types of action which characterize their behaviour and the particular beliefs and values which they possess. Actual individuals vary in the extent to which their activities are goal-rational, value-rational, affective or traditional. Clearly some element of calculative rationality is inevitable but equally indispensable is adoption by the individual of values which he may then pursue in a rational or affective manner.

There is at this point an existentialist element in Weber's theory of man, for he insists that there is an extensive range of values that the individual may choose to adopt. Like Nietszche, by whom Weber was greatly influenced, Weber sees the human condition as requiring the exercise of choice in relation to ultimate and incompatible ends of conduct, but he has a more open view than Nietszche of the possible ways in which men may affirm their existence and give meaning to their lives. And he does not believe in any universal set of values which human beings are bound to adopt. Man must, to an extent, choose his values and decide for himself how rational, emotional or traditional his actions are going to be.

The extent to which such existentialist choice occurs is, however, affected by the social relationships of the individual for Weber includes in his account of human nature the tendency to make value choices on the basis of the authority structure of the society in which the individual lives. His theory of man at this point becomes inseparable from his theory of society.

Weber's ideal types of action can be used to construct composite pictures of individual people according to the particular mix of ideal type activities which go to make up their actual behaviour, but Weber's own concern is to use his analyses of goal-rational, value-rational, affective and traditional action as the building blocks for thinking about society in terms of ideal types of social interactions and social groupings. His objective is to create a set of formal concepts which will enable him to organize empirical research so as to reach an understanding of the distinctive characteristics of modern society. He is particularly concerned to contrast traditional and rational types of society. To this end he develops ideal types of contemporary phenomena such as capitalism and bureaucracy, all of which are ultimately reducible to meaningful patterns of interactions between individuals.

The unit or irreducible 'atom' which carries social meaningfulness is the 'social relationship', a term Weber uses to 'denote the behaviour of a plurality of actors in so far as, in its meaningful content, the action of each takes account of that of the others and is oriented in these terms' (p. 118). Social relationships are analysed into three forms: conflict (or struggle), community, and association.

Conflict is a form of relationship in which action 'is oriented intentionally to carrying out the actor's own will against the resistance of the other party or parties' (p. 132). To do this successfully is to exercise 'power' and so achieve 'domination' or 'imperative control'. Conflict is in varying degrees a feature of all societies and varies from unregulated physical combat to carefully controlled competitive interactions. In each case the outcome depends on the qualities of individuals and groups and the nature of the conflict, but the end result is some form of social selection of the type best adapted to the conditions. Society as a whole is a complex balance of conflicting groups.

A social relationship is 'communal', if its orientation 'is based on a subjective feeling of the parties, whether affectual or traditional, that they belong together' (p. 136). Examples include family relationships and national communities. It is most typically found in small groups and traditional societies but is an element in nearly all social groupings.

Finally a social relationship is 'associative' when 'the orientation of social action within it rests on a rationally motivated adjustment of interests or similarly motivated agreement'. These interests may be anything from absolute values to pure expediency. Examples include 'rational free market exchange, which constitutes a compromise of opposed but complementary interests', and voluntary associations for the pursuit of some objective such as scientific research or to further 'some common absolute values' as in the case of commitment to a common cause. This form of social relationship is most characteristic of modern industrial society.

Actual social relationships involve some combination of these three ideal types. Weber takes it to be the sociologist's task to discover recurrent or uniform patterns in which one or other form of social relationship is dominant. These patterns may be the result of pure habit or of calculated self-interest but Weber's attention centres on the social 'order' which is based on a belief in the legitimacy or bindingness of rules.

The idea of valid norms or legitimate order is fundamental to Weber's theory of society. Some forms of conflict are unregulated except by the use of force and all patterns of cohesion are to an extent based on feelings of solidarity or mutual convenience, but settled forms of social organization all require a large measure of authority. Authority exists when the social actor behaves predictably because for some reason or other he believes in the legitimacy of certain rules or practices. Even physical power has most social significance when it is believed to be legitimate, as in the case of the political authority of the state with its monopoly of coercive force in a given territory.

Weber outlines three ideal types of legitimate order or authority. Traditional authority which rests on acceptance of the sanctity of rules because they have existed for a long time and in the legitimacy of those who have inherited the right to command under these rules. In traditional order the individual feels loyalty to the past and those who represent that past, a loyalty whose origin is often rooted in a belief in the sacredness of certain historical events.

Reverence for military and religious leaders of the past sometimes originates from charismatic authority. This type of order is legitimated by outstanding personal qualities of extraordinary individuals whose sanctity, heroism or virtue enables them to command large numbers of men and women in face-to-face relationships. Charisma is exemplified by the superhuman qualities attributed to prophets and military heroes which enable them to impose their own ideas and values on entire groups.

In complete contrast, rational or legal authority rests on a belief in the 'legality' of certain rules which means that those who issue the rules are entitled to do so according to yet further rules which lay down who has the right to command. In rational or legal order it is possible to know which rules are 'formally correct and have been imposed by an accepted procedure' (p. 131). It is an impersonal order which does not depend on the qualities of the individuals who create the rules or on their status as guardians of a tradition.

The significance of these distinctions can be brought out by noting that rulers must themselves remain within the confines of their order if they are to remain as rulers. Thus in a legal authority the ruler has to obey the law if he is not to lose the capacity to be obeyed; in a traditional authority the ruler is required to follow customary practice, and in the case of charismatic authority the leader must constantly demonstrate his outstanding capacities so that, for instance, a Chinese emperor would be deposed if there was extensive flooding, for which he would be blamed.

While legal and traditional forms of order are relatively stable and conservative, charismatic authority, like that of the Hebrew prophets, tends to be transient and revolutionary. But charisma is an important source of the values and ideals on which other types of order are based, for the charismatic leader is able to enact new laws on his own authority. Weber, therefore, attributes to the insights and ideas of particular individuals and particular historical movements considerable influence on the direction of social development. To have this influence these insights and ideas have to become incorporated in a more settled form of order through a process of 'routinization'.

The creative influence of self-appointed individual leaders in its pure form is incompatible with established social structures, but every charismatic leader eventually requires a band of followers or disciples. In order to retain his authority the leader has to go beyond the purely personal relationships he has with his followers, and develop an organization within his band of disciples so that there is a hierarchy of sub-leaders who are accepted as representatives of the leader in the community. This goes along with the systematic presentation of the leader's ideas and the development of a method of applying these to particular circumstances under the guidance of designated disciples or officials.

A vital stage in the routinization of charisma occurs when the leader loses his outstanding qualities or simply dies. His followers then have to provide some form of succession whereby the original leader's charisma is passed on, perhaps by invoking some magical sign or ritual ceremony or by the introduction of a hereditary principle. Whichever method is used the centrality of the personal qualities of the leader is merged with some concept of traditional authority which may involve either a 'patrimonial' administration under the control of a powerful king, or a feudal system in which authority is distributed to vassals in a series of voluntary agreements.

At the other extreme from charismatic 'order' with its band of followers personally devoted to the leader is the rational efficiency of the bureaucratic system with a fixed hierarchy of officials, each with a clearly defined and specialized sphere of authority within an established rule-governed chain of command which has strict rules of procedure, accurate records and centralized control. Each type of legitimate authority has its own type of administrative organization to maintain its dominance, and Weber goes on to specify the characteristic struggles for power within these different authority structures.

By drawing on his three ideal types of social relationships (conflict, communal and associative) and his three ideal types of legitimate authority (traditional, charismatic and legal) Weber is able to develop a whole range of further ideal types of social groupings which he then uses to characterize historically concrete societies so as to make their regular patterns of activity intelligible to us.

For instance Weber distinguished social relationships which are 'open' in that outsiders may enter into them and become participants if they so choose, and those which are 'closed' in that it is part of the subjective meaning of the relationship that it excludes certain people (on grounds of age, sex or nationality, for instance). He then applies this dichotomy along with his battery of ideal types to distinguish various sorts of social groupings. Thus he defines a 'corporate group' as any closed group whose order is enforced by a specialized functionary such as a chief with the support of administrative staff who, because of their representative function, are able to take 'corporate action'. Corporate groups may be communal as in the case of a family, or associational, as in the case of a business concern; conformity to its order can be traditional, or arise from affectual loyalty, or it may be based on the expediency of self-interested calculation. Further, associational corporate groups may be voluntary or compulsory in their origins and operations. Political groups are those whose orders are effective within a territorial area through the use or threat of force by their administrative staff, while religious corporate groups are 'hierocratic' if they use 'psychic' coercion to impose compulsory order.

The array of formal classifications which Weber is able to erect for his analyses of social organization is truly formidable, as is the range of his applications to actual social phenomena. One example is his study of the conflict between Junker (feudal landowners) and middle-class groups in nineteenth-century Prussia, which led him to make an important distinction between classes, in the Marxian sense of social groups with common economic interests dependent on productive factors, and status groups whose members share a common way of life which they value as a source of honour and prestige, rather than for material gain. The latter are more communal than associative. Weber gives an independent significance to status as opposed to economic class in the formation of social groups, particularly religiously based ones.

One thing which emerges from Weber's extensive empirical studies is his sensitivity to the peculiarities and historical uniqueness of specific cultures, but we can nevertheless discern certain very general theses about the main determinants of social relationships. Like Marx he gives centrality in his sociological explanations to economic activity which he defines as a form of rational activity whose 'subjective meaning . . . is concerned with the satisfaction of utilities' (p. 158). However, unlike Marx, he is aware of the value-relativity of the assumptions which lie behind the choice of economic objectives, and the tie-in between narrowly-defined rational economic action and the pursuit of values of no direct economic significance. Moreover he explicitly disputes the Marxian line on the intrinsic unimportance for causal explanation of developments in ideas and ideals. Uni-directional economic determinism is incompatible with the creative role which Weber allots to the influence of charismatic individuals and small groups. Weber's attempt to arrive at a compromise position between the materialistic determinism of the strict Marxian and the idealistic determinism of those who attribute all social change to autonomous intellectual and spiritual developments is most clearly seen in his treatment of the complex inter-relationships between Capitalism and Protestantism outlined in his famous book, *The Protestant Ethic and the Spirit of Capitalism.*

Weber's thesis is that the religious ideas of the Puritan sects had a significant influence on the development of small family capitalism in Europe from the seventeenth to the nineteenth centuries. He argues that the rejection of tradition, and the religious beliefs and practices of these sects, which he describes as worldly asceticism, were part of the psychological or spiritual background which engendered modern capitalist enterprise.

Capitalism, for Weber, as an ideal type, is exemplified in all human societies, since it is simply the use of enterprise or individual initiative in the provision of material needs. But modern capitalism is distinguished by the use of capital accounting to calculate the most profitable use of resources and the discipline of entrepreneurship which puts the systematic pursuit of long-term profit ahead of immediate self-gratification. The working of this system was, on Weber's view, greatly facilitated by the attitudes and way of life associated with the Puritan's frugal way of life and dedication to a 'vocation' in which he could find assurance that he was indeed one of the elect chosen for salvation through the grace of God. Worldly success was taken as one such sign of God's favour, thus giving a religious sanction to the dedicated pursuit of long-term wealth beyond that which is needed for the personal consumption, which was so essential to capitalist enterprise.

By demonstrating the meaningful connection between Puritan religious ideas and capitalist economic activity together with the empirical correlations between the distribution of Puritan sects and the geographical origins of modern capitalism, Weber seeks to establish an 'elective affinity' between these two apparently disparate social phenomena. In this way he makes clear the significant impact of material interests on religious belief, justifies the claim that the Protestant religion has facilitated the rise of capitalist society and does something to explain why capitalism did not emerge from ancient Chinese or Indian societies.

This fulfils his sociological aims of explaining a transition from traditional to rational society without assuming a fixed, universal and unilinear evolution of social types.

PRACTICAL IMPLICATIONS

On one reading of Weber his attempt to trace the development of modern capitalism through the influence of religious ideas, his account of the routinization of charisma, his preoccupation with the ideal type of the rational bureaucratic organization characteristic of modern capitalist states all demonstrate his commitment to the values of industrial capitalism. And certainly he regards the impersonal hierarchical form of legal order as the most intelligible of all social organization. Moreover he is anxious to discover how the stability of capitalist states can be maintained.

A more careful reading, however, shows that although Weber is interested in pin-pointing the distinctive features of modern society, he deplores as well as welcomes the cold rationality of the deferred gratification and military style discipline whose efficiency he so much admired. He regrets that the absence of emotion and tradition robs the bureaucratic life of much of its meaning and savour. Moreover his analysis of social class in terms of material life-chances enables him to see that large sections of the population are excluded from the material benefits of the system and that this undermines not only its stability but its acceptability.

To counter the drawbacks of the mechanistic depersonalization and dull routine of the life of the career bureaucrat who craves only for security and guaranteed status, and to balance the deprivations of the tightly organized military and industrial masses, Weber looks for a resurgence of the charismatic leadership he so much admired in the lives of the Hebrew prophets and the pioneering Puritans. This goes with his commitment to the nation as an affectual group. His patriotism leads him to encourage the development in Germany of a political class capable of leading the mass democratic movement which would imbue the people with spirit and breathe life into the impersonal rationality of its technological organization.

There is thus a romantic and existentialist aspect to Weber's social recommendations. He looks to the choices and leadership of exceptional individuals to provide the basis for a national life which has emotional meaningfulness and cohesion as well as the rational meaningfulness of routinized legal order. However this charismatic ideal is balanced by an admiration for the way in which democratic polities like Britain generate the popular support which enable a nation to compete effectively in the power struggle of international politics.

Evaluative criticism of Weber tends to centre on the charge that by stressing the role of highly relativistic values of charismatic origin he opens the way for those characteristically modern political movements, such as fascism, which deploy efficient organization in the cause of irrational ideals. But Weber is surely not to be blamed for drawing attention to what are better regarded as the non-rational (rather than irrational) bases of many forces at work in social relationships. Rather he is to be commended for resisting the easy retreat into a naturalistic ethic which simply endorses the dominant trends of modern society and avoiding the facile optimism which assumes the compatibility of rival interests. His perception of the importance of international competition for power and cultural prestige certainly demonstrates greater realism than we find in Marx.

Weber himself does not value destructive mass emotionalism for he is as much concerned for the freedom and meaningfulness of the life of each individual as for the value-basis of charismatic and legal orders. And while he admires the rationality of impersonal rule-based social organization, he denies that the objective of capitalist bureaucracy—the amassing of wealth—is itself justified by reason since it sacrifices present to future pleasure. The most that can be said is that he reveals his own evaluative concerns by selecting modern capitalism and the development from traditional to legal authority as the foci of his sociological interests but, as he himself insisted, this is compatible with value-neutrality in the treatment of his material.

Methodologically it is hard to dispute that Weber is right to emphasize that the theorist of society in his search for the uniform patterns of social organization has to take account of the historical particulars—whether they be the major personalities or significant events—that have shaped social realities and given to each society at least some of its distinctive features. And he must be right to say, against Marx, that economic factors are not always decisive in social causation.

Nor is it easy to reject Weber's view that we cannot begin to understand human society without reference to the meaningfulness of social interactions for their participants. And in this regard he performs valuable service in emphasizing the function of ideal types in capturing the meaningfulness of social interactions and organizations and in framing causal hypothesis about the relationships between social phenomena. Exception is taken, of course, to many of the details of his formal sociology, in particular pure unroutinized charisma seems more a type of power than of authority. But most criticisms of Weber's ideal types are based on the erroneous assumption that they are meant to be complete representations of actual historical realities.

It is less easy to be assured that the understanding of meaningful behaviour and the discovery of causal regularities go hand in hand as methods of sociological investigation. It seems too much of a coincidence that ideal types selected for their adequacy in capturing the meaningfulness of the social phenomena should fit so readily with yet further ideal types which generate causal hypotheses. In this respect Weber's method is as yet of unproved fruitfulness despite the impressive insights furnished by his own substantive sociological studies.

Despite the fact that Weber's causal analyses are as sophisticated as Durkheim's (both use the method of correlation), his chief impact stems from his reassertion of the idealist element in social theorizing with its stress on the distinctive place of the subjective element in social phenomena. This has had an enormous influence on a number of theorists.

To conclude this chapter we will look at Parsons's theory of society which seeks to combine the insights of Weber's action theory with the organic functionalism of Durkheim. In the next chapter we will examine the very different use made of Weber's ideas by Schutz.

TALCOTT PARSONS: STRUCTURAL-FUNCTIONALISM

In *The Structure of Social Action* (1937) Talcott Parsons sets out to demonstrate a convergence of ideas concerning the proper approach to the scientific study of society which he traced through the writings of Emile Durkheim and Max Weber, among others. He notes that these writers use a set of concepts, such as those of social action and social role, which could provide a skeleton outline of society as a system made up of identifiable and inter-related parts between which functional interrelationships can be discerned. Hence the twin ideas of social structure and social function.

In analysing social structure Parsons follows Weber in making the concept of 'action' fundamental. The 'unit-act' is said to be as basic to the social system as the particle is to classical mechanics; an act being a piece of behaviour which we can describe in terms of an actor selecting a means or method of obtaining some chosen 'end' or purpose. This Aristotelian starting point assumes that a society is built up from units which are both teleological (in that they involve the pursuit of an end) and subjective (the end is that which is envisaged by the actor himself and not by an external observer of his conduct). Every action takes place in a situation (the 'conditions' of action) over much of which the actor has no control. These conditions include other actions and each action may in turn become part of the conditions of yet further actions. In this way actions may be causally related to each other, thus making up what Parson calls an 'action system'; where these actions are social in the Weberian sense of being directed towards other people the resultant interactions make up a social system. Typically social action systems exhibit stable patterns which can be analysed into roles, that is expected repeated forms of behaviour by persons with a particular 'status', such as father or businessmen, which combine with other complementary expected forms exhibited by persons occupying other status positions, such as those of child or consumer. Any social system of 'status-roles' involves such interlocking sets of rule-governed expectations or collections of rights and duties setting out a 'normative' order to which individual role occupants must conform to a greater or lesser extent. The subjective element in social action and the centrality he gives to the idea of society as a normative structure place him well within the bounds of sociological idealism (see pp. 28f).

Provided there is minimal conformity to role expectations and sufficient agreement or consensus about what the obligations and rights are which attach to each status position, then there is a social system. However not all social systems are societies, for a number of interlocking sets of social action systems in combination is required to make up a society or 'total' social system, which must, like the Aristotle's polis, be self-sufficient, in that it has internal to itself all those social actions necessary for it to persist.

To explain the capacity of a total social system to sustain itself Parsons draws on Durkheim's functionalist concept of a society as an organic entity containing parts which contribute to the life of the whole. Here an organism is envisaged as a systematic unity of interacting parts which may be said to have a boundary between itself and its environment (like a fish and the water in which it swims). Across this boundary come various 'in-puts' (such as oxygen to the fish's gills) and 'out-puts' (such as the fish's eggs), and internal to the system are similar boundaries and exchanges between the parts of the organism (such as those between the fish's respiratory and digestive systems); the internal boundary exchanges enable the organism to survive in its environment by taking in and giving out that which it requires to maintain itself.

Following out this idea of the self-sufficiency of the total social system, Parsons argues that a society must have four subsystems (or major parts) which satisfy certain 'functional prerequisites', in that they each perform a task necessary to keep the system as a whole going:

(1) Goal attainment: the ways in which the members of a society, as individuals or role occupants are enabled to achieve their objectives, particularly their collective objectives; this is characteristically connected with the political aspect of social organization.

(2) Adaptation: the ways in which people, acting in their social roles, can adapt to their material environment by fitting in with it or using it to satisfy their needs. This is typically thought of as the economic sub-system.

(3) Integration: the various devices whereby individuals are brought into co-operative relationships and conflict minimized, such as law, administration and customary mores.

(4) Latency or Pattern Maintenance: the methods of ensuring that individuals internalize and voluntarily adhere to the norms of the society in which they have been brought up, such as the processes of socialization within families and educational organizations. The name 'latency' seems to have been suggested by the fact that this process was associated with 'tension management' which occurs in the privacy of domestic life when the individual's social being is 'latent' or inactive.

This is an abstract scheme in that any actual action or action-set can be part of more than one functional sub-system, but it helps to think of Parsons's analysis in terms of the political, the economic, the legal and the educational aspects of a total social system, although this is a serious over-simplification. The important thing to note is the accompanying claim that each sub-system contributes to and is supported by the other three. We have seen how Adam Smith pointed to the manner in which the administration of justice is required for the operations of a market economy and how that economy provides the material resources for the administration of justice. Such two-way exchanges are said, by Parsons, to take place between each sub-system. Obviously the economy provides material support for the other three but there are also exchanges of power (the use of sanctions and appeals to societal obligations) and of influence which are similar to the monetary exchanges which take place within the economy, so that every sub-system has an almost contractual relationship with the other in that each gives its support to the others only if it receives what it requires from them. Further, the values and expected behaviour in the four sub-systems must harmonize with one another so that, for instance, the values of the educational system fit its products for their tasks in the particular sort of economy existing in that society. So the various systems' problems are solved and the unit-acts of individuals are channelled into a complex pattern of complementary activities which furthers the survival of the individual by sustaining the total social system in which he lives.

Although empirical verification of the universal occurrence of these functional inter-relationships is lacking, Parsons's theory of society does indicate where research sociologists should look if they wish to discover the inner workings of a society. The explanatory scheme offered is attractive in that it commences with the readily intelligible idea of social actions and terminates in the idea of the necessity features of all social systems. Parsons claims to establish what must happen if a society is to exist and therefore seems to offer us an explanation of why each society has these structural features and functional inter-relationships. Thus the individual's choices and strivings are taken seriously but the existence of social order via the internalization of society's value system is explained.

One valuable set of ideas which Parsons develops from Weberian rather than Durkheimian sources is the notion of certain 'pattern variables' which he uses to characterize different sorts of society and to analyse social evolution (see *The Social System*, pp. 58–67).

These pattern variables are presented as contrasting pairs of attitudes which are embodied in different sets of role-statuses and their underlying values and so determine the type of social relationship which dominate in a particular society.

The first of the 'polar' alternatives are Affectivity *vs.* Affective Neutrality, which is roughly speaking the contrast between seeking immediate against deferred gratification. The second is the self-explanatory contrast of Self-orientation *vs.* Collectivity-orientation. The Third, Universalism *vs.* Particularism, opposes the principle that everyone is to be treated in the same way with the principle that special relationships, such as kinship, properly affect all social relationships. The fourth is Achievement *vs.* Ascription, the former stressing the performance of a role-incumbent while the latter emphasizes his attributes independently of his achievements. Finally, Specificity *vs.* Diffuseness opposes the attitude which treats social situations in closely defined and limited terms (e.g. as a purely economic matter) with that which regards each situation in the light of a wide range of social and moral considerations.

In these terms societies such as the United States are characterized by Affective Neutrality, Self-orientation, Universalism, Achievement and Specificity, The Universalism-Achievement pattern. In contrast traditional German society is described as fitting a Universalistic-Ascription pattern and classical Chinese social structure is said to follow a Particularistic-Achievement pattern, while Spanish-American societies are seen along Particularistic-Ascriptive lines. These analyses demonstrate how the social action aspect of Parsons's conceptual schemes works.

There are, however, many sources of dissatisfaction with the Parsonian scheme. In the first place it suffers from the intrinsic weaknesses of functionalist approaches, which apply also to Durkheim and—once divine planning is discounted—to Adam Smith as well.

It does help from the point of view of sociological description to know that one part or sub-system of an organism contributes something to the operations of other parts or sub-systems. And the explanation of how one sub-system keeps functioning is furthered by showing what supports it receives from outside its own boundaries. These relationships can be expressed in purely causal terms. But functionalism appears to be offering something more than this. The implication of saying that X is functional for Y is that this explains why X exists. But of course it does not do this unless we add further assumptions. In Smith's case these assumptions are theological: he assumes that X was created or planned by God in order to benefit Y. In biology the assumptions are those expressed in the theory of evolution that from the countless millions of organisms that develop through random genetic mutation, only those survive whose mutations enable them to maintain themselves and breed in a given environment. It is the combination of proven genetic theory and the principle of the survival of the fittest that makes the concept of function so explanatory in natural history.

Despite the efforts of Herbert Spencer (see p. 143) there is no equivalent evidence to support a theory of social evolution. True, Smith, Durkheim and Parsons all speak in their different ways of certain social phenomena being necessary for the survival of society, but all this comes down to is either the truism that if their institutions change societies will change (for societies unlike animals do not die they simply alter), or the highly unspecific claim that all societies of which we have knowledge have some sort of economic, educational and political systems. From this there follows little if anything about the closeness of the relationships which must exist between these systems (or sub-systems) or about their precise content. And so, while functionalism does help us to order causal statements about the relationships between parts of society in a vaguely illuminating way it does not keep its promise of explaining why the specific mechanisms of the social system are as they are.

Other doubts, which relate specifically to Parsons, concern his inability to demonstrate just where the 'boundaries' of his systems and sub-systems are to be located and his failure to clarify the nature of the alleged exchanges that take place over some of them. There is also considerable artificiality and arbitrariness in many of the complex schemata of sub-systems and their mutual interaction which Parsons develops.

Critics also say that Parsons follows Durkheim in over-emphasizing consensus and underplaying power. This, it is sometimes alleged, is part and parcel of the conservative implications of functionalism which tends to assume that existing social arrangements must be beneficial or else they would not have developed. But it is more likely related to Parsons's idealist model of society which emphasizes the role of norms and values in the determination of social organization.

For our present purpose, a more relevant criticism is that, despite the claim to establish a convergence of approaches in modern social theory, Parsons is left with an uneasy mix of 'action theory' with its stress on the meaningfulness of the individual's purposive behaviour, including the choices open to the actors, and 'system theory' with its stress on the order to which individuals must conform if they are to participate in the social process. True, the order is a normative one, to which individuals are only 'expected' to conform and may not in fact do so. But not only is a total social system constituted by the conformity of the occupants of status-roles to shared rules and values, it is actually assumed that since no society can survive without such a consensus it must in fact occur. Indeed this is what makes it possible to attain objective scientific knowledge of society. Paradoxically, therefore, although the idea of action and the choices it implies are the basic units of the social system, the genuineness of the choices and hence of the actions of individuals are called into question by the success of the social system in obtaining conformity to its norms. Structural-functionalism in its pursuit of a methodology for obtaining objective knowledge of society undermines its own postulates by failing to take seriously the actor's point of view, particularly his freedom. Social action may be voluntary but it follows the internalized norms of the social system. This, at least, is the feeling of those who have returned again to the Weberian starting point in protest against its emasculation in Parsons's systems theory, in which positivism is alleged to have won out over subjectivism and social action is swallowed up in the requirements of the total social system.

FOR FURTHER READING

Our text for Weber is *The Theory of Social and Economic Organisation*, edited with an introduction by Talcott Parsons (Free Press: Glencoe, 1947, paperback 1964). For selections from Weber see H. H. Gerth and C. Wright Mills, *From Max Weber* (Galaxy: New York, 1946) and W. G. Runciman, *Selections from Max Weber* (Cambridge University Press: Cambridge, 1979).

One brief introductory book in the Fontana Modern Masters series is by Donald MacRae, *Weber* (Collins: Glasgow, 1974). A more substantial work is Talcott Parsons's influential book *The Structure of Social Action* (Free Press: Glencoe, 1949) which has a long section on Weber.

See also Richard Bendix, *Max Weber, An Intellectual Portrait* (Doubleday: New York, 1962), J. Freund, *The Sociology of Max Weber* (Allen Lane: London, 1968). For the practical relevance of Weber's life and work see Anthony Giddens, *Politics and Sociology in the Thought of Max Weber* (Macmillan: London, 1972).

For Talcott Parsons, see his book *The Social System* (Free Press: Glencoe, 1951). Also *Essays in Sociological Theory* (Free Press: Glencoe, 1957). For commentary read Max Black (ed.), *The Social Theories of Talcott Parsons* (Prentice-Hall: New York, 1961). A highly critical discussion is contained in Alvin W. Gouldner, *The Coming Crisis of Western Sociology* (Heinemann: London, 1971). See also Ken Menzies, *Talcott Parsons and the Social Image of Man* (Routledge: London, 1977). For an excellent criticism of functionalism see Michael Lessnoff, *The Structure of Social Science* (Allen & Unwin: London, 1974).

CHAPTER 9

Alfred Schutz:
A Phenomenological
Approach

THE work of Alfred Schutz (1899–1959) exemplifies many of
the themes underlying a range of recent less traditional
approaches to the study of society, such as Symbolic Interactionism and Ethnomethodology. These approaches are
radical in that they reject many of the assumptions of the
reigning orthodoxy of 'structural-functionalism', the label
given to Talcott Parsons's synthesis of Durkheim's organicism
and Weber's social action theory which dominated social
theory after the end of the Second World War. In this chapter
the basic tenets of Parsons's system as outlined in the previous
chapter will be used as a background against which to
highlight the distinctive contribution of Schutz. We will then
take a look at some of the contemporary developments in
sociology which are in some way indebted to Schutz.

Schutz was a lawyer, economist, business man, and
philosopher. Born and brought up in Vienna during the early
1900s when that city was the capital of the vast Austro-
Hungarian Empire, he left his native country at the age of
thirty-eight during the build-up to the Nazi annexation. After
military service in the First World War he studied at Vienna
under the famous jurist, Hans Kelsen, and the economist
Ludwig von Mises, one of Max Weber's sternest critics.
Intellectually he was attracted by Weber's thought but sought
to clarify and develop it in the light of the 'phenomenological'
philosophy of Edmund Husserl whom he came to know
personally. His most comprehensive work, *The Phenomenology
of the Social World* (Northwestern University Press: Evanston,
1967), was first published (in German) in 1932, six years
before he left Austria to settle in New York where he worked at
the New School for Social Research and in business. Although
only a part-time academic, he wrote extensively in the

philosophy of social science, acting as a propagandist for phenomenological sociology and entering into fruitful dialogue with American scholars, particularly the disciples of George Herbert Mead (1863–1931), a Chicago philosopher whose psychological interpretation of social interactions has many similarities to Schutz's phenomenological approach. Much of Schutz's work has been published in the three-volume *Collected Papers* (Nijhoff: The Hague, 1962, 1964, and 1966). There is also the posthumous *Reflections on the Problem of Relevance* (Yale University Press: New Haven, 1970), part of a systematic theoretical work which he never completed.

Schutz's impact was comparatively slight during his lifetime but his lucid exposition of normally obscure and technical philosophical ideas and his persistent endeavours to deploy them in the understanding of what he called 'the social world', has made his work increasingly influential amongst those seeking novel ways of viewing social relationships.

SCHUTZ'S APPROACH

Despite Parsons's acknowledged debt to Weber and the centrality of the concept of action as the basic unit of his 'social system', the positivistic organicism of his overall theory often takes his analysis far away from the individual social actor. Schutz brings us right back to this starting point and builds his whole approach to society on the analysis of the individual's social experience. For him the Parsonian theoretical model of society is a fiction of the scientific observer's mind that distorts the reality of social life which is to be found only in the subjective experiences of the participants.

Schutz adopts what he takes to be the devices of Edmund Husserl's phenomenological philosophy. Husserl's method was to examine and analyse the individual's inner life, that is his experiences of phenomena or appearances as they occur in what is sometimes called the 'stream of consciousness'. He examines how the world looks or appears to the individual in abstraction from the cumulative assertions of science and received opinion, and avoiding ontological questions about what 'really exists'. Husserl starts from the assumption that experience is not simply 'given' to individuals but is 'intentional' in that it involves the person directing his attention to the 'objects' which make his experience what it is. These objects are perceived in the light of past experiences and acquired knowledge, resulting in what Husserl calls an 'apperception', or spontaneous attribution of meaning to what is given in sense perception. All consciousness is thus consciousness of an object and therefore in part a construct of the individual who directs his attention to the objects of his consciousness. Thus I see things, such as houses or cats, rather than a mass of unorganized shapes and colours which I may or may not then infer to be houses or cats. As it occurs in normal adult life, this experience—the subjective 'life-world' of the individual—is made up of a variety of elements, many of which can be stripped away by reflecting on experience, and noting, for instance, that we do not really 'see' a chair quite as common sense assumes it to be, but only a certain field of experience from which we select out objects. Husserl thinks that we can rid ourselves of our accumulated presuppositions about the world and reduce our experience to their basic elements and underlying structure.

Ultimately this process of reflection on the phenomena of everyday experience can rid us, Husserl says, of all 'presuppositions', but Schutz's interest focuses on the stage of phenomenological 'reduction' in which the philosopher rids himself of all his theoretical and scientific preconceptions about the world 'out there' and analyses the meaningfullness or 'sense' of the phenomena as experienced. Husserl goes on from there to 'purify' experience of all empirical elements including the individual's own contribution to his experiences, so uncovering the ultimate structure of consciousness in general. But Schutz remains at the level of psychological analysis, setting himself the task of analysing social experience—that is our experience of other people. His aim is to discover the elements of social life. His method is to reflect on social experience—the awareness of ourselves interacting with others or the 'intention' of social life. To do this we must put to one side or 'bracket' our belief in the reality of the world outside our experience, abandoning all presuppositions about what society is really like. It is not possible to do this in the midst of our experiences but, by reflecting on events which are past, we are able to analyse the world as it appears to our consciousness, identifying and examining the 'objects' by reference to which we can make sense of our experience. In this way, he thinks we can 'trace the roots of the problems of the social sciences directly back to the fundamental facts of conscious life' (*The Phenomenology of the Social World*, p. xxxii).

This sounds very like an idealist programme within methodological individualism in that the explanation of social life is ultimately located in the lived experiences of the individual but, as we shall see, social experience turns out to be irreducibly communal. Human consciousness presupposes the reality of other people and the individual's experiences are mediated by ways of thinking and feeling handed down through his social relationships. What appears to be a highly individualistic theory which seems to postulate that men infer the existence of others on the basis of their experience of their own selves is in fact designed to avoid having recourse to speculative empathy in the explanation of how it is that we come to have an understanding of the lives of others. This is what gives the theory much of its interest.

SCHUTZ'S THEORY OF MAN

Schutz does not have anything approaching a complete theory of human nature, but he locates the essence of the human condition in the subjective experience of acting in and adopting attitudes towards the everyday 'life-world'. For Schutz this is a world of practical activity. The key human capacities are to be discovered by the analysis of the elements of man's ongoing practical consciousness, the constant flow of action directed towards a series of objectives which enable us to regard life in terms of the 'projects' men pursue.

Although all action is meaningful in the important sense that it always consciously involves doing something, that is it is always directed towards the completion of an act which the actor projects in his own mind, Schutz follows Husserl in holding that the process of actually understanding our activity and attributing meaning to it is something that comes only through reflecting on our behaviour when it is past for such understanding entails dividing the stream of action up into a series of discrete acts with distinguishable objectives. Just as Adam Smith believes that an agent cannot take a detached and impartial view of his own behaviour while he is actually engaged in it, so that he must learn to become the observer of his own past behaviour if he is to arrive at the rules to which he should adhere in the moment of action, so Schutz maintains that we can only come to understand the meaning of our action as we look back on it in moments of reflection. We can then select out those elements of our experience which enable us to see our own behaviour as meaningful.

It is somewhat dismaying, therefore, to find that there are crucial aspects of everyday life which, according to Schutz, cannot be adequately grasped as we reflect on ourselves in action. Memory cannot recreate vivid lived experience (a fact Smith made use of to explain our lack of sympathy for those under the sway of strong emotions). Reflecting on our past behaviour we inevitably fail to capture its unique and essential elements, what it is really like at the time. Thus in retrospect I give meaning to my behaviour by splitting up the past into various separate times and moments, but in reality what I experienced was a constant flow of sensations merging into each other. The 'unreflected upon here and now' or 'stream of duration' of the actor is not reducible to the remembered series of distinct acts.

Nonetheless it is this 'pre-phenomenal' world of action that Schutz takes to be fundamental to human social life and which he therefore sets out to analyse as best he can. The 'life-world' of everyday experience is constituted, he suggests, by a continuing awareness of the persons and things with which the agent has to cope in order to achieve his flow of objectives and purposes. Although in some respects the individual is purely passive—as in physiological reflexes such as blushing—intentional experience or 'conduct' involves spontaneous activity. Agents are practical creatures whose 'natural' attitude is to take certain things for granted and set about changing others in a desired manner. Everyday life is thus a pragmatic orientation to the future. The assumption is that men have certain interests in terms of which they see and seek to alter their perceived world. Men are problem-setting and problem-solving animals—at least this is the consciousness of the active, working self in the unreflected upon 'Here and Now', the full reality of which cannot be recreated in memory. As lived through my activity has a unity because it is bound together by a sense of being mine, a 'primal' unity which is lost when we reflect on it but which is inseparable from the experience of activity itself.

To get by, the individual must 'define' his situation, that is he must establish or decide in what sort of situation he finds himself, what his problems are, and how he can go about gaining his objectives.

As a grown man living in a society he does this by drawing on a common 'stock of knowledge' about his world which he takes over and develops through his own experiences. His definition of his situation (e.g. 'I am in danger of being knocked down by a car') is thus 'biographically' determined—that is it depends on his own particular history as a man in his own particular society. This enables him to sort out those aspects of his situation which are fixed and ascertain what possibilities for action are open to him (e.g. 'the driver cannot stop the car so I had better run'). To do this he has to be able to identify things and events in his present situation as similar to previous occasions in a rough and ready way so that he can know what he may hope to achieve by way of satisfying his objectives. The nature of these objectives themselves is also affected by his inherited stock of knowledge.

This stock of knowledge which the individual brings to his situation and uses to 'define' it presupposes the ability to think of the world as made up of types of things. The process of abstraction and formalization by means of which we classify things as 'tables', 'cars', 'trees' and so on Schutz calls 'typification'. The inherited stock of knowledge comes as a collection of connected 'typifications' which enable us to recognize a situation as being of a certain kind and so know that certain techniques or recipes for dealing with it are appropriate. We are then able to see the work of everyday life in terms of 'meaningful configurations' and not as a disorganized mess. What the individual does is to construct a world—the world he 'intends' in his everyday consciousness—by using the typifications which are passed on to him by his social group.

In every situation certain things can be—and must be—taken for granted and certain things selected out as relevant to the individual's interests. So Schutz's individual sorts out his everyday world into 'domains of relevance', the primary domain being the immediate objects and events he can perceive, some of which he may hope to change. This is the only domain of which the individual requires detailed knowledge.

Having defined his situation and so orientated himself towards it by permitting his interests and desires to select the relevant 'typified' aspects of it, the individual may set himself to alter his situation by action. This involves him in anticipating in his mind possible ways of dealing with his situation as he perceives it. He fantasizes or imagines a project, or number of possible projects between which he then chooses. If these projects lead to action in which the agent purposes to bring into being a pre-conceived plan, Schutz calls this rational activity for it involves postulating means to the end in question. This is the motivated lived experience that represents the heart of subjective awareness.

The practical future-orientated directedness and expectations of the everyday life-world is expressed in what Schutz calls the 'in-order-to' motive. As actors we explain ourselves in terms of our own projects—the motivating lived experience—by saying that we do something (let us say, go to the store) 'in-order-to' achieve an objective (say, to buy food). This is possible because of the 'meaning-context' of the fantasies we have of ourselves of 'having done' things. Schutz notes that we can only do this on the basis of certain assumptions—for instance, that the future will resemble the past, and that what I have done before I can do again. These he regards as necessary conditions of the meaningfulness of an act to the actor.

This is, of course, derived from Weber, but Schutz argues that there is another meaning-context which Weber fails to distinguish. This comes into the picture only when we look back on our activities or those of others. It is the context of 'because' motives which we attribute to ourselves and others by hindsight through selecting out some features of the situation as it was before the action in question and then regarding these features as the reasons for—in the sense of causes of—the action. This is to explain action by reference to the past ('I hit him because I was very angry') rather than the future ('I hit him in order to teach him a lesson'). Schutz accurately points out that the difference is not merely a verbal one, for although it is true that I can use the word 'because' to assert an in-order-to motive ('I hit him because I wanted to get away') other 'because' statements ('genuine' ones) cannot be translated into in-order-to statements—thus we would not say 'I hit him in order to be angry'. The crucial difference is that a 'because' motive makes an essential reference to something preceding the act in question.

There is an important similarity between the two sorts of motives in that both refer to the past in one way or another. 'Because' motive statements refer straightforwardly to past events as the causes of action, while 'in-order-to' motive statements involve fantasizing the projected events as past—thus putting them, as he says, in the future perfect tense ('I will have done x or y'). This is something on which he has to insist on in order to retain the thesis that meaning is attributed to behaviour by looking back on it and not in the actual experiencing of it.

One important difference between the two types of motive statement, is that 'in-order-to' explanations allow for freedom of action whereas 'because' explanations are deterministic. Now it is a central part of Schutz's theory of man that although we inherit our stock of knowledge and cannot therefore control a great deal of our destiny, nevertheless we, to an extent, not only construct our own particular world out of our own particular experiences—no doubt on the ˙ basis of what we possess of the common stock of knowledge— but also act spontaneously both in our choices between projects and in adopting particular interests. Indeed this is essential to the subjective consciousness of the actor who views his world in 'in-order-to' terms. Schutz accepts that many 'relevances' (that is, interests which determine our selective awareness of the world) are 'imposed' by a social group but argues that there are 'intrinsic relevances' spontaneously chosen by the individual which alone give that individual a clear and comprehensible consciousness of his particular place in his world. Parsons's social structure is no more than a set of inherited typifications which the individual can use as a springboard for his own activities.

And so, while Schutz follows Parsons and Durkheim in believing that much of the individual's understanding of the world is given to him, he is not a determinist. Determinism may be the natural outlook in which to bring together 'because' motives but 'because' motives are extrinsic to the subjective experience of the actor whose orientation to the future is unalterably libertarian—'the actor always acts freely'. It is only in retrospect that conduct appears determined.

SCHUTZ'S THEORY OF SOCIETY

It has not been easy to present Schutz's theory of man without reference to his theory of society. By bringing in the idea of a largely inherited stock of knowledge, we have already dipped into Schutz's assumption that man is a social being. This follows from the fact that the consciousness of daily life is a social consciousness. This is so in two ways. First, consciousness takes for granted the existence and activities of other people as inhabitants of the same shared world. This is particularly apparent in specifically social action which takes into account the reactions of others, their assumed knowledge of the situation and so on.

Second, consciousness uses typifications which are created and communicated by groups of individuals in this shared world: a historically given world. This world is transmitted through the mother tongue of the group: the signs and symbols which embody sets of typifications and abstractions and standardizations setting forth the nature of the socio-cultural world itself. A society is a linguistic community. It exists through mutual symbols. Everyday consciousness is therefore the social or socially-derived consciousness of society. The individual's life-world is thus an 'inter-subjective' world with shared meanings and a sense of belonging to a group or groups. It is 'ours' not just 'mine'. We take for granted that we understand each other, see the world in the same way, and act within the same reality. All this requires no proof in normal life—it is part of the permanent reality of normal practical attitudes.

It is not claimed by Schutz that an individual has direct awareness of the experiences of others, or that he infers these experiences by empathy, rather each is aware of the other who is physically present to him as a being who is experiencing the same world as himself, and this includes experiencing a shared world of reciprocal perceptions (the mutual awareness of being perceived by the other person). Thus in the common vivid present of a conversation we have in Schutz's telling phrase 'the experience of growing old together'. This experience of 'we' is not present in all social relationships but occurs when one person is aware of himself simultaneously experiencing the same world as another, as when both persons are aware of each other watching a passing car. At times like this we cannot regard the other as a mere physical presence: we have a direct awareness of having an experience in common which, although it may be fleeting and fragmentary, is fundamental to social life.

This vivid present experience of the other's stream of consciousness which Schutz talk of as the general thesis of the alter-ego's existence, the grasp of the-other-I, involves an immediate grasp of the other person's motives (either in-order-to or because motives) and so enables us to understand these fellow community members, whom Schutz calls 'consociates'. Such consociates act reciprocally in that each can appreciate the other's because motives and incorporate them in his in-order-to motives which in turn provokes in response expected in-order-to motives (as in a process of question and answer).

In the we-relationship of consociates we have, for Schutz, the prototype of all social relationships or the 'basic structure of the world of daily life' in that other types of social relationships are 'derived' from it or presuppose it. Consociates regard their motives and their perspectives as interchangeable. There is mutual acceptance and understanding on the basis of simultaneous experience and shared typifications of the common world. The assumption that each sees the world in the same way Schutz calls the reciprocity of perspectives (*Collected Papers*, Vol. I, p. 316).

Although there is an element of this close-knit 'we-relationship'—the sense of a shared world—in all social relationships, it is characteristically dominant only in small settled communities or in existing groups which are self-selected and so consist of like-minded persons (what he calls 'voluntary groups'). 'We-relationships' require constant updating in face-to-face interactions. In one of Schutz's best-known essays, 'The Homecomer', he discusses the situation of a returning veteran who has sustained his desire for home through various memories of his previous way of life—the familiar sights and sounds and smells of his past. But he finds on his return that his memories have been left behind by the ongoing interactions of those left at home so that they are no longer accessible to him and he is not immediately intelligible to them. No longer do they have the same system of relevance and he does not fit readily back into his old assumed position in the community. Despite the fact that they have constantly thought of each other they have inevitably done so in terms of typification of each other's existing way of life and the lack of constant face-to-face experiences has undermined the we-relationship.

The veteran returns home incapacitated for accepting and being accepted in the same unthinking way as he was before he left the community. In this he is like the 'Stranger' (the title of another of Schutz's essays) who cannot fit naturally into the shared experiences of a community which he enters for the first time. However hard the Stranger tries to understand the ways of his adopted group, he can never accept these ways unquestioningly and fit into them spontaneously. He has to get at this new world by an abstract system of constructs which enable him to learn how to behave. This inevitably distances him from the group members and renders him an object of suspicion. The group will, for the Stranger, always be regarded in part as 'they' and not as 'we'.

Face-to-face communities are not, however, complete societies. The 'they-relationship' of the Stranger to the in-group is also characteristic of the relationship of community members to the wider society in which they live and holds for a good deal of social experience within normal communities.

As the Stranger has to take an objective view of the in-group in order to learn how they live and what they consider relevant or important, so the community members have to create a complex set of typifications in terms of which to operate in the society as a whole. This involves the development of common-sense knowledge of the patterns of behaviour followed by those of whom we have no direct knowledge. It is socially-derived typifications which provide us with the standard solutions to standard problems. The common stock of knowledge contains socially approved 'recipies' for dealing with recurrent problems. These typifications are absorbed through language and the institutionalized knowledge of society. Schutz illustrates this by pointing to the host of assumptions involved in the activity of mailing a letter. Such an act takes it for granted that there are certain types of persons—postmen, sorters etc.—who will process the letter in certain standard ways. This knowledge is objective in that it means thinking of others in the typology approved by our consociates. Such typologies are necessary presuppositions in the transaction of business beyond the community, as when we vote in an election or engage in trading. But typologies do not give us real understanding of the individual people who are assumed to follow these typical patterns. They are learned by a process of aculturation or socialization in which people come to construct patterns of the actors' motives and ends, and even of their characteristic attitudes and personalities. But this does not enable us to know these persons as individuals.

These typified patterns of the behaviour and characteristics of other people become motives for our own actions. By a process called 'self-typification' we learn to fit into the wider world by seeing ourselves as playing a set part in a typical situation (e.g. 'a person mailing a letter'). We are thus able to co-operate with people of whom we have no personal knowledge.

Taking the direct knowledge of the unique existence of the other as one extreme, Schutz traces out the various stages in which we move away from this to the opposite pole of social experience, the completely anonymous typification such as our idea of the army or the state. Closest to our shared experience with others are those relationships which involved a shared experience in the past although they do not do so now, or those in which we may have such shared experience in the future. These make up our relationships with what Schutz calls our 'contemporaries'.

Beyond this our social relationships become progressively less concrete or personal and more anonymous, covering eventually not simply remote contemporaries but our 'predecessors' and 'successors' with whom we have not had and will not have shared experiences. The cognitive awareness of these relationships depends on extremely abstract ideal types devoid of personal details or specific historical settings. And so our relationships may be *direct* or face-to-face, either in the past or in the present or only potentially, or they may be *indirect* as with those of our co-existing contemporaries whom we have not met and will not meet, or with our predecessors and successors.

The sum of such indirect or 'they-relationships' make up the totality of society. Society is a construct of ideal types defined according to the functions of the abstract individuals involved. And from a beginning in the immediacy of face-to-face relationships, sometimes of a very intimate personal kind, we arrive at the complete typification involved in our consciousness of the wider society. It is these typifications abstracted from direct experience of particular persons that constitute in the everyday world the objective social system by which people are able to deal with the socio-cultural world beyond that of their consociates. At this point the familiar scheme of rules, roles, status and institutions comes into play as the language which captures the abstract typifications in which we understand and cope with indirect social relationships. 'In order to find my bearings within the social group, I have to know the different ways of dressing and behaving, the manifold insignia, emblems, tools etc. which are considered by the group as indicating social status and are therefore socially approved as relevant' (*Collected Papers*, Vol. I, p. 350).

Are we not then, despite the brave beginnings with the subjective awareness of the other people, right back in a Parsonian-type scheme of social structure? To some extent this is so, although without the tight functional elements of Parson's scheme, and at this point Schutz does not present us with anything of startling originality. But the important aspect of Schutz's approach is the place which this type of awareness has in his scheme. The typifications of the social structure are simply one aspect of the individual's practical apprehension of the everyday world which he inherits and to an extent reconstructs in order to assist him to find his way around and so further his immediate purposes.

In Schutz's analysis of everyday consciousness, individuals have not only an ultimate sense of belonging to various groups—a 'we-ness' most clearly manifested in the life of a settled community—but also a reasonably developed social theory, that is a view of their society as a system of roles and institutions into which they must fit themselves. The abstract idea of society is thus in the first place an ordinary cultural product not a detached scientific scheme. Moreover this 'objective' typified social world, although it may be vital for the managing of everyday life, is removed from the reality of fundamental social experience in face-to-face social interaction and is not therefore basic to the individual's life. The more abstract and anonymous its content the further removed it is from the foundations of sociality.

And so while in all societies there will be a part of the common stock of knowledge which is a system of groupings on the basis of kin, age, sex, occupation, power and social status, this is primarily a construct adopted and adapted by the individual to serve his purposes rather than an accurate picture of the world. Schutz makes much of the idea of multiple realities. We view the world according to our different schemes and cannot assume, for instance, that our religious reality is the same as our aesthetic reality and so on. There is a similar divide between everyday experience and scientific activity, for the former is immediately practical while the latter is a detailed search for explanations. And yet in the social sciences the abstractions and objectifications of everyday life are accepted as the basis for scientific study of society and in it these typifications are used for quite different purposes, namely to observe rather than to change social reality. The disinterested observer who is doing his science abandons the practical realities and is therefore free from the anxiety of those who are participant in society. He 'brackets' his personal existence for the duration of his scientific work. In so doing he takes the ideal types of common experience and develops them into something more consistent and comprehensive.

Thus the social scientist, following the social participant, will make a distinction between course-of-action ideal types and personality ideal types. The former expresses a process or product such as stamping and delivering letters which has an objective meaning in that what is being done is a typical procedure for obtaining a particular end by a standard means. People use these course-of-action ideal types to help them solve standard problems in standard ways. Personality ideal types concern the assumed characteristics of the persons who are involved in such courses of action. That is, they assume that individuals in standard situations give certain subjective meanings to their actions so that we know something of the sort of person who typically behaves in a certain way and therefore can infer something of their motives and reasons. These 'puppets' are used by the social sciences to encapsule the characteristics of those who take part in the abstract scheme that is erected out of the agglomeration of ideal types. Personality ideal types thus represent the habitual paradigmatic motivations of individuals which are assumed by the social scientist. They may be applied to individuals or to collectives but not to concrete persons.

The objective is to interpret particular types of social reality without practical involvement, although the method is simply an extension of the way in which social actors understand each other in everyday life. The end product is referred to as a 'construct of constructs' which has as its ultimate reference the meaning which social life has for its actors but which involves taking these meanings out of their context and reifying them in order to find or establish a consistent and coherent picture of a society as a system.

This construct of constructs is not adequate to our knowledge of the existence of others for the we-relationships which we have for actual people are not relationships with ideal types. Actual people experience things with us and make choices for themselves. For the individual, the idea of society is a background only, against which he can act and which he can transcend. He can make something of the possibilities of his own self by using his inherited symbols to give meaning and significance to his own behaviour. The fact that this experience does not give us the so-called 'objective' knowledge of the external observer does not mean that social science can disprove the reality of the freedom which we have as individual actors, for its limited predictive power can establish only the probability of any particular action occurring.

How then are we to assess the value for social science of the ideal types which are developed from those used in everyday life? In the first place they must fit regular patterns which can be observed and so to some extent be verified, although only at the level of probability rather than of tight causal generalization. (This suggests that there is some real objectivity—in the sense of independence of human volition—expressed by the typified social order.) But they must also meet what is called the 'postulate of subjective interpretation' in that they must give intelligible explanations of actions. Here the relevant data are the actors' experiences and their own interpretations even although these are mediated through their inherited typifications. There is also the 'postulate of adequacy' which is that models must be understandable to the actor so that a descriptive or interpretative account of social action is acceptable only when it seems reasonable to the relevant social actors. In this way Schutz thinks that it is possible to attain approximate knowledge of society without ever penetrating through to the here and now of social experience. This means that we do not surrender the 'forgotten man' at the centre, the actor who is free to take what he can from the natural and culturally given world in which he finds himself by interpreting the authoritative social reality in accordance with his own typifications and so choose to follow out his own interests. For him 'society' is a pragmatic concept used to order his experiences in the light of his interests and in the hope of achieving the goals that he has at least to some extent set for himself.

IMPLICATIONS AND DEVELOPMENTS: SYMBOLIC INTERACTIONISM AND ETHNOMETHODOLOGY

Apart from such essays as 'The Homecomer' and 'The Stranger', Schutz's work is highly theoretical and has more to do with providing a philosophical background for the study of society than a full grown social theory. In this it is both more fundamental and more modest than most recent attempts to theorize about society as a whole. The implications of his interpretative idealism are mainly for the conduct of sociological investigation which, for Schutz, is not a sphere of immediate practical concern. I shall therefore examine some of the ways in which its influence has been felt among those practising sociologists who have taken up the detailed description of everyday small-scale social interactions rather than grand theorizing.

But the very modesty of Schutz's approach and the limited claims he makes for the validity of sociological method have their own implications for our understanding of ourselves. The idea that society is a monolithic coercive entity fulfilling essential functions and therefore beyond the control of the individual loses its hold before Schutz's image of an almost fictional construct which we use to help us solve some of our pressing practical problems. This serves as a base for radical criticism of the conservative orthodoxy of structural-functionalism for erroneously smothering the individual in a small-meshed net of natural necessity. By both starting out from, and also returning to, the consciousness of the individual and his 'in-order-to' motives, Schutz re-asserts human creativity and hence the dignity of the individual as an essential part of human life which is basic to our understanding of social interaction. Schutz's theory of society can therefore have a liberating effect on those who have taken too seriously the idea that society is an objective and fixed order to which the individual must conform.

To complete our survey of theories of society I shall take a very brief look at two modern schools of social theory—Symbolic Interactionism and Ethnomethodology—which owe something to the work of Schutz and illustrate the research implications of the ideas he helped to disseminate. Both schools have flourished in the post-war expansion of sociological studies and both go in for a regrettably large measure of the jargon which is a tiresome feature of so much recent work in social theory. However novel terminology is sometimes required to preserve and communicate new theoretical insights. It is therefore worth taking the trouble to appreciate the connotations of their specialist language while retaining a healthy scepticism about the metaphorical catch-phrases whose appeal is literary and journalistic rather than intellectual.

As a set of ideas Symbolic Interactionism owes as much to George Herbert Mead as to Alfred Schutz. Mead was a late nineteenth-century American social psychologist and philosopher who was influenced by Adam Smith's concept of the 'impartial spectator'. In Mead's hands Smith's spectator becomes the 'generalized other', the term he uses for that part of the 'self' which is an internalization of the attitudes of other people towards ourselves and our roles. The actual name 'Symbolic Interactionism' was coined by a disciple of Mead, Herbert Blumer, in 1937. It is intended to capture Mead's belief that social interaction involving the mutual understanding and interpretation of gestures and speech is the key to human society. Mead argues that the social structures of roles and institutions affect individual behaviour only through the common meanings expressed in the symbols of the group and the ways in which these are interpreted in exchanges between individuals.

In itself this does not take use much beyond Durkheim's collective representations and their function in cementing group membership and controlling individual behaviour. It also has something in common with Weber's insistence on seeing social relationships from the point of view of the actors involved. What distinguishes Symbolic Interactionism from its forerunners is the emphasis it places on the activity of the individual, or 'self', in using and manipulating the symbols of the group to participate in the creation of orderly social life. The Symbolic Interactionist draws on Mead's analysis of 'joint action' as a co-operative and creative enterprise to argue that Durkheim and Parsons present an 'over-socialized' view of man which neglects the activities of the conscious, self-reflective consciousness or 'self' in establishing the behaviour patterns of each social group. They do not deny that social customs, roles and institutions exist (although they do so in and through the consciousness of individuals) but note that all rules are to an extent vague and incomplete in that they do not detail everything that must be done. Social rules are only a framework. They leave interacting individuals room for manoeuvre so that they can extemporize when deciding which norms to follow, how these are to be interpreted and what to do about matters on which they are silent. Actual social relationships emerge from a complex process of give and take in which persons who are aware of themselves as one individual among others work out together how and to what extent they will co-operate or contest.

Symbolic Interactionists such as Anselm Strauss and Erving Goffman believe that men help to create their own interpretation of a social reality which is itself the outcome of prior interactions. On the basis of these interpretations men enter into certain types of social relationships. This is an inter-personal activity from which there emerges a degree of consensus as to what is 'going on' and who is playing what sort of part in the particular human drama concerned. It does not necessarily result in complete agreement of outlook since each conscious 'self' has his or her own views as to what is happening and how he or she wishes themselves and others to be regarded. As with Schutz there is a deliberate orientation of the individual towards a social situation as being of a certain type, but exactly how the situation is to be 'defined' depends on the individual actors and the parts they wish to be accepted as playing in that particular social 'game'.

This combination of Schutz's notion of defining a situation and Mead's idea of the self as an object of conscious reflection and a source of spontaneous activity is characteristic of Goffman's popular book *The Presentation of Self in Everyday Life* (Penguin: London, 1967) in which he stresses the idea of social life as a theatrical performance in which the actor presents himself to his audience using certain common techniques and signs which invite others to accept him as having a certain status and role. He cites Adam Smith's example of young aristocrats who adopt certain styles of dress and mannerisms in order to obtain the automatic respect of their social inferiors

(*Theory of Moral Sentiments*, I. iii.2.5, p. 54). Similar notions are to be seen in Peter Berger and Thomas Luckman, *The Social Construction of Reality* (Penguin: Harmondsworth, 1966). Berger and Luckman argue that men tend to forget that they are the authors of the social world and 'reify' social institutions by assuming that they have an objective reality beyond human control. To make this thesis convincing they deploy the phenomenological idea of 'sedimentation', a process whereby experiences are retained below the level of consciousness but, especially when they are the result of common intersubjective experiences, remain related to conscious behaviour through a sign system or language and so serve as the basis for institutional order.

A good example of the sort of sociological work which is inspired by such ideas of society is Goffman's *Asylums* (Penguin: Harmondsworth, 1968) in which he demonstrates how the perspectives of patients and staff in asylums differ and argues that the staff definitions of what is going on in such 'total institutions' (the term Goffman coined to describe institutions such as armies and prisons which encompass all aspects of the inmates' lives) is not intrinsically superior to that of the supposedly insane patients. Goffman points out that apparently crazy behaviour, such as hoarding seemingly useless items, is perfectly rational within an institution which denies individuals any privacy of possessions since people need to have something they can regard as their own.

Strauss has also used psychiatric hospitals to study how the formal rules of social institutions are only one of the elements which go to produce what he calls a 'negotiated order'; day to day relationships are the outcome of implicit bargaining conducted within the framework of official rules in accordance with the personal styles and capabilities of those involved. (Anselm Strauss *et al.*, *Psychiatric Institutions and Ideologies*, Free Press: Glencoe, 1964.)

This approach assumes with Schutz that social reality is a human achievement which needs the constant deployment of certain skills requiring the grasp of common symbols and a degree of self-awareness. 'Society' has reality, therefore, only in human consciousness. To any given individual social reality is an objective fact in that he has to take account of the attitudes and beliefs of other people when deciding how to act. He must adopt and internalize such attitudes in order to carry on routine relationships with others (this is the 'pragmatic' aspect of Symbolic Interactionism). But he need not wholly accept the outlooks of others, nor is he himself part of the interactions through which the standard interpretation of social reality is formed. Social meanings are widely shared group products arrived at collaboratively through the joint selection of those features of the external world which are to be deemed significant. Such a reality has the objectivity of being 'intersubjective' but it is not an existent reality beyond the consciousness of its creators or totally beyond their control.

The scope which this leaves to individual spontaneity is sufficient to make the appropriate metaphor for social life that of a 'game' (Mead's term) rather than a play. Individuals are free to extemporize and co-operate within flexible rules. They do not have to mouth fixed lines from predetermined postures. Societies are not, except in certain people's minds (such as those of confused social theorists) determinate objective and necessary structures but the outcome of joint actions entered into in an almost Hobbesian manner by partly socialized individuals who are prepared to compromise, bargain and use each other in order to play the serious games of life. The symbolic interactionist is concerned to describe and analyse these processes.

Ethnomethodologists share many of the preoccupations of Symbolic Interactionists. Both seek to change Durkheim's dictum about treating social facts as things into the maxim that social facts are to be treated as accomplishments. This is the expression used by the school's central figure, Harold Garfinkel, a self-acknowledged follower of Schutz. But the Ethnomethodologist goes further than the Symbolic Interactionist in denying the existence of a determinate set of common beliefs and values underlying all social cohesion. Although Symbolic Interactionists do not assume that there is a fixed and unanimously agreed social reality—indeed they stress that the world is made of 'multiple realities', even for each individual—nevertheless they do tend to accept at face value the meanings of the social interactions they describe (while not necessarily accepting the 'official' account of them). Ethnomethodologists are more radical. They contend that there is little cross-situation meaning in that how a situation appears to one participant or set of participants cannot be equated with the meaning it has for others in apparently similar situations. They therefore attempt to get behind the obvious consciously accepted meanings of social situations to the understandings which are presupposed in the explicitly formulated outlooks of social participants. This involves them in detailed study of the unthinking assumptions of everyday life.

One rather trivial example is given in Ryave's and Schenkein's 'Notes on the Art of Walking' (Roy Turner, *Ethnomethodology* (Penguin Books, 1974), pp. 265–74) where it is pointed out that 'doing walking', especially in a busy place, is a complex navigational skill. Walking has to be 'performed' within certain 'natural' boundaries in such a way as to 'manage' to avoid bumping into other people. The authors draw our attention to the fact that there is an important difference between 'walking-together' and 'walking-alone' which leads to different solutions to the navigational problem. They go on to suggest that their study of how people move their bodies from one place to another illustrates the fruitfulness of seeing social life as a problematic accomplishment.

The actual name 'ethnomethodology' was coined by Garfinkel to describe a commitment to the empirical study of practical reasoning, of how people make sense of what happens to them in social interactions, particularly in talking with each other. In *Studies in Methodology* (Prentice Hall: Englewood Cliffs, 1967), pp. 79–88 he describes an experiment used to demonstrate that social actors make use of what he calls the 'documentary method' whereby they take what is said to them as 'documenting' or pointing to an underlying pattern whose existence they presuppose. People take what is said to them as indicative of some sort of pattern, react to it accordingly, and so provide material for others to interpret as having an assumed meaning. Garfinkel shows that this occurs even when laboratory subjects are led into conversations about their private lives in which the experimenter offers advice in an entirely random manner. Even in such situations people attempt to make coherent sense out of the inconsistencies with which they are presented and look for an underlying pattern in what is in fact completely unpatterned.

Garfinkel contends that in social exchanges we are continually seeking to find out the patterns of thought of those with whom we interact. This is the context in which our notion of social reality is constructed and a shared understanding achieved. This reality cannot be generalized to other historically different situations since the meanings of each exchange are peculiar to that specific context. 'Indexicality' is the term given to the context-dependency of meaning. Garfinkel's point is that the meaning of what is said to us depends on our understanding of the particular situation we are in with all its nuances and peculiarities, so that the same words used in different situations have different meanings.

This can hardly mean that the Ethnomethodologist thinks that there is nothing in common between situations but his concern is to discover the differences which exist between meanings in different contexts. This has led to an interest in how the keeping of official documents in hospitals and other bureaucratic organisations, and therefore what those who provide the raw data for official statistics are really doing, is affected by the particular outlooks, and by the economic and the career prospects of those involved (See Aaron Cicourel 'Police Practices and Official Records' and David Sudnow 'Counting Deaths', both in Turner *op.cit.*) This concentration on the details of particular types of situations has much in common with the philosopher Wittgenstein's preoccupation with the details of ordinary linguistic usage in specific contexts and his idea that meaning is best explicated through examining the use to which expressions are put.

Another trend in modern linguistic philosophy is to regard speech as a type of act. The idea of 'speech acts' is put to good use by ethnomethodologists such as D. Lawrence Wilder who in his essay 'Telling the Code' argues that appealing to the accepted 'code' which holds among convicts (such as 'don't snitch' or 'grass') is used to exhibit rather than describe an existing social reality. 'Telling the code' is part of a self-elaborating schema whose meaning is to be understood through the use to which it is put by convicts to protect their interests and explain their behaviour. (See Taylor, *op.cit.* pp. 144–72).

The upshot of this approach is that the meaningfulness of social interaction is not to be seen as something which is simply given from outside a particular interaction. It is achieved and recreated in specific ways on each occasion. All that can be assumed is that in each situation the people involved will attempt to make sense out of what is going on in the light of their own presuppositions and interests. How they do this ought to be the subject of detailed empirical study. One method used in such studies, which is shared with the Interactionists, is that of 'participant observation'. This requires the experimenter to absorb himself in the situation he is seeking to study in order to learn how to use in its proper context the language of those with whom he participates. A more controversial method is that of staging experiments designed to disrupt everyday situations. By behaving in odd and zany ways and studying the confused and anxious reactions of those whose everyday assumptions are thus undermined it is thought that the assumptions of every day life will become apparent to the experimenter.

Ethnomethodology is in fact as significant for its methods as for its doctrines. Its experimental and first-hand gathering of information gives it a certain empirical standing. But the emphasis on the particular as against the general, and the stress on the accomplishment of social order in different circumstances, removes it from the more ambitious concerns of the traditional theories of society. If the only things that are real are particulars and if the abstractions of classical social theory do not really explain anything then these theories are clearly taking us in a helpful direction. But if society is at least in part still properly to be considered as a reality out there beyond the individual and no mere 'reification' projected onto the world, then Ethnomethodology is no more than a way of studying the limited extent to which the social agents modify and develop the 'givens' of the social situations in which they find themselves.

A severe critic would say that Ethnomethodologists make rather too much of the very ancient philosophical problem of how we are able to make general statements about particular situations. Their one-sided solution to the problem of 'universals', as it is known in the history of philosophy, is much too simple. And in practice the actual cash-value of the idea of 'indexicality' turns out to be little more than the assertion that there are neglected differences between broadly similar social situations.

Also Ethnomethodologists are rather too quick to move from the obvious point that the ideas upon which social relationships depend exist only in the minds of human beings to the far from obvious conclusion that the reality these ideas are about is entirely dependent on what human beings happen to think. The fact that social relationships involve thought does not entail that they are fictions.

More generally, common criticism of Schutz and his followers is that they are too naive in their acceptance of the common-sense assumptions about the world of inter-subjective social reality. The view that the analysis of everyday consciousness is the route to genuine social knowledge seems to involve an unjustified faith in our own uncritical outlooks. Epistemological problems about the trustworthiness of such assumptions are simply side-stepped. This has the dangerous methodological consequence of giving a spurious authority to the 'observations' of the practitioners of this particular form of social investigation whose intuitions lack the essential scientific standing of verifiability.

Schutz himself leaves obscure the relationship between the world-views of the agent and the observing scientist. The fact that the pragmatic typifications of everyday life are sometimes instrumental in successful activity indicates that they may have an objective validity beyond the inter-personal agreement. But how far the social scientist is able to arrive at genuinely objective truth in the sense that as an observer he is able to reach an accurate picture of what is going on in society is never made entirely clear. A crucial ambiguity remains between the use of 'objective' for a point of view (of the person reflecting on conduct) and for an epistomological status (a candidate for truth).

Nevertheless these recent developments and applications of Schutz's phenomenological approach to human society are a good deal more illuminating and, at the sociological level at least, more soundly based on empirical evidence, than the speculations of socio-biology which we looked at in Chapter 5 (see pp. 88–90). They do, however, lack the general explanatory power which a Hobbesian type of theory such as Edmund Wilson's would have were it congruent with the facts of human social life. Symbolic Interactionism and Ethnomethodology are plausible when identifying some of the processes of interaction formative of human culture seen as a set of partially shared values and norms which remain open to modification and manipulation by particular individuals in particular circumstances. These phenomena are clearly basic to the nature of human society. Ethnomethodology in particular is convincing in its critique of the structural-functional view of 'Society' as an objective reality which swallows up the individual into its holistic operations.

As overall theories, however, they are incomplete. They do not account for the emergence and re-emergence of certain similar social patterns through the interactions of different individuals as they seek to make sense of and mould their own particular lives. We have to ask, for instance, why men choose to present their selves as of one sort rather than another, and whether the attempt to make some sort of presentation is one of those irreducible elements of human life which we find in Hobbes or Smith. We have to explain why certain specific devices of self-presentation and reality construction are used and why particular types of assumption are made and patterns created. Some account is required of the relatively fixed and continuous aspects of different societies. Is some form of functionalist explanation required here? Or are we back in the realm of relatively permanent underlying psychological or material features of the human species? The metaphor of life as a drama or a game does not help us here.

The Marxian social theorist and others concerned with the large-scale trends in social development and general questions of social causation will find such preoccupations as those of the Ethnomethodologists' study of walking, and of such phenomena as conversational 'openings' and 'closings', trivial and beside the point. The Symbolic Interactionists' emphasis on the presentation of self can be similarly dismissed as the parochial concern of academic ideologues who are simply emphasizing the values of the market society with its stress on advertising and its assumption that everything, including the human personality, is something to be packaged, presented and sold. To describe what it is for convicts to 'tell the code', or even to point out, in the tradition of Durkheim, that to call someone a convict is simply to give them a socially convenient label, does little to explain why there are prisons and what might be done to eliminate them.

The fact that there are, as yet, no definitive answers, or even agreed approaches, to such larger questions and the co-existence of such very different theories of society as Ethno-methodology and Sociobiology, or Marxism and Structural-Functionalism, all of which are accepted as intellectually respectable by significant numbers of informed people, indicate the extent to which this area of human thought remains open to conjecture and speculation.

FOR FURTHER READING

The most accessible version of Schutz's writings is *On Phenomenology and Social Relations*, Selected Writings, ed. with an Introduction by Helmut R. Wagner (University of Chicago Press: Chicago and London, 1970). For further study see *Phenomenology and Social Reality: Essays in Memory of Alfred Schutz*, ed. M. Natanson (Nijhoff: The

Hague, 1970). In addition to the works referred to in the text (particularly *Ethnomethodology*, edited by Roy Turner) students of Symbolic Interactionism and Ethnomethodology should read *Understanding Everyday Life*, ed. J. Douglas (Aldine Publishing Company: Chicago, 1970) and *Phenomenology and Sociology*, ed. Thomas Luckmann (Penguin Books: Harmondsworth and New York, 1978).

PART THREE   Conclusion

CHAPTER 10   Outstanding
                     Problems

In this brief concluding chapter I shall make no attempt to summarize what has gone before or recommend the adoption of one type of theory or approach over another. The object in selecting and discussing seven theories of human society has been to introduce the reader to at least the main options open to the would-be social theorist and so provide an over-all frame of reference to assist him in making his own comparisons and assessments. In the course of such critical studies certain outstanding problems recur. These problems form the subject-matter of this chapter.

It will be obvious to the reader by now that it is arbitrary to pick out just seven theories of human society for attention. Indeed I have managed to slip in rather more than that under the guise of 'developments', and even then I have not been able to do more than mention several historically very important theorists, such as Spencer and Pareto. Nor have I been able to include the anthropological theories of Radcliffe-Brown, Malinowski and Claude Levi-Strauss. Many other contemporary social and political thinkers whose work is deserving of attention have not so far been mentioned. The work of George Homans, F. A. Hayek, Ralph Dahrendorf, Robert Merton, Louis Althusser and Alvin Gouldner, to mention a few, could easily have been incorporated had space permitted. However, the no doubt controversial selection of our seven chosen theorists has been made for the purpose of illustrating approaches rather than providing a comprehensive survey. And if it succeeds in its aim then this book should help the reader to assimilate the work of other social theorists by relating their ideas to some of the standard positions dealt with here.

It is, I have argued, always an over-simplification to classify any theorist as an individualist or a holist, a positivist or an interpretativist, a functionalist or an action theorist, and theories do not fall neatly into the boxes labelled conflict or consensus, materialist or idealist, descriptive or normative. But a certain amount of crude pigeon-holing is useful as a first stage in orienting ourselves to any set of social and political ideas, and an awareness of the strengths and weaknesses of these 'ideal types' of theories should at least have us asking the right sort of questions.

As he proceeds from classification to criticism the student of social theories must learn to distinguish between remediable deficiencies of detail and more fundamental inadequacies in a whole approach to and model of society. If Durkheim is wrong on some of his facts about Aboriginal religion this does not dispose of the whole functionalist theory of religion, and if Marx's predictions about the imminent downfall of capitalism in the nineteenth century have been falsified by events this does not necessarily undermine the value of approaching historical change in the terms of economic class conflict. The empirical correctness of particular studies is only indirectly a disproof of their broader factual assumptions about human nature and society and may have very little bearing on the validity of the methodology being used. One difficulty is to know at what point the accumulation of empirical evidence counts decisively against the basic postulates of a theory.

A classic example of this difficulty is the 'nature' versus 'nurture' debate concerning the relative importance of heredity and environment in the determination of conduct and character. This is one of the points of opposition between Hobbes and Durkheim (or between Smith and Marx for that matter). Despite the enormous quantity of evidence of the diversity of social customs and individual behaviour it remains possible to attempt to account for this diversity either in terms of (as yet largely unproven) innate differences between individuals and groups (such as races) or by attributing it to cultural conditioning shaped by different historical circumstances. Alternatively it is not difficult to counter the evidence of diversity by picking out some similarities between the social arrangements of different societies as evidence of an underlying uniformity in the human make-up. Clearly no simple set of empirical observations will settle such an issue, but equally clearly specific studies such as those carried out on the behaviour of identical twins raised in different environments (but *how* different?) are germaine to the dispute. In the end much depends on how we analyse such concepts as innateness and naturalness, and which human similarities and differences we consider significant. These matters cannot be settled by observation alone.

The nature versus nurture controversy may incline us to take the line that fixing on the 'best' social theory is a matter of adopting some sort of compromise between extremes. Surely the correct view on this issue is that social life depends in part on nature and in part on nurture, the problem being to determine what is the correct balance between the two types of in-put. Similarly we might assume that compromises can be struck between individualism and holism or between conflict and consensus theories, and that our task is to discover, for instance, the extent to which social science can be value-free. In this way we might hope to arrive at a theoretical amalgam which combines elements from each ideal type.

There is, however, no *a priori* reason why the truth should be anything like a bargain struck between competing views. Average opinions have not got a good record in the history of human thought. Nor is there any obvious way of making an impartial selection of the views between which compromises are to be negotiated. If there is anything at all in the idea that social outlooks are influenced by ideological considerations, then popularity is no signpost to validity in social theory. Moreover the same points which count against Aristotle's theory of the moral 'mean' (see p. 68) warn us about opting for any easy consensus position.

In any case it is doubtful whether some fundamental assumptions admit of much in the way of compromise. Once it is allowed, for instance, that the free choices of individuals have significant consequences for the nature and operation of social institutions then the whole positivist approach to history is undermined, for it will never then be possible to know whether a particular piece of evidence is a disproof of a causal law or an instance of uncaused human choice. Similarly once value judgements are admitted into the substance of social theorizing it is hard to see how this can be reconciled with positivism without distorting either the nature of value judgements or the notion of scientific truth. And the naturalistic fallacy remains the Achilles heel of all attempts to revive a natural law approach to social science.

And even if value judgements are excluded from social theory we are still faced with the problem of deciding what constitutes a good explanation in social science. Is it or is it not important that a theory accord with the subjective interpretations of those involved? No empirical evidence will settle this question and yet on its solution depends what is to count as relevant evidence for or against a sociological hypothesis. A Marxist can discount a capitalist's assertions that he is motivated by benevolence towards his employees and that he looks upon them as if they were members of his own family. A Durkheimian can endeavour to reinterpret such claims as expressions of some shared secular norm functional to the cohesion of that society. Certain action theorists on the other hand would be committed to accepting them as perfectly valid views which needs to be incorporated into social theory without being explained away or reduced to something else. There is no simple solution to this sort of radical disagreement.

Perhaps the most intractable tension is that between verifiability and intelligibility. The pursuit of 'objective' in the sense of observable scientific data is the constant obsession of those social theorists who long for the certainty and intellectual respectability of the natural sciences. This goal does hold out the best prospect of escaping from the dangers of ideological bias, but as a method it tends to distort social reality as it is actually experienced. The visible and the measurable are selected for their methodological convenience whether or not they have human significance. On the other hand the bare analysis of social experience from the subjective point of view lacks testability, and perhaps even explanatory power, despite its immediate 'intelligibility'. To know the reasons people have for doing what they do is always informative and may be illuminating but we may still wish to have an explanation for the recurrence and potency of these reasons.

In reflecting on the history of social thought it is difficult to know whether those who emphasize the subjective point of view and the notion of meaningful action do so out of idealist conviction and because they believe that this affords us a trustworthy route to the explanation of social phenomena which is not available to the less fortunate natural scientist, or is merely a matter of settling for a scientific second best to fill the void created by the almost total absence of proven sociological laws. For some people reasons may not be as sociologically definitive as causes but at least they are better than nothing. For others the knowledge of human motivations and intentions gives us an account of social phenomena far more fundamental than that which we could ever have of natural events.

More generally the choice between positivism and inter-pretativism remains to date largely a matter of faith. The continuing radical disagreements between, for instance, Marx-ists who fasten on the economic dimension of social processes as causally overriding, and those more idealistically inclined positivists who attribute independent force to religious and moral factors, or the controversies between those who rate biological over psychological or sociological factors in the causal analysis of behaviour, can be seen as an indication of immature science, as Thomas Kuhn argues in *The Structure of Scientific Revolutions* (Chicago University Press: Chicago, 1970). But these disagreements may also be taken as the inevitable result of the pursuit of a misguided intellectual objective. In this situation it is equally rational to continue along the positivist's path in the anticipation of eventual scientific success on the model of the natural sciences, or to adopt alternative criteria of explanatory adequacy.

The point of these remarks is to indicate the philosophical nature of many of the issues which remain outstanding after our examination of theories of human society. These issues are philosophical because there is at present no way in which they can be settled by an appeal to observable facts or adequately testable theories, but they remain, nevertheless, appropriate topics for rational discussion. Perhaps in time other solutions will become apparent through the development of social science (although there will always be the danger of acquiescing in a consensus on social theory which is based on ideological rather than rational factors). But it may be that the really divisive intellectual questions in social theory are inherently and ineradicable contentious and insoluble in that equally well informed, impartial and intelligent persons may reasonably disagree about them.

In either case it may be helpful to conclude this book by making a few points about some of the perennial philosophical issues which have bearing on the choice between competing approaches to social theory. The three related issues are (1) freewill versus determinism, (2) the nature of explanation, and (3) the objectivity of value judgements.

Determinism is the theory that every event (including every human thought and action) is caused. This entails the view that whatever happens has to happen and cannot happen otherwise unless the events and conditions which cause it are different. Such a theory is clearly in line with the positivist's programme for explaining human behaviour in terms of causal regularities. In contrast the doctrine of free will is that at least some events, namely human choices, are uncaused and therefore free in that there is no set of pre-existing circumstances which force a person to make one choice rather than another.

The strength of the free will (or libertarian) position is that, as Schutz notes, it is the unshakable assumption of people as they make choices and act intentionally. When we act in order to do something we believe that we could act otherwise if we chose to do so. But equally when we observe phenomena and attempt to explain any event, human or otherwise, we find it hard (particularly in a scientific age) not to assume that it has a cause. The quick libertarian response to the assumption of total causality is to say that this cannot be proved since it is not possible to investigate all events to see if they are caused, but the determinist can point to the constant progress of science in discovering more and yet more causal laws as a ground for holding to the assumption that all events have causes.

For social theory the argument centres on the notion of social action. The libertarian insists that only the belief in freewill is compatible with our everyday assumptions about men's responsibility for their acts. It would be irrational, he argues, to blame or praise someone for his actions if he could not have behaved otherwise: determinism and responsibility are incompatible notions. On the contrary, the determinist replies, it is only if we can believe that an agent's actions are his own, and this means that they are caused by something in *him*, that it makes sense to hold him accountable. If acts are uncaused then they are the products of chance, and it is irrational to praise or blame people because of how they chanced to choose. Indeed we could not hope to alter behaviour by praise and blame, or reward and punishment, if acts are not open to causal influence. Thus many determinists adopt the position of Hobbes in *Leviathan* (chapter 21) and argue that freedom and necessity are compatible and that men may be free in the same way as a falling stone is free when its movement is not impeded.

The libertarian is not impressed by the notion of self-causation since it leaves no room for the belief that the individual can at least sometimes act differently even if everything else had been the same. Nor does he accept that an uncaused act must be a random one since men choose for reasons and reason is the opposite of caprice or chance.

Here we reach a real impasse and at the same time one possible explanation of why the free will-determinist debate cannot be settled by empirical observation: regularity in conduct could be the result either of rational choice or of causal factors. Within limited circumstances we are able to make rough predictions about a good deal of human behaviour: we can, for instance, be reasonably certain that nearly everyone will get up in the morning and go to bed at night. This may seem to favour the causal theory since knowledge of causal regularities enables us to predict future events. But rational behaviour is also predictable. Rational people follow rules; and they consider that a good reason in a particular situation remains a good reason in all similar situations. This leads them to make the same type of response to similar situations. Further, most people would be most surprised to learn that such regularities are causally determined if this carries the implication that rational consistency amounts to causal necessity. Most of us take it for granted that we could stay in bed in the morning even when we choose, with good reason, not to do so. Of course this does not prove that we are in fact free, but the libertarian can, by appealing to the concept of rational action provide an alternative account of regularity in human behaviour and thus undercut one of the determinist's main points.

Much, however, depends on what is involved in the concept of rational action, and this takes us on to our second intractable philosophical issue, namely the nature of explanation. The only real rival to the positivist's causal model of explanation is one which appeals to the intelligibility of action, a matter of which, as we have seen, much is made by action theorists. In order to offer a really distinctive contrast between explanation in the natural and in the social sciences it is necessary to go beyond the contention that human beings are aware of the motives for their actions. That we can introspect the occurrence of the desires which move us to act may seem to open up an avenue for the explanation of human behaviour which is not available to the natural scientist in his study of inanimate entities. But introspection may simply be a way of identifying the causes of action. By observing that desires of a certain sort (e.g. hunger) always precede actions of a certain sort (e.g. eating) we may conclude that hunger causes men to eat. But there is nothing different in principle here from the causal explanation of non-human events. The only difference is that we have, in the case of human behaviour, a special way (introspection) of making the observations on which the causal generalisations are based.

The genuine alternative to the causal type of explanation is the thesis that, when acting, men choose between objectives on criteria other than the relative strength of their existing desires, and that they adopt such methods of reaching these objectives as seems to them most likely to succeed. On this theory men draw on their knowledge of how the world works (including their causal knowledge) and their perception of the circumstances in which they are set, to select the means to their freely chosen ends. The basic insight here is that it is always intelligible and explanatory to say that a person acted as he did because he thought that this would have the results he wished to see realized. The 'because' here is not a causal one. It is not implied that when men act rationally they have to do what they do. We therefore have a form of explanation which is intellectually satisfying but non-causal.

If we then press the issue of why a person adopts particular ends it may be satisfactory enough to be told that these are of a type with which we are familiar. To know that a person is, for instance, acting in order to obtain food, or recognition, or rest, may explain his actions to us because we know what it is to want these things. And neither the intellectual satisfaction nor the truth of such explanations requires the assumption that people cannot equally well adopt other familiar and hence intelligible objectives. The weakness of this position is that familiarity removes only the psychological not the intellectual need for further explanations.

Certainly there are limitations to the range of such interpretative explanations since this method works less well, if it works at all, when we seek to understand the behaviour of those who live in very different cultures from our own. It is hard, for instance, for us to accept what we regard as superstitious beliefs as satisfactory ingredients in a sociological explanation because we cannot enter into and so understand such beliefs. Some would even go so far as to say that we cannot understand a belief which we do not share. This makes cross-cultural understanding virtually impossible.

Many other aspects of the philosophy of social explanation require exploration. I have said only a little, for instance, about the controversial status of functional explanations (see pp. 110 and 194) but the problematic nature of the topics that have already been mentioned is enough to be going on with, for complexity is compounded by the consideration of our third philosophical topic, the debatable objectivity of value judgements.

The determined determinist, when confronted with the analysis of action deployed by the libertarian in support of an interpretative form of social explanation, can always take the Hobbesian line of attempting to reduce the processes of thought and choice to mechanistic and hence causal terms. But conscious and deliberate choices, particularly reflective moral decisions, are among the human phenomena most recalcitrant to such mechanistic reductionism. The experience of actually making moral choices is hard to reconcile with the idea that we always act in accordance with our strongest desire. Most people believe, at least sometimes, that they ought to do things that they do not wish to do, and often they act on such beliefs: temptation, it appears, can be resisted. But if we can know what is right and good and if we can sometimes act on that knowledge then determinism and positivism are vulnerable.

Moreover if moral values are independent of human choices and moral judgements can be true or false in the same way as statements of fact can be true or false, then this provides a basis for an important type of interpretative explanation of human conduct (for it must then be accounted rational to do what is right and choose what is good). Further, a belief in the objectivity of moral values encourages us to incorporate value judgements into social theory.

If, on the other hand, moral judgements are no more than expressions of human desires and emotions then our moral convictions are more likely to be seen as candidates for causal explanation than as a frame of reference for interpretative explanations. Further, subjectivism in morals is one of the main justifications for attempting the difficult task of rendering theories of society value-free. Mere personal preference is manifestly out of place in an objective academic study.

There is, however, no more open question in philosophy than that of the epistemology or truth-value of moral judgements. On the one hand it is argued that moral discourse has many features similar to the forms of speech which we use to make factual statements (for instance conflicting moral judgements are assumed to contradict each other), and it remains the unshakeable conviction of most people that at least some types of conduct must be accepted as good or evil by every rational being. (Can any sane person, for instance, really not believe that killing an innocent person is wrong, or think that to say that murder is evil is no more than to express a strong feeling of dislike for it?)

On the other hand the ineradicable nature of moral disagreement between equally informed and impartial persons, the evidence of the diversity of moral beliefs in different societies, classes and historical periods, and the intellectual difficulty of making clear what sort of objective reality values could have, all these combine to produce scepticism about the very idea of moral truth and falsehood.

These arguments must be pondered by everone concerned with the nature of human conduct and so of human society. In this chapter I have scarcely been able to do more than stress the importance of a few fundamental philosophical issues for the study of social theory. The fact that we must end here, on the verge of such major intellectual problems, indicates both the enormity and the interest of the task of theorizing about human society.

FOR FURTHER READING

There are a number of excellent bcoks on the philosophy of social science. In addition to those already mentioned (see pp. 23 and 50) see M. Brodbeck, *Readings in the Philosophy of the Social Sciences* (Macmillan: London 1968), A. Ryan, *The Philosophy of the Social Sciences* (Macmillan: London, 1970) and H. P. Rickman, *Understand-*

ing and the Human Studies (Heinemann: London, 1967). Ryan has also edited a useful collection of essays, *The Philosophy of Social Explanation*, (Oxford University Press: London, 1973). See also Roger Beehler and Alan R. Drengson (eds.), *The Philosophy of Society* (Methuen: London, 1978) and Charles W. Smith, *A Critique of Sociological Reasoning* (Blackwell: Oxford, 1979).

On the more general philosophical topics, see Peter Winch, *The Idea of a Social Science* (Routledge: London, 1958), Anthony Kenny, *Will, Freedom and Power* (Blackwell: Oxford, 1975); R. M. Hare, *Freedom and Reason* (Oxford University Press: Oxford, 1963) and J. L. Mackie, *Ethics* (Penguin Books: Harmondsworth, 1977).

Index